Bookkeeping For Canadians

FOR

DUMMIES®

2ND EDITION

by Lita Epstein, MBA
and Cécile Laurin, CA

WILEY

John Wiley & Sons Canada, Ltd.

Bookkeeping For Canadians For Dummies,® 2nd Edition

Published by
John Wiley & Sons Canada, Ltd.
6045 Freemont Blvd.
Mississauga, ON L5R 4J3
www.wiley.com

Library and Archives Canada Cataloguing in Publication Data

Epstein, Lita
      Bookkeeping for Canadians for dummies / Lita Epstein
and Cécile Laurin.

 Issued also in electronic format.
ISBN 978-1-11847-808-0
      1. Bookkeeping –Canada. I. Laurin, Cécile II. Title.

 HF5616.C3E67 2012   657'.20971   C2012-906464-5

ISBN 978-1-118-47826-4 (ebk); 978-1-118-47828-8 (ebk); 978-1-118-47827-1 (ebk)

Printed in the United States

 2 3 4 5 BRR 15 14

WILEY

About the Authors

Lita Epstein earned her MBA from Emory University's Goizueta Business School. She designs and teaches online courses on topics such as investing for retirement, getting ready for tax time, and finance and investing for women. She's written more than ten books, including *Streetwise Retirement Planning* and *Trading For Dummies*.

Lita was the content director for a financial services website, http://MostChoice.com, and managed the website Investing for Women. As a Congressional press secretary, Lita gained firsthand knowledge about how to work within and around the federal bureaucracy, which gives her great insight into how government programs work. In the past, Lita has been a daily newspaper reporter, magazine editor, and fundraiser for the international activities of former president Jimmy Carter through The Carter Center.

Cécile Laurin, CA is a professor of accounting and coordinator at Algonquin College of Applied Arts and Technology in Ottawa. She has also taught at the University of Ottawa. Her career began in public accounting, performing audits with the firm now known as KPMG. She then became the chief financial officer of three engineering firms and the international law firm Gowling Lafleur Henderson LLP. She obtained a Bachelor of Administration and a Bachelor of Commerce (Honours) from the University of Ottawa and is a member of the Institute of Chartered Accountants of Ontario and the Canadian Institute of Chartered Accountants. She is the co-author of *Accounting For Canadians For Dummies* and has written several learning tools for professors and students in accounting. Cécile has also developed several distance-learning courses offered through Algonquin College.

Dedication

Lita: To my father, Jerome Kirschbrown, who taught me the importance of accounting, bookkeeping, and watching every detail.

Cécile: For my son, Marc, and my daughter, Marie.

Authors' Acknowledgments

Lita: I want to take this opportunity to thank all the people who have helped make this book a reality. In particular, I want to thank the wonderful folks at Wiley who shepherded this project to completion — Stacy Kennedy and Kelly Ewing, as well as my copy editor, Elizabeth Rea. I also want to thank my technical advisor, Shellie Moore, who is a CPA and made sure that all the bookkeeping and accounting details were accurate. Finally, I want to thank my agent Jessica Faust at BookEnds, who helps find all my book projects.

Cécile: I would like to thank Anam Ahmed, my editor, Andrea Douglas, my copy editor, and Pauline Ricablanca, production editor, as well as the many other behind-the-scenes people at Wiley for making this experience enjoyable and low-stress. I learned a lot through this experience, and my students will be the beneficiaries, now and into the future.

Publisher's Acknowledgments

We're proud of this book; please send us your comments through our online registration form located at `http://dummies.custhelp.com`. For other comments, please contact our Customer Care Department within the U.S. at 877-762-2974, outside the U.S. at 317-572-3993, or fax 317-572-4002.

Some of the people who helped bring this book to market include the following:

Acquisitions and Editorial

Associate Acquisitions Editor: Anam Ahmed

Production Editor: Pauline Ricablanca

U.S. Project Editor: Kelly Ewing

Copy Editor: Andrea Douglas

Editorial Assistant: Kathy Deady

Cartoons: Rich Tennant
(`http://www.the5thwave.com`)

Cover photo: © DNY59

Composition Services

Project Coordinator: Kristie Rees

Layout and Graphics: Joyce Haughey

Proofreaders: Melissa Cossell, Penny L. Stuart

Indexer: BIM Indexing & Proofreading Services

John Wiley & Sons Canada, Ltd.

>   **Deborah Barton,** Vice President and Director of Operations

>   **Jennifer Smith,** Vice-President and Publisher, Professional & Trade Division

>   **Alison Maclean,** Managing Editor

Publishing and Editorial for Consumer Dummies

>   **Kathleen Nebenhaus,** Vice President and Executive Publisher

>   **David Palmer,** Associate Publisher

>   **Kristin Ferguson-Wagstaffe,** Product Development Director

Publishing for Technology Dummies

>   **Andy Cummings,** Vice President and Publisher

Composition Services

>   **Debbie Stailey,** Director of Composition Services

Contents at a Glance

Table of Contents

Introduction

Bookkeepers take care of all the financial data for small businesses. If you subscribe to the idea that information is power (which we do), you must then agree that the bookkeeper has a tremendous amount of power within a business. Information tracked in the books helps business owners make key decisions that involve sales planning and product offerings, as well as the management of many other financial aspects of their business.

If it weren't for the hard work of bookkeepers, businesses wouldn't have any clue about what happens with their financial transactions. Without accurate financial bookkeeping, a business owner wouldn't know how many sales her business made, how much cash it collected, or how much cash it paid for the products it sold to customers during the year. She also wouldn't know how much cash her business paid to employees or how much cash it spent on other business expenses throughout the year.

Accurate and complete financial bookkeeping is crucial to any business owner, but it's also important to those who work with the business, such as investors, financial institutions, and employees. People both inside the business (managers, owners, and employees) and outside the business (investors, lenders, and the government) all depend on the bookkeeper to accurately record financial transactions.

To perform the bookkeeper's crucial job well, you need certain skills and talents. Bookkeepers must be detailed-oriented, enjoy working with numbers, and be meticulous about accurately entering those numbers in the books. They must vigilantly keep a paper or electronic trail, as well as filing and storing all needed backup information about the financial transactions entered into the books.

Whether you're a business owner keeping the books yourself or an employee keeping the books for a small-business owner, the smooth financial operation of the business depends on your job as bookkeeper.

About This Book

In this book, we introduce you to the key aspects of bookkeeping and how to set up and use your financial books. We walk you through the basics of book-keeping, starting with the process of setting up your business's books and developing

- ✔ A list of your business's accounts, called the Chart of Accounts
- ✔ Your business's General Ledger, which summarizes all the activity in a business's accounts
- ✔ Your business's journals, which give details about all your business's financial transactions

Then, we take you through the process of recording all your transactions — sales, purchases, and other financial activity. We also talk about how to manage payroll, governmental reporting, and external financial reporting.

Finally, we show you how to start the yearly cycle all over again by closing (or emptying out) the necessary accounts for the current year so that you can start with zero balances in those accounts in the next year.

Bookkeeping is a continuous cycle, starting with financial transactions, recording those transactions in journals, posting those transactions to the General Ledger, testing your books to be sure that they're in balance, making any necessary adjustments or corrections to the books (to keep them com-plete, accurate, and in balance), preparing financial statements and reports to understand how well the business did during the year, and finally getting ready to start the process all over again for the next year.

You can find out all about this cycle, starting with Chapter 2 and following the bookkeeping journey through closing out the year and getting ready for the next year in Chapter 22.

Conventions Used in This Book

We use QuickBooks throughout this book to show you how to create a set of records for a business, enter information, and generate a variety of book-keeping reports.

Foolish Assumptions

While writing this book, we made some key assumptions about who you are and why you've picked up this book to get a better understanding of bookkeeping. We assume that you're one of the following types of people:

- A business owner who wants to know how to do your own books. You have a good understanding of business and its terminology, but you have little or no knowledge of bookkeeping and accounting.

- A person who does bookkeeping or plans to do bookkeeping for a small business and needs to know more about how to set up and keep the books. You have some basic knowledge of business terminology but don't know much about bookkeeping or accounting.

- A staff person in a small business who's just been asked to take over the business's bookkeeping duties. You need to know more about how transactions are entered into the books, how to prove out transactions so that you can be sure you're making entries correctly and accurately, and how to prepare financial statements and reports by using the data you collect.

- A student who wants to get an overview of bookkeeping so that you can apply these skills to your studies and to your intended profession.

What You Don't Have to Read

Throughout *Bookkeeping For Canadians For Dummies,* 2nd Edition, we include a number of examples that show how to apply the basics of bookkeeping to real-life situations. If you're primarily reading this book to gain a general knowledge of the subject and don't need to delve into all the nitty-gritty, day-to-day aspects of bookkeeping, you may want to skip over the paragraphs marked with the Example icon (see the section "Icons Used in This Book," later in this Introduction). Skipping the examples shouldn't interfere with your grasp on the key aspects of how to keep the books.

How This Book Is Organized

Bookkeeping For Canadians For Dummies is divided into six parts, which we outline in the following sections.

Part I: Basic Bookkeeping: Why You Need It

In Part I, we discuss the importance of bookkeeping, explain how it works, and help you get started with setting up your business's books. We also touch on the terms that are unique to bookkeeping and tell you how to set up the roadmap for your books, the Chart of Accounts.

Part II: Keeping a Paper or Electronic Trail

In Part II, we explain how you enter your financial transactions in the books, how you post transactions to your General Ledger (the granddaddy of your bookkeeping system), and how you track all the transaction details in your journals. We also give tips about how to develop a good internal control system for managing your books and your business's cash, as well as talk about your options if you decide to computerize your bookkeeping.

Part III: Tracking Day-to-Day Business Operations with Your Books

In Part III, we show you how to track your day-to-day business operations, including recording sales and purchases with applicable sales taxes as well as any adjustments to those sales and purchases, such as discounts, returns, and allowances. In addition, we talk about the basics of setting up and managing employee payroll, as well as all the government paperwork that you need to complete as soon as you decide to hire employees.

Part IV: Preparing the Books for Year's (Or Month's) End

In Part IV, we introduce you to the process of adjusting your books at the end of an accounting period, whether it's the end of a month or the end of a year. These key adjustments include recording depreciation of your fixed assets, calculating and recording your interest payments and receipts in your books, accruing expenses and service revenue, and possibly adjusting for unearned revenue. This part also covers various aspects of proving out your books, from checking your cash and testing the balance of your books to making any needed adjustments or corrections.

Part V: Reporting Results and Starting Over

In Part V, we tell you how to use all the information in your books to prepare financial statements and reports that show how well your business did during the month, quarter, or year. We also lay out all the paperwork that you have to deal with, including year-end government reports and CRA forms. Finally, you can find out how to close out the books at year-end and get ready for the next year.

Part VI: The Part of Tens

The Part of Tens is the hallmark of the *For Dummies* series. In this part, we highlight the ten ways you can efficiently manage your business's cash by using your books and the top ten accounts that you need to know how to manage.

Icons Used in This Book

For Dummies books use little pictures, called *icons,* to flag certain chunks of text that either you shouldn't miss or you're free to skip. The icons in *Bookkeeping For Canadians For Dummies* are

Look to this icon for ideas about how to improve your bookkeeping processes and how to use the information in the books to manage your business.

This icon marks anything that we want you to recall about bookkeeping after you finish reading this book.

This icon points out any aspect of bookkeeping that comes with dangers or perils that may hurt the accuracy of your entries or the way in which you use your financial information in the future. We also use this icon to mark certain things that can get you into trouble with the government, your lenders, your vendors, your employees, or your investors.

This icon points to real-life specifics about how to do a particular bookkeeping function.

Where to Go from Here

Can you feel the excitement? You're now ready to enter the world of book-keeping! Because of the way *Bookkeeping For Canadians For Dummies* is set up, you can start anywhere you want.

If you need the basics — or if you're a little rusty and want to refresh your knowledge of bookkeeping — start with Part I. However, if you already know bookkeeping basics, are familiar with the key terminology, and know how to set up a Chart of Accounts, consider diving in at Part II.

If you've set up your books already and feel comfortable with the basics of bookkeeping, you may want to start with Part III and how to enter various transactions. On the other hand, if your priority is using the financial information that you've already collected, check out the financial reporting options in Part V.

Part I

Basic Bookkeeping: Why You Need It

In this part . . .

Not sure why bookkeeping is important? In this part, we explain the basics of how bookkeeping works and help you get started with the task of setting up your books.

This part also exposes you to terms that you may already know but that have a unique meaning in the world of bookkeeping, such as ledger, journal, posting, debit, and credit. Finally, we start you on your bookkeeping journey by showing you how to set up the roadmap for your books, the Chart of Accounts.

Chapter 1

So You Want to Do the Books

*F*ew small-business owners actually hire accountants to work full time for them because, for a small business, that expense is probably excessive. So, instead, the owner hires a *bookkeeper* who serves as the business accountant's eyes and ears. In return, the accountant helps the bookkeeper develop good bookkeeping practices and reviews his or her work periodically (usually monthly).

In this chapter, we provide an overview of a bookkeeper's work. If you're just starting a business, you may be your own bookkeeper for a while until you can afford to hire one, so think of this chapter as your to-do list.

Delving into Bookkeeping Basics

Like most businesspeople, you probably have great ideas for running your own business and just want to get started. You don't want to sweat the small stuff, such as keeping detailed records of every penny spent; you just want to quickly build a business that can make a lot of money.

Well, slow down — starting a business isn't a race! If you don't carefully plan your bookkeeping operation and figure out exactly what financial detail you want to track, and how, you have absolutely no way to measure the success (or failure, unfortunately) of your business efforts.

Bookkeeping, when done properly, gives you an excellent gauge of how well your business is doing. When done in a timely manner, bookkeeping gives you quick feedback on how your business is doing. It also provides you with a lot of information throughout the year so that you can test the financial success of your business strategies and make course corrections as soon as possible, if and when necessary, to ensure that you reach your year-end profit goals.

Bookkeeping can become your best friend when it comes to managing your financial assets, meeting your obligations, and testing your business strategies, so don't short-change it. Take the time to develop your bookkeeping system with your accountant before you even open your business's doors and make your first sale.

Picking your accounting method

You can't keep books unless you know how you want to go about doing so. The two basic accounting methods you have to choose from are *cash-basis accounting* and *accrual accounting.* The key difference between these two accounting methods is the point at which you record sales and purchases in your books. If you choose cash-basis accounting, you record transactions only when cash changes hands. (Only a very limited number of Canadian businesses are allowed to use cash-basis accounting.) If you use accrual accounting, you record a transaction when the products are delivered or services are provided, even if cash doesn't change hands.

For example, suppose your business buys products to sell from a vendor but doesn't actually pay for those products for 30 days. If you're using cash-basis accounting, you don't record the purchase until you actually lay out the cash to the vendor. If you're using accrual accounting, you record the purchase when you receive the products, and you also record the obligation to pay the vendor in an account called Accounts Payable.

We talk about the pros and cons of each type of accounting method in Chapter 2.

Understanding assets, liabilities, and equity

Every business has three key financial parts that you must keep in balance: assets, liabilities, and equity. *Assets* include everything the business owns and uses, such as cash, inventory, buildings, equipment, and vehicles. *Liabilities* include everything the business owes to others, such as vendor bills, credit card balances, and bank loans. *Equity* includes the claims that owners have on the assets, based on each owner's portion of ownership in the business.

The formula for keeping your books in balance involves these three elements:

Assets = Liabilities + Equity

Because balancing your books is so important, we talk a lot about how to keep your books and accounting records in balance throughout this book. You can find an initial introduction to this concept in Chapter 2.

Introducing debits and credits

To keep the books, you need to revise your thinking about two common financial terms: debits and credits. Most non-bookkeepers and non-accountants think of debits as subtractions from their bank accounts. The opposite is true with credits — people usually see credits as additions to their accounts, in most cases, in the form of refunds or corrections in favour of the account holders.

Well, forget all you thought you knew about debits and credits. Debits and credits are totally different animals in the world of bookkeeping. Because keeping the books involves a method called *double-entry bookkeeping*, you have to make a least two entries — a debit and a credit — into your bookkeeping system for every transaction. Whether that debit or credit adds or subtracts from an account depends solely on the type of account.

We know all this debit, credit, and double-entry stuff sounds confusing, but we promise you can understand it if you work through this book. We start explaining this critical, yet somewhat confusing, concept in Chapter 2.

Charting your bookkeeping course

You can't just enter transactions in the books willy-nilly. You need to know where exactly those transactions fit into the larger bookkeeping system. That's where your *Chart of Accounts* comes in; it's essentially a list of all the accounts your business has and what types of transactions go into each account.

We talk more about the Chart of Accounts in Chapter 3.

Recognizing the Importance of an Accurate Electronic or Paper Trail

To keep the books, you need to create an accurate electronic or paper trail. You want to track all your business's financial transactions so that if a question comes up at a later date, you can turn to the books to figure out what went wrong, or answer a particular query about an amount or balance reported in your books.

An accurate electronic or paper trail is the only way to track your financial successes and review your financial failures, tasks that are vitally important in order to grow your business. You need to know what works successfully so that you can repeat it in the future and build on your success. On the other hand, you need to know what failed so that you can correct it and prevent making the same mistake again.

In the General Ledger you summarize all your business's financial transactions, and you use journals to keep track of the tiniest details of each transaction. You can make your information-gathering more effective by using a computerized accounting system, which gives you access to your financial information in many different formats. Controlling who enters this financial information into your books and who can access it afterwards is smart business and involves critical planning on your part. We address all these concepts in the following sections.

Maintaining a ledger

The granddaddy of your bookkeeping system is the General Ledger. In this ledger, you keep a summary of all your accounts and the financial activities that took place involving those accounts throughout the year.

You draw upon the General Ledger's account balances to develop your financial statements and reports on a monthly, quarterly, or annual basis. You can also use these account balances to develop internal reports that help you make key business decisions. We talk more about developing and maintaining the General Ledger in Chapter 4.

Keeping journals

Small businesses conduct hundreds, if not thousands, of transactions each year. If you recorded every transaction in the General Ledger, that record would become unwieldy and difficult to use. Instead, most businesses keep a series of journals that detail activity in their most active accounts.

For example, almost every business has a Cash Receipts Journal in which to keep the detail for all incoming cash and a Cash Disbursements Journal in which to keep the detail for all outgoing cash. Other journals can detail sales, purchases, customer accounts, vendor accounts, and any other key accounts that see significant activity.

You decide which accounts you want to create journals for based on your business operation and your need for information about key financial transactions. We talk more about the importance of journals, the accounts commonly journalized, and the process of maintaining journals in Chapter 5.

Considering computerizing

Most businesses today use computerized accounting systems to keep their books. You should consider using one of these systems, rather than trying to keep your books on paper. Your bookkeeping takes less time and is probably more accurate with a computerized system, as compared to the old pen-and-paper method.

In addition to increasing accuracy and cutting the time it takes to do your bookkeeping, computerized accounting also makes designing reports easier. You can then use these reports to help make business decisions. Your computerized accounting system stores detailed information about every transaction, so you can group that detail in any way that may assist your decision making. We talk more about computerized accounting systems in Chapter 6.

Instituting internal controls

Every business owner needs to be concerned with keeping tight controls on the business's cash and how it's used. One way to institute this control is to place internal restrictions on who has access to the cash, who can enter information into your books, and who has access to use that information.

You also need to carefully control who has the ability to accept cash receipts and who has the ability to pay out your business's cash. Appropriately separating duties helps you protect your business's assets from error, theft, and fraud. We talk more about controlling your cash and protecting your financial records in Chapter 7.

Using Bookkeeping's Tools to Manage Daily Finances

After you set up your business's books and put in place your internal controls, you're ready to use the systems you established to manage the day-to-day operations of your business. You can quickly see how a well-designed bookkeeping system can make the job of managing your business's finances much easier.

Maintaining inventory

If your business keeps inventory on hand or in warehouses, you need to track the costs of the products you plan to sell in order to manage your profit potential. If you see inventory costs trending upward, you may need to adjust your own selling prices in order to maintain your profit margin. You certainly don't want to wait until the end of the year to find out how much your inventory cost you.

You also must keep careful watch on how much inventory you have on hand and how much you've sold. Inventory can get damaged, discarded, or stolen, meaning that your physical inventory on hand may differ from the amounts you have reported in your books. Do a physical count periodically — at least monthly for most businesses, and possibly daily for active retail stores where inventory is turned over and sold quickly.

In addition to watching for signs of theft or poor handling of inventory, make sure you have enough inventory on hand to satisfy your customers' needs. We talk more about how to use your bookkeeping system to manage inventory in Chapter 8.

Tracking sales

Everyone wants to know how well sales are doing. If you keep your books up to date and accurate, you can get those numbers very easily on a daily basis. You can also watch sales trends as often as you think necessary, whether that's daily, weekly, or monthly.

Use the information collected by your bookkeeping system to monitor sales, review discounts granted to customers for quick payments, and track the return of product and allowances granted to customers because of product defects. You need to know all three elements to gauge the success of the sales of your products.

If you find you need to offer price reductions more frequently in order to encourage sales, you may need to review your pricing, and you definitely need to research market conditions to determine the cause of this sales weakness. New activities by an aggressive competitor or simply a slow market period may be causing the sales slump. Either way, you need to understand the weakness and figure out how to maintain your profit goals in spite of any obstacles.

When tracking sales reveals an increase in the number of your products being returned, you need to research the issue and find the reason for the increase. Do the same if you find you need to grant your customers larger or more frequent sales allowances. Perhaps the quality of the product you're selling is declining, or contains defects and you need to find a new supplier. Whatever the reason, an increased number of product returns usually gives you a sign of a problem that you need to research and correct.

We talk more about how to use the bookkeeping system to track sales, discounts, returns, and allowances in Chapter 9.

Handling payroll

Many businesses find payroll a huge nightmare. Payroll requires you to comply with a lot of government regulations and fill out a lot of government paperwork. You also have to worry about collecting payroll taxes and paying the employer's share of those taxes. And if you pay employee benefits, you have yet another layer of record keeping to deal with.

We talk more about managing payroll and government requirements in Chapters 10 and 11. We also talk about year-end payroll reporting obligations in Chapter 20.

Running Tests for Accuracy

You can waste all the time it takes to track your transactions if you don't periodically test to be sure you've entered those transactions accurately. The old adage "Garbage in, garbage out" holds very true for bookkeeping: If the numbers you put into your bookkeeping system are garbage, the reports you develop from those numbers are garbage, as well.

Proving out your cash

The first step in testing out your books includes proving that you accurately recorded your cash transactions. This process involves checking a number of different transactions, including the cash taken in on a daily basis by your cashiers and the accuracy of your checking account. We talk about all the steps that you need to take to prove out your cash in Chapter 14.

Testing your balance

After you prove out your cash (see Chapter 14), you can check that you've recorded everything else in your books just as precisely. Review the accounts for any glaring errors and then test whether they're in balance by preparing a trial balance. You can find out more about trial balances in Chapter 16.

Doing bookkeeping corrections

You may not find your books in balance the first time you do a trial balance, but don't worry. People rarely find their books in balance on the first try. In Chapter 17, we explain common adjustments that you may need to make while you prove out your books at the end of an accounting period, and we also explain how to make the necessary corrections and adjustments.

Finally Showing Off Your Financial Success

Proving out your books and ensuring their balance means you finally get to show what your business has accomplished financially by developing reports to present to others. It's almost like putting your business on a stage and taking a bow — well . . . at least, you hope you've done well enough to take a bow.

If you take advantage of your bookkeeping information by reviewing and consulting it throughout the year, you'll have a good idea of how well your business is doing. You also can take any course corrections throughout the year to ensure that your end-of-the-year reports look great.

Preparing financial statements

Most businesses prepare at least two key financial statements, the balance sheet and the income statement, which you can show to outsiders, including the bank from which your business borrows money and your business's investors.

The balance sheet is a snapshot of your business's financial health as of a particular date. The balance sheet should show that your business's assets are equal to the combined value of your liabilities and your equity. It's called a *balance sheet* because it's based on a balanced formula:

Assets = Liabilities + Equity

The income statement summarizes your business's financial transactions for a particular time period, such as a month, quarter, or year. This financial statement starts with your revenues and sales, subtracts the costs of goods sold, and then subtracts any expenses incurred in operating the business. The bottom line of the income statement shows how much profit your business made during the accounting period. If you haven't done well, the income statement shows how much you've lost.

We explain how to prepare a balance sheet in Chapter 18, and we talk more about developing an income statement in Chapter 19. If you haven't seen them before, you may want to take a peek at what these documents look like now because it is always good to keep the end product of your bookkeeping efforts in mind.

Paying income taxes

Most small businesses don't have to pay income taxes. Instead, the business's owners report the business's profits on their personal tax returns, whether the business is owned by one person (a *sole proprietorship*) or two or more people (a *partnership*). Only a company that is *incorporated* pays income taxes because it is a separate legal entity in which investors buy shares (which we explain further in Chapter 21).

We talk more about business structures and how their income is taxed in Chapter 21.

Getting a Business Number (BN)

Any business that deals with payroll taxes, goods and services tax or harmonized sales tax (GST/HST) collection, or importing or exporting goods requires a nine-digit business number (BN), which the Canada Revenue Agency (CRA) issues. Your BN is the root number for all your accounts with the federal government.

Each sole proprietorship, partnership, or corporation in Canada must get a BN. Sole proprietors get one BN for all their businesses, if they own more than one. Other organizations, such as trusts, clubs, and charities, may also get a BN if, for example, they have to register for GST/HST. (We discuss GST/HST in Chapter 5.) To register online or to find out more about online registration, visit www.businessregistration.gc.ca.

Québec has its own equivalent of the BN, the NEQ, which stands for the Québec enterprise number. If you need to register in Québec, check out www.registreentreprises.gouv.qc.ca/en/demarrer/immatriculer. Because you are operating in Québec, you use your NEQ to register your payroll, import-export, or corporate income tax accounts, and you must still contact the CRA for a BN.

Before you register your BN number, you need to make some important decisions about the business you plan to operate. You must know

- The name of the business
- Its physical location
- Its *legal structure* (whether it's a sole proprietorship, partnership, or corporation)
- Its fiscal year-end
- The estimated amount of its sales in a year

Figures 1-1 through 1-5 show the form RC1 Request for a Business Number (BN).

Figure 1-1:
Page 1
of the
Request for
a Business
Number
form.

Canada Revenue Agency / Agence du revenu du Canada

REQUEST FOR A BUSINESS NUMBER (BN)

BN | | | | | | | | | |

FOR OFFICE USE

Complete this form to apply for a business number (BN). If you are a sole proprietor with more than one business, your BN will apply to all your businesses. **All businesses have to complete parts A and F.** Once completed, send this form to your local tax centre. The tax centres are listed at **www.cra-arc.gc.ca/cntct/tso-bsf-eng.html** or in Pamphlet RC2, *The Business Number and Your Canada Revenue Agency Program Accounts*. If you need more information, visit **www.cra.gc.ca/bn** or call us at **1-800-959-5525**.

Note: If your business is in the province of Quebec and you want to register for the goods and services tax/harmonized sales tax (GST/HST), do not use this form. Contact Revenu Québec. However, if you want to register for any of the other three accounts listed below, complete the appropriate part indicated in the following instructions:
• To open a GST/HST account, complete parts A, B, and F.
• To open a payroll account, complete parts A, C, and F.
• To open an import/export account, complete parts A, D, and F.
• To open a corporation income tax account, complete parts A, E, and F.

Part A – General information

A1 | Ownership type and Operation type

☐ Individual ☐ Partnership ☐ Trust ☐ Corporation ☐ Other (specify: _____)

Are you incorporated? ☐ Yes ☐ No **(All Canadian corporations have to provide a copy of the certificate of incorporation or amalgamation or complete the information requested in Part E.)**

Tick the box below that best describes your type of operation (if none apply, leave this section blank):

☐ Sole proprietor
☐ Society
☐ Employer of a domestic
☐ Foster parent
☐ Religious body
☐ Hospital

☐ Federal government (publicly funded)
☐ Federal government (not publicly funded)
☐ Provincial government
☐ Municipal government
☐ Financial institution
☐ Employer-sponsored plan

☐ Other government body
☐ Strata condo corporation
☐ Association
☐ University/school
☐ Union
☐ Diplomat

A2 | **Owner(s) information** – Complete this part to provide information for the individual owner, partner(s), corporation director(s), or officer(s) of the business. If you need more space, include the information on a separate piece of paper. The social insurance number (SIN) is mandatory for individuals (sole proprietors) applying to register for a GST/HST account (Social Insurance Number Disclosure Regulations, *Excise Tax Act*).

Social insurance number (SIN)	First name	Last name
Title	Work phone number	Work fax number
Occupation	Home phone number	Home fax number
	Cellular phone number	Pager number

Social insurance number (SIN)	First name	Last name
Title	Work phone number	Work fax number
Occupation	Home phone number	Home fax number
	Cellular phone number	Pager number

Contact Person – Please provide the name of a contact for registration purposes only (the contact name provided will not be considered an authorized representative. If you wish to authorize a representative to speak on your behalf about your BN program account(s), complete Form RC59, *Business Consent form*. For more information, see Pamphlet RC2, *The Business Number and Your Canada Revenue Agency Program Accounts*.

Title	First name	Last name
	Work phone number	Work fax number
	Cellular phone number	Pager number

RC1 E (11)

(Vous pouvez obtenir ce formulaire en français à **www.arc.gc.ca** ou au **1-800-959-3376**.)

Page 1 of 5

Canadä

© Canada Revenue Agency. Reproduced with permission of the Minister of Public Works and Government Services Canada, 2012

A3	Identification of business

Name

Physical business location | Postal or zip code

Mailing address (if different from the physical business location)
c/o | Postal or zip code

Operating / Trade name

Language of preference ☐ English ☐ French

Are you a third party requesting the registration? ☐ Yes (If **yes**, enter your name and company name below.) ☐ No

Your name: _____

Company name: _____

A4	Major business activity

Clearly describe your major business activity. Give as much detail as possible using at least one noun, a verb, and an adjective.
Example: Construction – Installing residential hardwood flooring.

_____

_____

Specify up to three main products or services that you provide or contract, and the estimated percentage of revenue they each represent.

_____ _____ %

_____ _____ %

_____ _____ %

A5	GST/HST information – For more information, see Pamphlet RC2, *The Business Number and Your Canada Revenue Agency Program Accounts.*

Do you provide or plan to provide goods or services in Canada or to export outside Canada? If **no**, you generally cannot register for GST/HST. However, certain businesses may be able to register. For details, see Pamphlet RC2.	☐ Yes	☐ No
Are your annual worldwide GST/HST taxable sales, including those of any associates, more than $30,000? If **yes**, you **have** to register for GST/HST. **Note:** Special rules apply to charities and public institutions. For details, see Pamphlet RC2.	☐ Yes	☐ No
Are you a public service body (PSB) whose annual worldwide GST/HST taxable sales are more than $50,000? If **yes**, you **have** to register for GST/HST. **Note:** Special rules apply to charities and public institutions. See Pamphlet RC2 for details.	☐ Yes	☐ No
Are all the goods/services you sell/provide exempt from GST/HST?	☐ Yes	☐ No
Do you operate a taxi or limousine service? If **yes**, you **have** to register for GST/HST regardless of your revenue.	☐ Yes	☐ No
Are you an individual whose sole activity subject to GST/HST is from commercial rental income?	☐ Yes	☐ No
Are you a non-resident?	☐ Yes	☐ No
Are you a non-resident who charges admission directly to audiences at activities or events in Canada? If **yes**, you **have** to register for GST/HST, regardless of your revenue.	☐ Yes	☐ No
Do you want to register voluntarily? By registering voluntarily, you **must** begin to charge GST/HST and file returns even if your worldwide GST/HST taxable sales are $30,000 or less ($50,000 or less if you are a public service body). For details, see Pamphlet RC2.	☐ Yes	☐ No

Figure 1-2:
Page 2
of the
Request for
a Business
Number
form.

Page 2 of 5

Part B – GST/HST account information – Complete a separate form for each division of your corporation that requires a GST/HST account.

B1 | GST/HST account identification – If the information is the same as in Part A3, tick the box. ☐

Account name

Physical business location	Postal or zip code

Mailing address (if different from the physical business location) for GST/HST purposes c/o	Postal or zip code

B2 | Filing information – For more information, see Pamphlet RC2, *The Business Number and Your Canada Revenue Agency Program Accounts.*

Enter the amount of your **sales in Canada** (dollar amount only) $ _____   (If you have no sales enter $0)

Enter the amount of your **worldwide sales** (dollar amount only) $ _____   (If you have no sales enter $0)

Enter the fiscal year-end for GST/HST purposes.
If you do not enter a date, we will enter December 31.   Month Day

Do you want to make an election to change the fiscal year-end for GST/HST purposes?   ☐ Yes   ☐ No

If **yes**, enter the date you would like to use.   Month Day

Enter the effective date of registration for GST/HST purposes.   Year Month Day   For information about when to register for GST/HST, see Pamphlet RC2.

B3 | Reporting period

Unless you are a charity or a financial institution, we will assign you a reporting period based on your total annual GST/HST taxable sales in Canada (including those of your associates) for the **preceding year**. If you do not have annual sales from the preceding year, your sales are $0. If you want to elect for a different reporting period, your options, if any, are listed below. Please indicate in the right column which option you want to elect. For more information, see Pamphlet RC2, *The Business Number and Your Canada Revenue Agency Program Accounts.*

Reporting period election
Select **yes** if you want to file more frequently than the reporting period assigned to you.   ☐ Yes   ☐ No

Total annual GST/HST taxable sales in Canada (including those of your associates)	Reporting period assigned to you, unless you choose to change it (see next column)	Options
☐ More than $6,000,000	Monthly	No options available
☐ More than $1,500,000 up to $6,000,000	Quarterly	☐ Monthly
☐ $1,500,000 or less	Annual	☐ Monthly **or** ☐ Quarterly
☐ Charities	Annual	☐ Monthly **or** ☐ Quarterly
☐ Financial institutions	Annual	☐ Monthly **or** ☐ Quarterly

B4 | Direct deposit information – The account holder identified below requests and authorizes the Minister of National Revenue to directly deposit into the Canadian financial institution's account identified below, amounts payable to the account holder under Part IX of the *Excise Tax Act*.

Complete the information area below or attach a blank cheque and write "VOID" across the front. This method provides a faster, more convenient, and dependable way of receiving refunds. The CRA will deposit your GST/HST refund into your Canadian financial institution's account.

Branch number   Institution number   Account number

Name(s) of account holder(s):

Figure 1-3: Page 3 of the Request for a Business Number form.

Page 3 of 5

Part C – Payroll account information – Complete parts C1 and C2 if you need a payroll account.

C1 | **Payroll account identification** – If the information is the same as in Part A3, tick the box. ☐

Account name

Physical business location | Postal or zip code

Mailing address (if different from the physical business location)
c/o | Postal or zip code

Language of preference ☐ English ☐ French

C2 | **General information**

a) What type of payment are you making?

☐ Payroll ☐ Registered retirement savings plan

☐ Registered retirement income fund ☐ Other (specify) _____

b) How often will you pay your employees or payees? Please tick the pay period(s) that apply.

☐ Daily ☐ Weekly ☐ Bi-weekly ☐ Semi-monthly

☐ Monthly ☐ Annually ☐ Other (specify) _____

c) What is the maximum number of employees you expect to have working for you at any time in the next 12 months? _____

d) When will you make the first payment to your employees or payees? | | | | | | | |
Year   Month   Day

e) Duration of business: ☐ Year-round ☐ Seasonal

If seasonal, tick month(s) of operation: J F M A M J J A S O N D

f) If the business is a corporation, is it a subsidiary or an affiliate of a foreign corporation? ☐ Yes ☐ No

If **yes**, enter country: _____

g) Are you a franchisee? ☐ Yes ☐ No

If **yes**, enter the name and country of the franchisor: _____

Part D – Import/export account information – If you need an import/export account for commercial purposes (you do not need to register for an import/export account for personal importation), complete D1 and D2. Complete a separate form for each branch or division of your corporation that needs an import/export account for commercial purposes.

D1 | **Import/export account identification** – If the information is the same as in Part A3, tick the box. ☐

Account name

Physical business location | Postal or zip code

Mailing address (if different from the physical business location)
c/o | Postal or zip code

Language of preference ☐ English ☐ French

Do you want us to send you import/export account information? ☐ Yes ☐ No

Page 4 of 5

Figure 1-4:
Page 4
of the
Request for
a Business
Number
form.

D2	Import/export information

Type of account: ☐ Importer ☐ Exporter ☐ Both importer/exporter ☐ Meeting, convention, and incentive travel

If you are applying for an exporter account, you **must** enter all of the following requested information.

Enter the type of goods you are or will be exporting:

Enter the estimated annual value of goods you are or will be exporting. $ _____

Part E – Corporation income tax account information – If you need a corporation income tax account, complete Part E1. If you have not provided your certificate of incorporation or amalgamation you have to complete Parts E2 and E3.

E1	Corporation income tax account identification – If the information is the same as in Part A3, tick the box. ☐

Name (as listed on your certificate of incorporation)

Physical business location	Postal or zip code

Mailing address (if different from the physical business location) c/o	Postal or zip code

Language of preference ☐ English ☐ French

E2	Complete this part if you have not provided a copy of your Canadian certificate of incorporation or amalgamation.

Certificate Number _____
Date of Incorporation _____
Date of Amalgamation _____

E3	Indicate the jurisdiction of your business.

☐ Federal
☐ Provincial _____ (province)
☐ Foreign _____ (country/state)

Part F – Certification
All businesses have to complete and sign this part. You are authorized to sign this form if you are an individual, a partner, an officer of your business or a corporation director. If the direct deposit information is entered, an authorized representative **may not** sign this form.

The person signing this form is the: ☐ Owner ☐ Partner ☐ Corporation director ☐ Officer ☐ Authorized representative

I certify that the information given on this form is, to the best of my knowledge, true and complete.

_____
First and last names (print)

_____
Signature

Title
_____
| | | | | | | |
Year   Month   Day

Note: After you register your new business number or CRA program account (e.g. GST/HST) we may contact you to confirm the information you provided. At that time we may ask you to provide more information. Having complete and valid information on file for your business allows us to serve you better.

Figure 1-5:
Page 5
of the
Request for
a Business
Number
form.

You can get the scoop on the requirements and obligations of operating a payroll in Chapter 10, and how to remit payroll-related taxes and benefits in Chapter 11. We look at the requirements and obligations concerning GST/HST in Chapter 5, and explore how to remit GST/HST and PST in Chapter 21.

Because the rules around importing and exporting are very complex, we don't explore that aspect of your responsibilities to the CRA. Consult with your accountant if that need comes up for your business.

Chapter 2

Getting Down to Bookkeeping Basics

. . . .

In This Chapter

▶ Keeping business books and records

▶ Defining bookkeeping terms

▶ Navigating the accounting cycle

▶ Choosing accrual accounting, rather than cash-basis accounting

▶ Deciphering double-entry bookkeeping

▶ Knowing your debits from your credits

. . . .

All businesses need to keep track of their financial transactions — that's why bookkeeping and bookkeepers are so important. Without accurate books and records, how can you tell whether your business is making a profit or taking a loss?

In this chapter, we cover the key parts of bookkeeping by introducing you to the language of bookkeeping, familiarizing you with how bookkeepers manage the accounting cycle, and showing you how to understand the most difficult type of bookkeeping — double-entry bookkeeping.

Bookkeepers: The Record Keepers of the Business World

Bookkeeping, the methodical way in which businesses track their financial transactions, is rooted in accounting. *Accounting* is the total structure of records and procedures used to record, classify, and report information about a business's financial transactions. Bookkeeping involves the recording of that financial information into the accounting system while maintaining adherence to solid accounting principles.

Bookkeepers are the ones who toil day in and day out to ensure that transactions are captured and accurately recorded. Bookkeepers need to be very detail-oriented and love to work with numbers, because numbers and the accounts they go into are just about all these people see all day. Bookkeepers don't need to have a professional accounting designation.

Many small-business owners who are just starting up their businesses initially serve as their own bookkeepers until their businesses grow large enough to hire someone dedicated to keeping the books. Few small businesses have accountants on staff to check the books and prepare official financial reports; instead, they have a bookkeeper on staff who serves as the outside accountant's eyes and ears. Most businesses do seek an accountant who has a professional designation to perform all the necessary duties and responsibilities as required by the business owners and by the different Canadian laws.

In many small businesses today, a bookkeeper enters the business transactions on a daily basis while working inside the business. At the end of each month or quarter, the bookkeeper sends summary reports to the accountant, who checks the transactions for accuracy and completeness and then prepares financial statements.

In most cases, an accountant initially helps set up the accounting system so that the business owner can be sure it uses solid accounting principles. That accountant periodically stops by the office and reviews how the business uses the system to be sure the business is handling transactions properly.

Creating accurate financial reports is the only way you can know how your business is doing. The business develops these reports by using the information you, as the bookkeeper, enter into your accounting system. If that information isn't accurate, your financial reports are meaningless. As the old adage goes,

Wading through Basic Bookkeeping Lingo

Before you can take on bookkeeping and start keeping the books, you must get a handle on some key accounting terms. The following sections include lists of terms that all bookkeepers use on a daily basis.

Note: These sections don't give you an exhaustive list of all the unique terms you need to know as a bookkeeper. For full coverage of bookkeeping terminology, turn to the glossary at the back of this book.

Accounts for the balance sheet

Here are a few terms you need to know to understand the common elements of all balance sheets:

✔ **Balance sheet:** The financial statement that presents a snapshot of the business's financial position (assets, liabilities, and equity) as of a particular date in time. It's called a *balance sheet* because the things owned by the business (assets) must equal the claims against those assets (liabilities and equity). Sometimes, accountants call this statement the Statement of Financial Position, which gives more emphasis to the fact that the amounts presented are a snapshot of a particular point in time.

On a proper balance sheet, the total assets should equal the total liabilities plus the total equity. If your numbers fit this formula, the business's books are in balance. (We discuss the balance sheet in greater detail in Chapter 18.)

✔ **Assets:** All the things a business owns in order to successfully run, such as cash, accounts receivable, inventory, buildings, land, tools, equipment, vehicles, and furniture.

✔ **Liabilities:** All the debts the business owes, such as bank loans, credit card balances, and unpaid bills.

✔ **Equity:** All the money invested in the business by its owners. In a small business owned by one person, the owner's equity appears in a single Capital account named after the owner. In a partnership, you need several Capital accounts — one for each partner. In a larger business that's incorporated, owners' equity appears in shares of stock usually referred to as common shares. Another key Equity account is *Retained Earnings,* which tracks all the profits, net of any losses that the owners of the business have chosen to reinvest into the business, instead of paying out equity to the business's shareholders. Small unincorporated businesses track money paid out to owners in Drawings accounts, whereas incorporated businesses dole out money to owners by paying *dividends* (a portion of the business's profits paid by common share for the quarter or year).

Accounts for the income statement or Statement of Earnings

Here are a few terms related to the income statement that you should know:

- ✓ **Income statement:** The financial statement that presents a summary of the business's financial activity over a certain period of time, such as a month, quarter, or year. The statement starts with revenue earned, subtracts out the costs of goods sold and the expenses, and ends with the bottom line — net profit or loss. This end result is where most people get the short term *P&L* for this statement. P&L stands for "profit and loss." (We show you how to develop an income statement in Chapter 19.)

- ✓ **Revenue:** All money collected in the process of selling the business's goods and services. Those who are in the business of selling goods generally use the term *sales*. Besides providing a good or service, some businesses also collect revenue through other means, such as collecting rent or earning interest by offering short-term loans to other businesses. (We discuss how to track revenue in Chapter 9.)

- ✓ **Costs of goods sold:** All money spent to purchase or make the goods or services that a business plans to sell to its customers. (We talk about purchasing goods for sale to customers in Chapter 8.)

- ✓ **Expenses:** All money spent to operate the business that's not directly related to the sale of individual goods or services. (We review common types of expenses in Chapter 3.)

- ✓ **Gains and losses**: Certain transactions are recorded as gains and losses rather than revenues and expenses to indicate they did not result from the main activities of the business. Selling assets that the business no longer needs is an example of this type of transaction.

Other common terms

Some other common bookkeeping terms include the following:

- ✓ **Accounting period:** The time during which you track financial information. Most businesses track their financial results on a monthly basis, so each accounting period equals one month. Some businesses choose to do financial reports on a quarterly basis, so the accounting periods are three months in length. Other businesses look at their results only on a yearly basis, so their accounting periods are 12 months long. Businesses that track their financial activities monthly usually also create quarterly and *annual reports* (a year-end summary of the business's activities and financial results) based on the information they gather.

✔ **Accounts Receivable:** The account used to track all customer sales that are made on credit (or on account). The terms *credit sales* and *sales on account* do not refer to credit card sales. Customers establish credit with the business directly and promise to pay for their purchases at an agreed-upon later date. (We discuss how to monitor Accounts Receivable in Chapter 9.)

✔ **Accounts Payable:** The account used to track all outstanding bills from vendors or suppliers, contractors, consultants, and any other companies or individuals from whom the business buys goods or services on credit. (We talk about managing Accounts Payable in Chapter 8.)

✔ **Depreciation:** An accounting method used to track the aging and use of property, plant, and equipment assets. Accountants use the term *property, plant, and equipment* for a category of assets that the business finds useful for more than one year. For example, if you own a car, you know that each year you use the car, its book value is reduced. Every major asset a business owns ages, gets used up, and eventually needs to be replaced, including buildings, factories, equipment, and other key assets. (We discuss how you monitor depreciation in Chapter 12.)

✔ **General Ledger:** Where all the business's accounts are summarized. The General Ledger is the granddaddy of the bookkeeping system. (We discuss posting to the General Ledger in Chapter 4.)

✔ **Interest:** The money that a business needs to pay if it borrows money from a bank or other business, in addition to the original sum borrowed. For example, when you buy a car by using a car loan, you must pay not only the amount you borrowed but also additional money (interest) based on a percent of the amount you borrowed and have not yet repaid. (We discuss how to track interest expenses in a business's books in Chapter 13.)

✔ **Inventory:** The account that tracks all products that you plan to sell to customers. (We review inventory valuation and control in Chapter 8.)

✔ **Journals:** Where bookkeepers keep records (in chronological order) of daily business transactions. Each of the most active accounts — including Cash, Accounts Payable, and Accounts Receivable — has its own journal. (We discuss entering information into journals in Chapter 5.)

✔ **Payroll:** The way a business pays its employees. Managing payroll is a key function of the bookkeeper and involves reporting many aspects of payroll to the government, including taxes and benefits to be paid on behalf of the employee for Canada Pension Plan, Employment Insurance, and worker's compensation premiums. (We discuss employee payroll in Chapter 10, and the government side of payroll reporting in Chapter 11.)

✔ **Trial balance:** How you determine whether the books are in balance before you pull together information for the financial reports and close the books for the accounting period. (We discuss how to do a trial balance in Chapter 16.)

Pedalling through the Accounting Cycle

As a bookkeeper, you do your work by completing the tasks of the accounting cycle. It's called a cycle because the workflow is circular: entering transactions, adjusting the account balances, closing the books at the end of the accounting year, and then starting the entire cycle again for the next accounting cycle.

The accounting cycle has eight basic steps, which you can see in Figure 2-1.

The Accounting Cycle

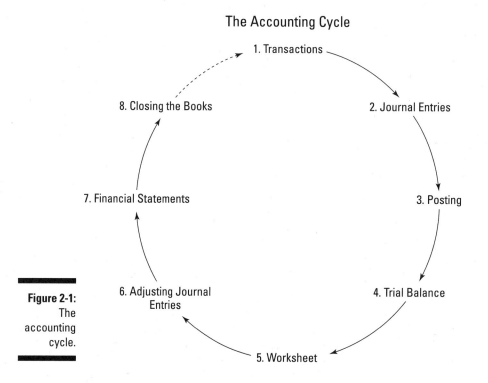

Figure 2-1:
The
accounting
cycle.

Here's a breakdown of each step in this cycle:

1. **Transactions:** Financial transactions start the process. Transactions can include the sale or return of a product, the purchase of supplies for business activities, or any other financial activity that involves the exchange of the business's assets, the establishment or payoff of a debt, or the deposit from or payout of money to the business's owners. All sales and expenses are transactions that you must record. We cover transactions

in greater detail throughout the book while we discuss how to record the basics of business activities — recording sales of inventory, purchases of inventory or other assets, taking on new debt, or paying off debt.

2. **Journal entries:** You list the transaction in the appropriate journal, maintaining the journal's chronological order of transactions. (Accountants also call the journal the book of original entry, and it's the first place you record a transaction.) We talk more about journal entries in Chapter 5.

3. **Posting:** You post each transaction to the account that is affected by the transaction. These accounts are part of the General Ledger, where you can find a summary of all the business's accounts. We discuss posting in Chapters 4 and 5.

4. **Trial balance:** At the end of the accounting period (which may be a month, quarter, or year, depending on your business's practices), you prepare a trial balance from the General Ledger. (Your accounting software may produce this trial balance automatically.)

5. **Worksheet:** Unfortunately, if you are preparing a trial balance manually, your first result may show that the books aren't in balance. If that's the case, you must first look for errors and make any necessary corrections. After your trial balance is in balance, you need to record additional transactions called *adjustments,* which you can track on a worksheet. (You can skip using a worksheet if only a few adjusting entries are needed.) You make adjustments directly to the accounts affected in the General Ledger. Typical adjustments include recording the depreciation of assets and adjusting for one-time payments (such as insurance) at the end of an accounting cycle. These adjustments are needed to more accurately match monthly expenses with monthly revenues. You may also make adjustments to record revenues that the business has earned by providing services for which the business hasn't yet billed customers. After you make and record adjustments, you take another trial balance to make sure the accounts remain in balance. (Some bookkeepers and accountants feel that this last step can be optional if you record the adjusting journal entries directly into the General Ledger.)

6. **Adjusting journal entries:** Some bookkeepers find using a worksheet is a good way of coming up with all the necessary corrections and adjustments to the trial balance. You don't need to record the adjusting entries into the General Ledger until you have arrived at the adjusted trial balance on the worksheet. If, on the other hand, you opted to skip using a worksheet, you need to post your adjusting journal entries directly into the General Ledger.

7. **Financial statements:** You prepare the balance sheet and income statement by using the corrected General Ledger account balances.

8. **Closing:** You close the books for the Revenue, Expense, and Drawings accounts, and then begin the entire cycle again with zero balances in those last three types of accounts.

As a businessperson, you want to be able to gauge your profit or loss on month-by-month, quarter-by-quarter, and year-by-year bases. Revenue, Expense, and Drawings accounts must start with zero balances at the beginning of each year. In contrast, you carry over Asset, Liability, and Equity account balances from year to year because the business doesn't start with nothing at the beginning of each year. Assets, Liabilities, and Equity account balances carry forward and continue into the next year. Accounts receivable get collected, outstanding bills and debt get paid, and so on. You carry forward the balances of these three types of accounts from year to year until you sell the business or wind it up.

Exploring Cash and Accrual Accounting

Small businesses often run their operations on a *cash basis,* meaning they never buy or sell on credit (often referred to as *on account*). Some owners essentially measure their financial performance based on how much money they have in the bank account. Although cash basis provides a very simple business model, it doesn't take long before it isn't practical. The other danger is that not all transactions are taken into account. When the business starts to send out invoices on account, or when it starts to deal with suppliers on credit, you need to adopt accrual accounting. In the following sections, we look at both methods.

Cash-basis accounting

With *cash-basis accounting,* you record all transactions in the books when cash actually changes hands, meaning when the business receives cash payment from customers or pays out cash for purchases or other services. Cash receipt or payment can be in the form of cash, cheque, credit card, debit card, electronic fund payments, or other means used to pay for an item.

You can't use cash-basis accounting if your store sells products on account and bills the customer, who then pays at a later date. The cash-basis accounting method has no means to record and track money due from customers.

With the cash-basis accounting method, the business records the purchase of supplies or goods that you plan to sell only when you actually pay cash for those supplies or goods. If you buy goods on credit, which you plan to pay later, you don't record the transaction until you actually pay out the cash.

Although cash-basis accounting is easy, the Canada Revenue Agency (CRA) doesn't like it, allowing only certain select businesses to use it for reporting taxable income. Businesses involved in farming and the fishing industries can report income on a cash basis. The rest of the businesses must follow the accrual accounting method.

Cash-basis accounting does a good job of tracking cash flow, but it does a poor job of matching revenues earned with expenses incurred. You may find this deficiency a problem if, as it often happens, your business buys products in one month and sells those products in the next month. For example, you buy products in June with the intent to sell, and you pay $1,000 cash for those products. You don't sell the products until July, and that's when you receive cash for the sales. When you close the books at the end of June, you have to show the $1,000 expense with no revenue to offset it, meaning you have a loss that month. When you sell the products for $1,500 in July, you have a $1,500 profit. So, your monthly report for June shows a $1,000 loss, and your monthly report for July shows a $1,500 profit, when in actuality, you had net revenues of $500 over the two-month period.

In this book, we concentrate on the accrual accounting method. If you choose to use cash-basis accounting, don't panic: You can still find most of the book-keeping information in here useful, but you don't need to maintain some of the accounts we list, such as Accounts Receivable and Accounts Payable, because you don't record transactions until cash actually changes hands. If you're using a cash-basis accounting system and sell things on credit, though, you need to have a way to track what people owe you — particularly for tax-reporting purposes.

Recording by using accrual accounting

With *accrual accounting,* you record all transactions in the books when those transactions occur, even if no cash changes hands. For example, if you sell on account, you record the transaction immediately and enter it into an Accounts Receivable account until you receive payment. If you buy goods on account, you immediately enter the transaction into an Accounts Payable account until you pay out cash.

Accrual accounting is based on the *generally accepted accounting principles* (GAAP), the authoritative standards and rules that govern financial account-ing and financial reporting. We don't go into all the technical jargon of the rules, but we need to point out that GAAP is very important to businesses, and users of financial information such as lenders and CRA. Businesses that are incorporated and intend to have their shares traded on a stock market (such as the Toronto Stock Exchange (TSX)) must follow the GAAP rules based on the International Financial Reporting Standards (IFRS) and have their financial statements audited every year. The GAAP for all businesses, not just public companies, maintain that accrual accounting presents a fairer picture of the financial performance of a business than cash-basis account-ing. (Refer to the preceding section for a look at the problems that crop up when you use cash-basis accounting.)

Like cash-basis accounting, accrual accounting has its drawbacks. It does a good job of matching revenues and expenses within the same accounting period, but it does a poor job of getting you to pay attention to cash. Because you record revenue when the transaction occurs and not when you collect the cash, your attention may be diverted from the all-important cash collection. If your customers are slow to pay, you may end up with a lot of revenue and little cash. But don't worry just yet; in Chapter 9, we tell you how to manage Accounts Receivable so that you don't run out of cash because of slow-paying customers.

Many businesses that use the accrual accounting method monitor cash flow on a weekly basis to be sure that they have enough cash on hand to operate the business. If your business is seasonal, such as a landscaping business that has little to do during the winter months, you can establish short-term lines of credit through your bank to maintain cash flow through the lean times.

Seeing Double with Double-Entry Bookkeeping

All businesses use double-entry bookkeeping to keep their books. A practice that helps minimize errors and increases the chance that your books bal-ance, *double-entry bookkeeping* gets its name because you enter all transac-tions with two sides, using a minimum of two accounts.

When it comes to double-entry bookkeeping, the key formula for the balance sheet (Assets = Liabilities + Equity) plays a major role. Accountants call this formula the *accounting equation*.

In order to adjust the balance of accounts in the bookkeeping world, you use a combination of debits and credits. You may think of a *debit* as a subtraction because debits usually mean a decrease in your bank balance. On the other hand, you've probably been excited to find unexpected *credits* in your bank account or on your credit card, which mean you've received more money in the account. Now, forget all that you've ever heard about debits or credits. In the world of bookkeeping, their meanings aren't so simple.

The only definite thing when it comes to debits and credits in the bookkeeping world is that a debit is on the left side of a transaction and a credit is on the right side of a transaction. Everything beyond that can get very muddled. We show you the basics of debits and credits in this chapter, but don't worry if you're finding this concept very difficult to grasp. You get plenty of practice in using these concepts throughout this book.

Before we get into all the technical mumbo jumbo of double-entry bookkeeping, here's an example of the practice in action. Suppose you purchase a new desk that costs $1,500 for your office. This transaction actually has two parts: You spend an asset — cash — to buy another asset — furniture. So, you must adjust two accounts in your business's books: the Cash account and the Furniture account. Here's what the transaction looks like in a bookkeeping entry (we talk more about how to do initial bookkeeping entries in Chapter 4):

Account	Debit	Credit
Furniture	$1,500	
Cash		$1,500

To purchase a new desk for the office with cash.

Handwritten note:
- Cash is an asset acct; bc it was decreased, this is a credit.
- furniture is an asset acct too.

In this transaction, you record tohe accounts affected by the transaction. The debit increases the amount of the Furniture account, and the credit decreases the amount in the Cash account. For this transaction, both affected accounts are asset accounts, so if you look at how the balance sheet is affected, you can see that the only changes are to the asset side of the balance sheet equation:

Assets = Liabilities + Equity

Furniture increase = No change to this side of the equation

Cash decrease

In this case, the books stay in balance because the exact dollar amount that increases the amount of your Furniture account decreases the amount of your Cash account. At the bottom of any journal entry, you should include a brief explanation of the purpose for the entry. In the first example, we indicate this entry was "To purchase a new desk for the office with cash."

To show you how to record a transaction if it affects both sides of the balance sheet equation, here's an example that shows how to record the purchase of inventory on account. Suppose that you purchase $5,000 worth of widgets on credit. (Haven't you always wondered what widgets are? We can't help you there. They're just commonly used in accounting examples to represent something that's purchased and sold.) These new widgets add more costs to your Inventory asset account and also add to your obligations in your Accounts

Payable account. (Remember, the Accounts Payable account is a Liability account in which you track bills that you need to pay at some point in the future.) Here's how the bookkeeping transaction for your widget purchase looks:

Account	Debit	Credit
Inventory	$5,000	
Accounts Payable		$5,000

Asset → Inventory
Liability → Accounts Payable

Purchase on account widgets for sale to customers.

Here's how this transaction affects the balance sheet equation:

Assets = Liabilities + Equity

Inventory increases = Accounts Payable increases + No change

In this case, the books stay in balance because both sides of the accounting equation increase by $5,000.

You can see from the two preceding example transactions how double-entry bookkeeping helps to keep your books in balance — as long as you make sure each entry into the books is balanced. Balancing your entries may look simple here, but sometimes bookkeeping entries can get very complex when the transaction affects more than two accounts.

Don't worry; you don't have to understand it totally now. We show you how to enter transactions throughout the book, depending on the type of transaction that you're recording. We're just giving you a quick overview to introduce the subject right now.

Double-entry bookkeeping goes way back

No one's really sure who invented double-entry bookkeeping. The first person to put the practice on paper was Benedetto Cotrugli in 1458, but mathematician and Franciscan monk Luca Pacioli is most often credited with developing double-entry bookkeeping. Although Pacioli's called the "father of accounting," accounting actually occupies only one of five sections of his book *Everything About Arithmetic, Geometry and Proportions,* which was published in 1494. Pacioli didn't actually *invent* double-entry bookkeeping; he just described the method used by merchants in Venice during the Italian Renaissance period. He's most famous for his warning to bookkeepers: "A person should not go to sleep at night until the debits equalled the credits!"

Differentiating Debits and Credits

Because bookkeeping's debits and credits are different than the ones you're used to encountering in everyday life, you're probably wondering how you're supposed to know whether a debit or credit will increase or decrease an account. Believe it or not, identifying the difference becomes second nature when you start making regular entries in your bookkeeping system. But to make things easier for you, Table 2-1 gives you a chart that's commonly used by all bookkeepers and accountants. Yep, everyone needs help sometimes.

Table 2-1	How Credits and Debits Affect Your Accounts	
Account Type	**Debits**	**Credits**
Assets	Increase	Decrease
Liabilities	Decrease	Increase
Equity	Decrease	Increase
Drawings	Increase	Decrease
Revenue	Decrease	Increase
Expenses	Increase	Decrease

Copy Table 2-1 and post it on an index card at your desk when you start keeping your own books. We guarantee it can help you keep your debits and credits straight.

Assets = Liabilities + Equity.

Acct	Dr	Cr
Inventory	—	
Cash (RBCchq)		—

Chapter 3

Outlining Your Financial Roadmap with a Chart of Accounts

In This Chapter

▶ Introducing the Chart of Accounts

▶ Breaking down the balance sheet accounts

▶ Examining the income statement accounts

▶ Creating your own Chart of Accounts

Can you imagine the mess your personal records would be if you didn't keep track of each electronic bill payment you made, cash withdrawal made at an ATM, or each cheque you wrote? Like us, you've probably lost track, but you certainly learn your lesson when you realize that an important payment bounces as a result. Yikes!

Keeping the books of a business can be a lot more difficult than maintaining a personal chequebook. You must carefully record each business transaction to make sure that it goes into the right account. This careful bookkeeping gives you an effective tool for figuring out how well the business is doing financially.

As a bookkeeper, you need a roadmap to help you determine where to record the effect of all those transactions. This roadmap is called the Chart of Accounts. In this chapter, we tell you how to set up the Chart of Accounts, which includes many different accounts. We also review the types of transactions you enter into each type of account in order to track the key parts of any business — assets, liabilities, equity, revenue, and expenses.

Getting to Know the Chart of Accounts

The *Chart of Accounts* is the roadmap that a business creates to organize its financial transactions. After all, you can't record a transaction until you know where to put it! Essentially, this chart is a list of all the accounts a business has, organized in a specific order. Each account has a description that includes the type of account and the types of transactions that should be entered into that account. Every business creates its own Chart of Accounts based on how the business is operated, so you're unlikely to find two businesses with the exact same Chart of Accounts.

However, some basic organizational and structural characteristics are common to all Charts of Accounts. The organization and structure are designed around two key financial statements: the *balance sheet,* which shows what your business owns and what it owes, and the *income statement,* which shows how much money your business took in from sales and revenue, and how much money it spent on expenses to generate those sales. (You can find out more about balance sheets in Chapter 18 and income statements in Chapter 19.)

The Chart of Accounts starts first with the balance sheet accounts, which include

- **Current Assets:** All accounts that track things the business owns and expects to use in the next 12 months, such as cash, accounts receivable (money not yet collected from customers), and inventory.

- **Long-Term Assets:** All accounts that track things the business owns that have a lifespan or usefulness to the business of more than 12 months, such as buildings, furniture, equipment, intangible assets, or long-term investments.

- **Current Liabilities:** All accounts that track debts the business must pay over the next 12 months, such as accounts payable (bills from vendors and suppliers, contractors, and consultants), interest payable, credit cards payable, and any amounts owing from payroll transactions, such as amounts taken off employees' pay for income taxes.

- **Long-Term Liabilities:** All accounts that track debts the business must pay over a period of time longer than the next 12 months, such as mortgages payable and long-term bank loans.

- **Equity:** All accounts that track the owners' transactions directly with the business and their claims against the business's assets, which include any money invested in the business, any money taken out of the business, and any earnings that the owners have reinvested in the business.

Income statement accounts, which include the following, fill the rest of the chart:

- ✔ **Revenues:** All accounts that track sales of goods and services, as well as revenue generated for the business by other means, such as lending money.

- ✔ **Cost of Goods Sold:** All accounts that track the direct costs of goods the business has sold (only used by businesses selling goods).

- ✔ **Expenses:** All accounts that track expenses related to running the business that aren't directly tied to the sale of individual products or services.

When developing the Chart of Accounts, start by listing all the Asset accounts, the Liability accounts, the Equity accounts, the Drawings accounts (if applicable for unincorporated businesses), the Revenue accounts, and finally, the Expense accounts. All these accounts come from two places: the balance sheet and the income statement.

In this chapter, we review the key account types found in most businesses, but this list isn't cast in stone. You need to develop an account list that makes the most sense for operating your business and giving you the financial information you want to track. While we explore the various accounts that make up the Chart of Accounts in this chapter, we point out how the structure may differ for different types of businesses.

The Chart of Accounts is a money-management tool that helps you track your business transactions, so set it up in a way that provides you with the financial information you need to make smart business decisions. You'll probably end up tweaking the accounts in your chart annually, and you may add accounts during the year if you find something for which you want more detailed tracking. We discuss adding and eliminating accounts from your books in Chapter 17.

Starting with the Balance Sheet Accounts

The first part of the Chart of Accounts is made up of balance sheet accounts, which break down into the following three categories:

- ✔ **Asset:** These accounts track what the business owns. Assets include cash on hand, inventory, furniture, buildings, vehicles, and so on.

- ✔ **Liability:** These accounts track what the business owes, or more specifically, the claims that lenders have against the business's assets. For example, mortgages on buildings and lines of credit with the bank are two common types of liabilities.

✔ **Equity:** These accounts track what the owners put into the business and the claims that the owners have against the business's assets. For example, shareholders are business owners who have claims against the business's assets.

The balance sheet accounts, and the financial report they make up, are so called because they have to *balance* out. The reported book value of the assets must be equal to the claims made against those assets. (Remember, these claims are liabilities made by lenders and equity belonging to owners.)

We discuss the balance sheet in greater detail in Chapter 18, including how you prepare and use it. The following sections, however, examine the basic components of the balance sheet, as reflected in the Chart of Accounts.

Tackling assets

First on the chart are always the accounts that track what the business owns — its assets. The two types of Asset accounts are Current Assets and Long-Term Assets.

Current assets

Current assets are the key assets that your business uses up during a 12-month period, so those assets likely won't be available the next year — or, at least, will be replaced by new assets by that time. The accounts that reflect current assets on the Chart of Accounts are

✔ **Cash in Chequing:** Any business's primary account is the chequing account used for operating activities, to deposit revenues collected, and to pay expenses and debt. Some businesses have more than one operating account in this category; for example, a business that has many divisions or locations may have an operating account for each division or location.

✔ **Cash in Savings:** This account is used for surplus cash. Any cash for which the business has no immediate plan is deposited in an interest-earning savings account so that it can at least earn interest while the business decides what to do with it.

✔ **Cash on Hand:** This account tracks any cash kept at retail stores or in the office. In retail stores, cash must be kept as floats in registers in order to provide change to customers (see Chapter 7). In the office, businesses often keep petty cash around for immediate cash needs that pop up from time to time. The Cash on Hand account helps you keep track of the cash held by the business outside a bank.

✔ **Accounts Receivable:** If you offer your products or services to customers on account (meaning on *your* credit system), then you need this account to track the customers who buy on your dime.

You don't use Accounts Receivable to track purchases made by customers on bank credit cards because in that case your business gets paid directly by the banks, not by the customers. Refer to Chapter 9 to read more about this scenario and the corresponding type of account.

✔ **Inventory:** This account tracks the cost of products that you have on hand to sell to your customers. The cost of the assets in this account varies, depending on the cost formula you decide to use to track the flow of inventory into and out of the business. We discuss inventory valuation and tracking in greater detail in Chapter 8.

✔ **Prepaid Insurance:** This account tracks insurance you paid earlier in the year in advance. Later on, you reduce the prepaid insurance each month with a credit to show that month's insurance coverage as an insurance expense because the portion of the asset has been used up.

Depending on the type of business you're setting up, you may have other Current Asset accounts that you decide to track. For example, if you're starting a service business, you may want to have a Supplies account.

Long-term assets

Long-term assets are assets that your business plans to use for more than 12 months. This list includes some of the most common long-term assets, starting with the key accounts related to buildings and factories owned by the business:

✔ **Land:** This account tracks the land owned by the business. The value of the land is based on the cost of purchasing it. Land value is tracked separately from the value of any buildings standing on that land because land doesn't depreciate in the books, but buildings do. *Depreciation* is an accounting method that shows an asset is being used up. We talk more about depreciation in Chapter 12.

✔ **Buildings:** This account tracks the value of any buildings that a business owns. Like with land, the value of the building is based on the cost of purchasing it. The key difference between buildings and land is that the accountant depreciates the building.

✔ **Accumulated Depreciation — Buildings:** This account tracks the cumulative amount the accountant has recorded as depreciation for a building over its useful lifespan. We talk more about how to calculate depreciation in Chapter 12.

✓ **Leasehold Improvements:** This account tracks the value of long-lasting improvements made to buildings or other facilities that a business leases, rather than purchases. Frequently, when a business leases a property, the business must pay for any improvements necessary in order to use that property the way the business needs to use it. For example, if a business leases a store in a strip mall, the space leased is probably either an empty shell or filled with shelving and other items that may not match the particular needs of the business. Like with buildings, the accountant depreciates leasehold improvements while the asset gets used up.

✓ **Accumulated Depreciation — Leasehold Improvements:** This account tracks the cumulative amount the accountant depreciates leasehold improvements.

Your business may also have extra cash that it invests in the shares of other businesses, in long-term investments in land, or in other types of assets that may earn some interest income. If your business intends to hold these assets for long periods of time, as part of the required classification of accounts inside your balance sheet, you need to add another title and sub-total for long-term investments. You also need to create and track additional accounts in the General Ledger.

The following list includes the types of accounts for small long-term assets, such as vehicles and furniture:

✓ **Vehicles:** This account tracks any cars, trucks, or other vehicles owned by the business. You list the initial book value of any vehicle in this account based on the total cost paid to put the vehicle in service. Sometimes, this book value can become greater than the purchase price if you need to make alterations or additions to make the vehicle usable for your particular type of business. For example, if a business provides transportation for people living with disabilities and must add additional equipment to a vehicle in order to serve the needs of its customers, the business adds that additional equipment cost to the book value of the vehicle. Vehicles depreciate through their useful lifespan.

✓ **Accumulated Depreciation — Vehicles:** This account tracks the depreciation of all vehicles owned by the business.

✓ **Furniture and Fixtures:** This account tracks any furniture or fixtures purchased for use in the business. The account includes the value of all chairs, desks, store fixtures, and shelving needed to operate the business. You base the value of the furniture and fixtures in this account on the cost of purchasing these items. These items depreciate during their useful lifespan.

✔ **Accumulated Depreciation — Furniture and Fixtures:** This account tracks the accumulated depreciation of all furniture and fixtures.

✔ **Equipment:** This account tracks equipment that you purchase for use for more than one year, such as computers, copiers, tools, and cash registers. You base the value of the equipment on the cost to purchase these items. Equipment also depreciates to show that over time, the asset reaches the point where you must replace it.

✔ **Accumulated Depreciation — Equipment:** This account tracks the accumulated depreciation of all the equipment.

The following accounts track the long-term assets that you can't touch but that still represent things of value owned and used by the business, such as patents and copyrights. These assets are called *intangible assets,* and the accounts that track them include

✔ **Patents:** This account tracks the costs associated with *patents,* which are grants made by governments that guarantee to the inventor or the owner of the patent of a product or process the exclusive right to make, use, and sell that product or process over a set period of time. Patent costs are amortized (see Chapter 12). You base the value of this asset on the expenses that the business incurs to get the right to patent the product or the cost of purchasing that patent.

✔ **Amortization — Patents:** This account tracks the accumulated amortization of a business's patents. Amortization is very much like depreciation, but it is a term that is used for intangible assets while depreciation is typically used for tangible, depreciable long-term assets.

✔ **Copyrights:** This account tracks the costs incurred to establish *copyrights,* the legal rights given to an author, playwright, publisher, or any other distributor of a publication or production for a unique work of literature, music, drama, or art. This legal right expires after a set number of years, so amortization is recorded only up until the business reaches that limit or when a choice is made to stop using the copyright, whichever comes first.

✔ **Goodwill:** You need this account only if your business buys another business for more than the fair value of its *net assets* (assets minus liabilities). Goodwill reflects the intangible value of this purchase for assets not on the balance sheet of the seller, such as business reputation, store locations, customer base, and other items that increase the value of the business bought as a going concern.

If you hold a lot of assets that don't fit within the categories we list in this section, you can also set up an Other Assets account to track those assets. While time goes by, the purpose of owning a particular asset may change. For example, say you purchase some land with the intention of building a factory.

Before construction, economic changes cause you to revise your plans, and you now need to put the land up for sale. The asset may then rightfully belong to another asset category. If that happens, you can move that particular asset to the appropriate category or group. So, in this example, the land goes from the Land account classified under long-term assets to the Land Available for Sale account because the land has become an investment. Your change in the intended use of the asset may mean that you need to add another account to your Chart of Accounts to accommodate this change. We discuss adjusting the Chart of Accounts in Chapter 17.

Laying out your liabilities

After you cover assets, the next stop on the bookkeeping highway is the accounts that track what your business owes to others. These others can include vendors and suppliers from whom you buy products or supplies on account, banks from which you borrow money, and anyone else who lends money to your business or to whom the business needs to make a payment to settle an obligation, such as credit card companies, employees, or the Canada Revenue Agency (CRA). Like assets, you lump liabilities into two types: current liabilities and long-term liabilities (sometimes also called *long-term debt*).

Current liabilities

Current liabilities are debts due to be paid in the next 12 months. Some of the most common types of Current Liabilities accounts that appear on the Chart of Accounts are

- ✔ **Accounts Payable:** This account tracks money owed that the business must pay in less than a year to vendors, contractors, suppliers, and consultants. The business must pay most of these liabilities in 30 to 60 days from the date of their invoices, depending on the terms you have negotiated.

- ✔ **Goods and Services Tax Payable and Retail Taxes Payable:** You may not think of goods and services tax or harmonized sales tax (GST/HST) and provincial sales tax (PST) as liabilities. But because your business collects taxes from your customers and doesn't pay those taxes immediately to the government entities, the taxes collected become a liability tracked in these accounts. A business usually charges the sales tax throughout the month, and then pays the tax to the appropriate provincial or federal government on a monthly basis. We discuss paying GST/HST and PST in greater detail in Chapters 5 and 21.

✔ **Accrued Payroll Taxes:** This account tracks payroll taxes collected from employees to pay combined federal and provincial income taxes, as well as Canada Pension Plan (CPP) and Employment Insurance (EI) contributions. Businesses don't have to pay these taxes to the government entities immediately, so depending on the size of the payroll, businesses may pay payroll taxes on a monthly or quarterly basis. We discuss how to handle payroll taxes in Chapter 10.

✔ **Credit Cards Payable:** This account tracks all accounts with credit card companies to which the business owes money. Most businesses use credit cards as short-term debt and pay off the balance owed completely at the end of each month. Some smaller businesses carry credit card balances over a longer period of time. Because credit cards often have a much higher interest rate than lines of credit, most businesses transfer any credit card debt that they can't pay entirely at the end of a month to a line of credit at a bank. When it comes to your Chart of Accounts, you can set up one Credit Card Payable account, but you may want to set up a separate account for each card your business holds to improve your ability to track credit card usage.

How you set up your current liabilities and how many individual accounts you establish depends on how detailed you want to make each type of liability tracking. For example, you can set up separate current liability accounts for major vendors if that approach provides you with a better money-management tool. Suppose that a small hardware retail store buys most of the tools it sells from Snap-On Tools. To keep better control of its purchases from Snap-On Tools, the bookkeeper sets up a specific account called Accounts Payable — Snap-On Tools, which she uses for tracking invoices and payments to that vendor only. In this example, the bookkeeper tracks all other invoices and payments to other vendors and suppliers in the general Accounts Payable account.

Long-term liabilities

Long-term liabilities are debts due in more than 12 months. The number of long-term liability accounts you maintain on your Chart of Accounts depends on your debt structure. The two most common types of long-term liability accounts are

✔ **Loans Payable:** This account tracks any long-term loans, such as a mortgage on your business building. Most businesses have separate Loans Payable accounts for each of their long-term loans. For example, you could have Loans Payable — Mortgage for your building and Loans Payable — Car for your vehicle loan.

✔ **Notes Payable:** Some businesses borrow money from other businesses using *promissory notes,* a method of borrowing that doesn't require the business to put up an asset as collateral, which you need to do with a mortgage on a building. The promissory note documents a formal promise to repay the loan, plus interest, at a specified future date. The Notes Payable account tracks any notes due.

Eyeing the equity

Every business is owned by somebody. *Equity accounts* track owners' contributions to the business, as well as their share of ownership. For a corporation, you track ownership by the sale of individual shares because each shareholder owns a portion of the business. In smaller businesses that are owned by one person or a group of people, you track equity by using Capital and Drawings accounts. Here are the basic Equity accounts that appear in the Chart of Accounts:

✔ **Common Shares:** This account reflects the book value of outstanding shares sold to investors. The amount in this account corresponds to the amount paid by the original investors. Only corporations need to establish this account. If an original investor resells his shares to another investor, that transaction does not affect the recorded value in the Common Shares account of the corporation.

✔ **Retained Earnings:** This account, exclusive to corporations, tracks the profits or losses accumulated since a business opened. At the end of each year, the profit or loss calculated on the income statement is closed to this account. For example, if your business made a $100,000 profit in the past year, you increase the Retained Earnings account by that amount; if the business lost $100,000, then you subtract that amount from this account.

✔ **Capital:** Only unincorporated businesses need this account. The Capital account reflects the amount of initial money the business owner contributed to the business, as well as owner contributions made after initial start-up. You base the book value of this account on cash contributions and other assets contributed by the business owner, such as equipment, vehicles, or buildings invested at their fair market value. If a small business has several different partners, then each partner gets her own Capital account to track her contributions. Similar to Retained Earnings, the Capital account increases for profits and decreases for any losses accumulated since the business opened.

✔ **Drawings:** Only businesses that aren't incorporated need this account. The Drawings account tracks any money or other assets that a business owner takes out of the business. If the business has several partners, each partner gets his own Drawings account to track what he takes out of the business.

Drawings by an owner are not a salary. Owners often make the mistake of thinking that the cash they draw from their business is the amount on which they have to pay income taxes. Not so. The amount reported on the personal income tax return of the owner of an unincorporated business is the amount of the owner's share of profit of that business. We describe in more detail the reporting of income to CRA in Chapter 21.

Tracking the Income Statement Accounts

Two types of accounts make up the income statement:

- ✔ **Revenues:** These accounts track all money coming into the business, including sales, services rendered, rents, dividends from investments, interest earned on savings, and any other methods used to generate income.

- ✔ **Expenses:** These accounts track all money that a business spends in order to earn revenues. You include in expenses the depreciation that doesn't directly involve cash spent during the year.

The bottom line of the income statement shows whether your business made a profit or suffered a loss for a specified period of time. We discuss how to prepare and use an income statement in greater detail in Chapter 19.

The following sections examine the various accounts that make up the income statement portion of the Chart of Accounts.

Recording the money you make

First up in the income statement portion of the Chart of Accounts are accounts that track revenue. If you choose to offer discounts, accept returns, or possibly grant allowances, that activity also falls within the revenue group. The most common income accounts are

- ✔ **Sales and Service Revenue:** These accounts, which appear at the top of every income statement, track all the money that the business earns by selling its products, services, or both.

- ✔ **Sales Discounts:** Because most businesses offer discounts to encourage quick payments, this account tracks any reductions to the full price of merchandise.

- ✔ **Volume Discounts:** This account keeps track of reductions in your selling price to foster relationships with key customers or to encourage large orders from your customers. Some computer software packages don't keep track of volume discounts.

✔ **Sales Returns and Allowances:** This account tracks transactions related to *returns* — when customers bring products back to your business because they're unhappy with them for some reason — and *allowances* — which are reductions to the price of goods that you make because of defects in the products. With allowances, the customer doesn't return the goods.

When you examine an income statement from a business other than the one you own or are working for, you usually see the following accounts summarized as one line item called Revenue or Net Revenue. Because sales of products or services don't generate all income, other income accounts that may appear on a Chart of Accounts include

✔ **Other Income:** If a business takes in income from a source other than its primary business activity, you record that income in this account. For example, a business that encourages recycling and earns income from the items recycled records that income in this account.

✔ **Interest Income:** This account tracks any income earned by collecting interest on a business's savings accounts, promissory notes receivable, or long-term investments. If the business loans money to another business and earns interest on that money, you record that interest in this account, as well.

✔ **Rent Revenue:** Occasionally, a business may have extra office or warehouse space that it rents out to tenants. Although this source of cash might not represent a large amount of revenue, you need to track it in its own account in your bookkeeping.

✔ **Gain or Loss on Sale of Fixed Assets:** Any time your business sells a fixed asset, such as a car or furniture, you record any gain or loss made from the sale in this account. A business should record only revenue remaining after subtracting the accumulated depreciation from the original cost of the asset. The CRA calculates and taxes these gains and losses in a different way from other revenues, so identifying what the amounts are every year is important.

Tracking the cost of sales

Of course, before you can sell a product, you must spend some money to either buy or make that product. The type of account used to track the money spent is called a Cost of Goods Sold account. The most common Cost of Goods Sold accounts are

- **Purchases:** This account tracks the purchases of all items you plan to sell.

- **Purchase Discount:** This account tracks the discounts you may receive from vendors if you pay for your purchase quickly. For example, a business may give you a 2 percent discount on your purchase if you pay the bill in 10 days, rather than wait until the end of the 30-day payment term originally negotiated.

- **Purchase Returns and Allowances:** If you're unhappy with a product you buy, record the cost of any items you return to the vendor in this account. You also use this account to record any *purchase allowances* — allowances given to you by the vendor as reductions in the purchase price you pay for defective goods that you're willing to keep.

- **Freight-In Charges:** You track any charges related to shipping items that you purchase for later sale in this account.

Acknowledging the money you spend

Expense accounts take the cake for the longest list of individual accounts. Any money you spend on the business that you can't tie directly to the sale of an individual product falls under the Expense account category. For example, advertising a storewide sale isn't directly tied to the sale of any one product, so the costs associated with advertising go into an Expense account.

The Chart of Accounts mirrors your business operations, so deciding how much detail you want to keep in your Expense accounts is up to you. Most businesses have expenses that are unique to their operations, so your list is probably longer than the one we present here. However, you may find that you don't need some of the accounts we suggest.

On your Chart of Accounts, the Expense accounts don't have to appear in any specific order, so we list them here alphabetically. The most common Expense accounts are

- **Advertising:** This account tracks all expenses involved in promoting a business or its products. You record money spent on newspaper, television, Internet, magazine, and radio advertising in this account, as well as any money spent to print flyers and mailings to customers.

- **Automotive Expenses:** This account tracks expenses related to the operation of business vehicles.

- **Bank Service Charges:** This account tracks any charges made by a bank to service a business's bank accounts.

✔ **Depreciation and Amortization:** These accounts track the cost of property, plant, and equipment, as well as intangible assets that the business uses.

✔ **Dues and Subscriptions:** This account tracks expenses related to memberships, professional associations, or subscriptions to magazines for the business.

✔ **Equipment Rental:** This account tracks expenses related to renting equipment for a short-term project. For example, a business that needs to rent a truck to pick up some new fixtures for its store records that truck rental cost in this account.

✔ **Interest:** This account tracks all the interest paid by the business on borrowed money.

✔ **Insurance:** This account tracks any money paid for insurance. Many businesses break insurance costs down into several accounts, such as Insurance — Casualty, which tracks the coverage for any damages to property, or Insurance — Officers' Life, which tracks money spent to buy insurance to protect the lives of key managers or officers of the business. Businesses often insure their key executives because an unexpected death, especially for a small business, may mean facing many expenses in order to keep the business's doors open. In such a case, you can use the insurance proceeds to cover those expenses.

✔ **Legal and Accounting:** This account tracks any money that a business pays for legal or accounting advice.

✔ **Maintenance and Repairs:** This account tracks any payments to keep the property, plant, and equipment, or the rented premises, in good working order.

✔ **Miscellaneous Expenses:** A catchall account for expenses that don't fit into one of a business's established accounts. If certain miscellaneous expenses occur frequently, a business may choose to add an account to the Chart of Accounts to better keep track of the particular expense. The bookkeeper then moves the related expenses into that new account by subtracting all related transactions from the Miscellaneous Expenses account and adding them to the new account. If you do this shuffle, you need to carefully balance out the adjusting transaction to prevent any errors or double counting.

✔ **Office Expense:** This account tracks the cost of items used to run an office. For example, office supplies (such as paper, pens, or business cards) fit in this account. As with the Miscellaneous Expenses, a business may choose to track some office expense items in their own accounts. For example, if your office uses a lot of copy paper and you want to track that separately, you set up a Copy Paper Expense account. Just be sure you really need the detail, because the number of accounts can get unwieldy and hard to manage.

✓ **Payroll Benefits:** This account tracks any payments for employee benefits, such as the employer's share of Canada Pension Plan (CPP), Employment Insurance (EI), and worker's compensation.

✓ **Postage and Delivery:** This account tracks any money spent on stamps, express package shipping, and other shipping. If a business does a large amount of shipping through vendors such as UPS or Purolator, it may want to track that spending in separate accounts for each vendor. This option is particularly helpful for small businesses that sell over the Internet or through catalogue sales. Don't confuse the delivery costs tracked here with the freight costs paid to purchase inventory for resale. We explain in the preceding section that freight-in costs get grouped with purchases to become Costs of Goods Sold.

✓ **Rent Expense:** This account tracks rental costs for a business's office, storage, or retail space.

✓ **Salaries and Wages:** This account tracks any money paid to employees as salary or wages. You may want a separate account to track vacation pay.

✓ **Supplies:** This account tracks any business supplies that don't fit into the category of office expenses. For example, you track supplies needed for the operation of retail stores, such as shopping bags, by using this account. You can also create separate Supplies accounts for services that your business provides. An example would be grease used by a business providing oil changes for vehicles.

✓ **Travel and Entertainment:** This account tracks money spent for business purposes on travel or entertainment. Some businesses separate these expenses into several accounts, such as Travel and Entertainment — Meals, Travel and Entertainment — Travel, and Travel and Entertainment — Entertainment, to keep a closer watch on these costs.

✓ **Telephone and Internet:** This account tracks all business expenses related to using telephones and the Internet.

✓ **Utilities:** This account tracks money paid for utilities, such as electricity, gas, and water.

Setting Up your Chart of Accounts

You can use the lists upon lists of accounts provided in this chapter to get started setting up your business's own Chart of Accounts. You don't need to know a secret method to make your own chart — just make a list of the accounts that apply to your business.

When first setting up your Chart of Accounts, don't panic if you can't think of every type of account you may need for your business. You can very easily add to the Chart of Accounts at any time. Just add the account to the list and distribute the revised list to any employees that use the Chart of Accounts for recording transactions into the bookkeeping system. (Even employees not involved in bookkeeping need a copy of your Chart of Accounts if they are responsible for telling the bookkeeper to which account transactions should be recorded.)

The Chart of Accounts usually includes at least three columns:

- **Account:** Lists the account names
- **Type:** Lists the types of accounts — Asset, Liability, Equity, Revenue, Cost of Goods Sold, or other Expenses
- **Description:** Contains a description of the type of transaction that you should record in the account

Many businesses also assign numbers to the accounts that you can use for coding charges. If your business is using a computerized system, the computer automatically assigns the account number. Otherwise, you need to plan out your own numbering system. The most common number system is

- **Asset accounts:** 1,000 to 1,999
- **Liability accounts:** 2,000 to 2,999
- **Equity accounts:** 3,000 to 3,999
- **Sales accounts:** 4,000 to 4,999
- **Cost of Goods Sold accounts:** 5,000 to 5,999
- **Expense accounts:** 6,000 to 6,999

This type of numbering system matches the one used by computerized accounting systems, making it easy for a business to transition if at some future time it decides to automate its books by using a computerized accounting system.

One major advantage of using a computerized accounting system is that most accounting software allows you to customize it with a number of different Charts of Accounts based on the type of business you plan to run. When you get your computerized system, whichever accounting software you decide to use, you just need to review the list of business-type chart options included with that software, delete any accounts that you don't want, and add any new accounts that fit your business plan.

TIP

If you're setting up your Chart of Accounts manually, be sure to leave a lot of room between accounts to add new accounts. For example, number your Cash account 1,000 and your Accounts Receivable account 1,100. That numbering leaves you plenty of room to add other accounts that track cash.

Figure 3-1 is a sample Chart of Accounts for H.G.'s Cheesecake Shop that we developed by using QuickBooks. Note that in QuickBooks, the General Ledger accounts aren't necessarily assigned account numbers. You will also note the column for the type of account each General Ledger account belongs to. For example, when you choose Long-Term Liability for a loan, this means that the principal payments on the loan will come due in more than 12 months, as described earlier in this chapter. This choice of type determines where QuickBooks places the debt on your balance sheet. We discuss how to prepare a balance sheet in Chapter 18.

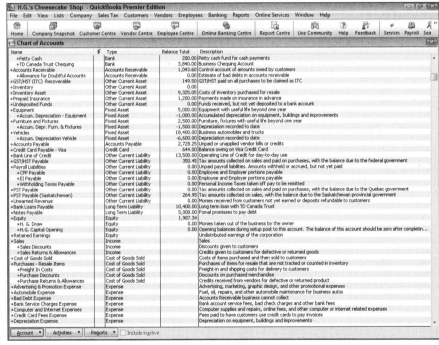

Figure 3-1:
The top portion of a sample Chart of Accounts.

Part II
Keeping a Paper or Electronic Trail

The 5th Wave   By Rich Tennant

In this part . . .

*B*elieve it or not, correctly entering your financial transactions in the books is a science. This part introduces you to the basics of entering financial transactions, posting transactions to your General Ledger (the granddaddy of your bookkeeping system), and tracking all the transaction details in your journals.

Any bookkeeping system must have good internal controls, so we tell you how to set them in place so that you can be sure you not only enter all your financial transactions into the books but also enter them correctly. In addition, you want to be sure that cash coming into and going out of the company is properly handled, so we provide recommendations for how to separate various money-related duties.

Finally, we introduce you to your options when it comes to computerized accounting systems and share the benefits of using these types of systems to keep your business's books.

Chapter 4

Ledgers: A One-Stop Summary of Your Business Transactions

As a bookkeeper, you may be dreaming of having one source that you can turn to when you need to review all entries that impact your business's accounts. (Okay, so maybe that's not exactly what you're dreaming about. Just work with us here.) The General Ledger is your dream come true. In it, you can find a summary of transactions and a record of the accounts that those transactions affect.

In this chapter, you can discover the purpose of the General Ledger. We tell you how to not only develop entries for the Ledger but also enter (or post) them. In addition, we explain how you can change already posted information or correct entries in the Ledger, and how this entire process is streamlined when you use a computerized accounting system.

The Eyes and Ears of a Business

We're not using eyes and ears literally here because, of course, the book known as the General Ledger isn't alive, so it can't see or hear. But wouldn't it be nice if the ledger could just tell you all its secrets about what happens with your money? You could certainly much more easily track down any bookkeeping problems or errors.

Instead, the General Ledger serves as the figurative eyes and ears of book-keepers and accountants who want to know what financial transactions have taken place historically in a business. By reading the General Ledger — not exactly interesting reading, unless you love numbers — you can see, account by account, every transaction that has taken place in the business. (And to uncover more details about those transactions, you can turn to your business's journals, where you record transactions on a daily basis. See Chapter 5 for the lowdown on journals.)

The General Ledger is the granddaddy of your business. You can find all the transactions that ever occurred in the history of the business in the General Ledger account. You can go to this one place to find transactions that impact Cash, Inventory, Accounts Receivable, Accounts Payable, and any other account included in your business's Chart of Accounts. (Refer to Chapter 3 for more information about setting up the Chart of Accounts and the kind of transactions you can find in each kind of account.)

Developing Summary Entries for the General Ledger

Because you first enter your business's transactions into journals, you develop many of the entries for the General Ledger based on information pulled from the appropriate journal. For example, you list cash receipts and the accounts that are affected by those receipts in the Cash Receipts journal. You list cash disbursements and the accounts affected by those disbursements in the Cash Disbursements journal. You do the same for transactions found in the Sales journal, Purchases journal, General journal, and any other special journals you may be using in your business.

At the end of each month, you summarize each journal by adding up the columns and then use the totals to post to the General Ledger. Believe us; this process takes a lot less time than entering every transaction in the General Ledger.

We introduce you to the process of entering transactions into the different journals in Chapter 5. Next, we outline the step-by-step process of posting entries to customer accounts, to vendor accounts, and to the General Ledger. We use the Cash Receipt journal to demonstrate all the steps involved in posting.

All entries posted to the General Ledger must be balanced entries. That's the cardinal rule of double-entry bookkeeping. For more detail about double-entry bookkeeping, read Chapter 2.

Figures 4-1 to 4-4 summarize the remaining journal pages that we prepare in Chapter 5 and include:

✔ Figure 4-1: Summarized Cash Disbursements journal

✔ Figure 4-2: Summarized Sales journal

✔ Figure 4-3: Summarized Purchases journal

✔ Figure 4-4: General journal

Figure 4-1 shows the details and summary of the Cash Disbursements journal for a business.

Figure 4-1:
A Cash Disbursements journal keeps track of all cash transactions involving cash sent out of the business. This figure shows how to summarize those transactions so that they can be posted to the General Ledger.

Handwritten annotations:
Assets
Dr - increase
Cr - decrease.

(Expenses:
Dr - increase
Cr - decrease)

H.G.'s Cheesecake Shop
Cash Disbursements Journal
June 2013

CD-12

Handwritten: Expense acct (above Account Debited); asset acct (above Cash Credit)

Date		Account Debited	Cheque number	PR	General Debit	Accounts Payable Debit	Salaries Debit	Cash Credit
June	1	Rent Expense - Cohen	951	√	1,000.00			1,000.00
	3	Acc. Pay. Henry's B.S.	952	√		500.00		500.00
	4	Acc. Pay. Helen's P.G.	953	√		220.00		220.00
	5	Employee Name	954				350.00	350.00
	10	Credit Card Payable	955	√	270.00			270.00
						720.00	350.00	2,340.00
						√	√	

Handwritten at bottom:
Acct   Dr   Cr
Rent   —
Cash   —

The table that follows lists the accounts of the General Ledger that are affected by the summarized transactions recorded in the Cash Disbursements journal that appears in Figure 4-1:

Debit		**Credit**	
Rent Expense	$1,000	Cash	$2,340
Accounts Payable	$720		
Salaries Expense	$350		
Credit Card Payable	$270		
Total debits	$2,340	Total credits	$2,340

The table demonstrates how the amounts posted to the General Ledger balance out at $2,340 each for the debits and credits. The Cash account is decreased to show the cash outlay, the Rent Expense and Salaries Expense accounts are increased to show the additional expenses, and the Accounts Payable and Credit Card Payable accounts are decreased to show that the business paid the bills, so they're no longer due.

Figure 4-2 shows the Sales journal for a sample business.

Figure 4-2:
A Sales journal keeps track of sales transactions on account. This figure shows how to summarize those transactions so that you can post them to the General Ledger.

					H.G.'s Cheesecake Shop Sales Journal June 2013		
							S - 20
Date		Customer Account Debited	PR	Invoice Number	Accounts Receivable Debit	Sales Credit
June	1	Sandra Smith	√	443	236.00	236.00
	4	Charlie's Garage	√	444	140.00	140.00
	4	Patricia Perry	√	445	320.00	320.00
	7	Jack Jones	√	446	190.00	190.00
					886.00	886.00
					√	√

The table that follows lists the accounts of the General Ledger that are affected by the summarized transactions recorded in the Sales journal that appears in Figure 4-2:

Debit		**Credit**	
Accounts Receivable	$886	Sales	$886
Total debits	$886	Total credits	$886

The table demonstrates how the amounts posted keep the General Ledger in balance. The Accounts Receivable account is increased to show that customers owe the business money because they bought items on account. The Sales account is increased to show that even though no cash changed hands, the business in Figure 4-2 took in revenue. Cash will be collected when the customers pay their bills.

The business needs to add a few columns to the Sales journal to accommodate the goods and services tax or harmonized sales tax (GST/HST), as well as provincial sales tax or retail sales tax (PST/RST). We discuss this requirement to charge taxes on your sales at the end of Chapter 5. We left out the taxes in the sample journal entries in Figures 4-1 through 4-4 in order to keep things simple.

Figure 4-3 shows the business's Purchases journal for the first few days of the month June.

Figure 4-3: A Purchases journal keeps track of all purchases of goods that a business plans to sell. This figure shows how to summarize those transactions so that you can post them to the General Ledger.

		H.G.'s Cheesecake Shop				
		Purchases Journal				
		June 2013				P - 19
Date		Vendor Account Debited	PR	Invoice Number	Purchases Debit	Accounts Payable Credit
June	1	Henry's Baking Supplies	√	H - 492	750.00	750.00
	6	Plates Unlimited	√	10 - 140	100.00	100.00
	8	Helen's Paper Goods	√	1497	75.00	75.00
					925.00	925.00
					√	√

The table that follows lists the accounts of the General Ledger that have been affected by the summarized transactions recorded in the Purchases journal that appears in Figure 4-3.

	Debit			*Credit*	
Purchases	$925		Accounts Payable	$925	
Total debits	$925		Total credits	$925	

The table demonstrates how the posted amounts continue to keep the General Ledger in balance. The Accounts Payable account increases to show that money is due to vendors, and the Purchases account also increases to show that goods held for resale were purchased.

Figure 4-4 shows the General journal for a sample business.

The three entries recorded in the General journal, shown in Figure 4-4, show how six accounts in the General Ledger are affected by the transactions. The Sales Return and Purchase Return accounts increase to show additional returns. The Accounts Payable and Accounts Receivable accounts both decrease to show that the business no longer owes or is owed that money. The Vehicles account increases to show new business assets, and the H.G. Capital account (which is where the owner's deposits into the business are tracked) increases because of an owner investment into the business.

Figure 4-4:
A General journal keeps track of all miscellaneous transactions that aren't tracked in a specific journal, such as a Sales journal or a Purchases journal. This figure shows three transactions so that you can post them to the General Ledger.

H.G.'s Cheesecake Shop
General Journal
June 2013

GJ 16

Date		Account Title and Explanation	PR	General Debit	General Credit
June	5	Sales Return	√	60.00	
		Accounts Receivable - S. Smith	√√		60.00
		Credit memo No. 123			
	9	Accounts Payable	√√	200.00	
		Purchase Returns	√		200.00
		Debit memo No. 346			
	10	Vehicles	√	10,000.00	
		H. G. Capital	√		10,000.00
		H.G. Invests car into the business			

Posting Entries to the General Ledger

After you summarize your journals, you post your entries into the General Ledger accounts.

When posting to the General Ledger, include transaction dollar amounts, as well as references to where you originally entered material into the books so that you can track a transaction back if a question arises later. For example, you may wonder why an account has a high balance, your boss or the owner may wonder why the business spent certain money, or an *auditor* (an outside accountant who checks your work for accuracy) may raise a question.

Whatever the reason someone questions a balance or a specific item in the General Ledger, you definitely want to be able to find the point of original entry for every transaction in every account. Use the reference information that you record in the General Ledger to guide you to the original detail about the transaction in the journals so that you can answer any question that arises.

For the business example we use in this chapter, three of the accounts — Cash, Accounts Receivable, and Accounts Payable — are carried over month to month, so each has an opening balance. Just to keep things simple, in this example we start each account with a $2,000 balance. These three accounts appear on the balance sheet, and so they never get closed. We talk more about which accounts are closed at the end of each year and which accounts remain open, as well as why that's the case, in Chapter 22.

For the purposes of this example, we assume that the transactions are from the first month of the fiscal year. And in the figures that follow, we give examples for only the first ten days of this first month.

The figures for the various accounts in this example show that the balance of some accounts increases when a debit is recorded and decreases when a credit is recorded. Others increase when a credit is recorded and decrease when a debit is recorded. That's the mystery of debits, credits, and double-entry accounting. For more about this accounting rule, flip to Chapter 2.

The Cash account (see Figure 4-5) increases with debits and decreases with credits. Ideally, the Cash account always ends with a debit balance, which means you still have money in the account. A credit balance in the cash account indicates that the business is overdrawn, and you know what that means — your cheques get returned because of insufficient funds in the account.

Getting over overdraft problems

Here's a possible way out of an overdraft problem: Consider getting the business owner to secure a permission with your business's bank to go into a temporary bank overdraft position.

Of course, the bank charges your business interest for any overdraft. But at least your cheques don't bounce!

H.G.'s Cheesecake Shop Cash						
Date		Description	Ref.	Debit	Credit	Balance
June	1	Beginning Balance				2,000.00
	30	Cash Receipts	CR 17	3,260.00		5,260.00
	30	Cash Disbursements	CD 12		2,340.00	2,920.00

Figure 4-5: The Cash account in the General Ledger.

The Accounts Receivable account (see Figure 4-6) increases with debits and decreases with credits. Ideally, this account also has a debit balance that indicates the amount still due from customer purchases. If no money is due from customers, the account balance is zero. A zero balance isn't necessarily a bad thing if all customers have paid their bills. However, a zero balance may be a sign that your sales have slumped, which can be bad news.

H.G.'s Cheesecake Shop Accounts Receivable						
Date		Description	Ref.	Debit	Credit	Balance
June	1	Beginning Balance				2,000.00
	5	Credit memo No. 123	GJ 16		60.00	1,940.00
	30	Sales	S 20	886.00		2,826.00
	30	Cash Receipts	CR 17		530.00	2,296.00

Figure 4-6: The Accounts Receivable account in the General Ledger.

The Accounts Payable account (see Figure 4-7) increases with credits and decreases with debits. Normally, this account has a credit balance because the business still owes money to vendors, contractors, and others. A zero balance here equals no outstanding bills.

Figure 4-7:
The Accounts Payable account in the General Ledger.

	Date		Description	Ref.	Debit	Credit	Balance
			H.G.'s Cheesecake Shop				
			Accounts Payable				
	June	1	Beginning Balance				2,000.00
		9	Debit memo No. 346	GJ 16	200.00		1,800.00
		30	Purchases	P 19		925.00	2,725.00
		30	Cash Disbursements	CR 12	720.00		2,005.00

These three accounts — Cash, Accounts Receivable, and Accounts Payable — are part of the balance sheet, which we explain fully in Chapter 18. Asset accounts on the balance sheet usually carry debit balances because they reflect assets (in this case, cash) owned by the business. Cash and Accounts Receivable are asset accounts. Liability and Equity accounts usually carry credit balances because Liability accounts show claims made by creditors (in other words, money that the business owes to banks, vendors, or others), and Equity accounts show claims made by owners (in other words, how much money the owners have put into or reinvested into the business). Accounts Payable is a Liability account.

⟜ The Sales account (see Figure 4-8) isn't a balance sheet account. Instead, you use it to develop the income statement, which shows whether a business earned revenue in the period you're examining. (For the lowdown on income statements, see Chapter 19.) Credits and debits are pretty straightforward when it comes to the Sales account: Credits increase the account, and debits decrease it. The Sales account usually carries a credit balance, which is a good thing because it means the business has earned income.

What's that, you say? The Sales account should carry a credit balance? That may sound strange, so let us explain the relationship between the Sales account and the balance sheet. The Sales account is one of the accounts that feed the bottom line of the income statement, which shows whether your business made a profit or suffered a loss. A profit means that you earned more through sales than you paid out in costs or expenses. Expense and Cost accounts usually carry a debit balance.

| H.G.'s Cheesecake Shop | | | | | |
| Sales | | | | | |
Date	Description	Ref.	Debit	Credit	Balance
June 1	Beginning Balance				0
30	Sales	S 20		886.00	886.00
30	Cash Receipts	CR 17		1,230.00	2,116.00

Figure 4-8:
The Sales account in the General Ledger.

The income statement's bottom-line figure shows whether the business made a profit. If Sales account credits exceed Expense and Cost account debits, then the business made a profit. You add that profit in the form of a credit to the Equity account called Capital (Retained Earnings in the case of an incorporated business), which tracks how much of your business's profits the owners reinvested into the business to grow the business. If the business lost money and the bottom line of the income statement shows that cost and expenses exceeded sales, then the bottom-line number is a debit. You subtract that debit from the balance in the Capital or the Retained Earnings account to show the reduction to profits reinvested in the business.

If your business earns a profit at the end of the accounting period, the Capital or the Retained Earnings account increases thanks to a credit from the Sales account. If you lose money, your Equity account decreases.

Because the Capital or the Retained Earnings accounts are Equity accounts and Equity accounts usually carry credit balances, Capital and Retained Earnings usually carry credit balances, as well.

After you post all the General Ledger entries, you need to record details about where you posted the transactions on the journal pages. We show you how to record those details in Chapter 5.

All Equity accounts end up increasing for business profits and decreasing for business losses. The Equity account in an incorporated business is called the Retained Earnings account. In the case of H.G.'s Cheesecake Shop, the business's Equity account is a single Capital account, called H.G. Capital, created for the owner: H.G. H.G.'s Cheesecake Shop needs only one Equity account because the business is a sole proprietorship. If a business is either a sole proprietorship or a partnership, it doesn't need a Retained Earnings account for equity.

Adjusting Entries and Accrual Accounting

Your entries in the General Ledger aren't cast in stone. If necessary, you can always change or correct an entry by using an *adjusting entry*. You can also use adjusting entries to implement accrual accounting. We discuss the need for accrual accounting in Chapter 2. Four of the most common reasons for General Ledger adjustments are

- ✔ **Depreciation expense:** A business shows the aging of its assets through depreciation. Each year, you write off a portion of the original cost of an asset as an expense, and you note that change as an adjusting entry. Determining how much you should expense is a complicated process that we explain in greater detail in Chapter 12.

- ✔ **Prepaid expenses:** You allocate expenses that your business pays up front, such as a year's worth of insurance, by the month by using an adjusting entry at the end of an accounting period. We show you how to develop entries related to prepaid expenses in Chapter 17.

- ✔ **Adding an account:** You can add accounts by using adjusting entries at any time during the year. If you're creating the new account to track transactions separately that used to appear in another account, you must move all transactions already in the books to the new account. You do this transfer with an adjusting entry to reflect the change.

- ✔ **Deleting and inactivating an account:** Delete accounts only if they've never been used in transactions. Instead of deleting an account in your chart, you should inactivate it. We show you how to view entries you make in the General Ledger in the following section.

Keep your records of past transactions intact. The Canada Revenue Agency (CRA) may be paying you a visit in the future to perform an audit on your income tax return. You don't want to be in a position where you can't show how you arrived at balances in your tax return because you deleted the accounts that you used to reach that balance. For this primary reason, we recommend you inactivate, rather than delete, accounts that you don't plan to use any longer.

We talk more about adjusting entries and how you can use them in Chapter 17.

Using Computerized Transactions to Post and Adjust in the General Ledger

If you keep your books by using a computerized accounting system, your accounting software actually posts to the General Ledger behind the scenes. You can view your transactions right on the screen. We show you how to view transactions onscreen by following two simple steps in QuickBooks:

1. **Click Company from the top menu bar, and then click the Chart of Accounts selection (see Figure 4-9).**

2. **Double-click the account for which you want more detail.**

   In Figure 4-10, we look into Accounts Payable and see the transactions for May that were entered when the business paid the bills.

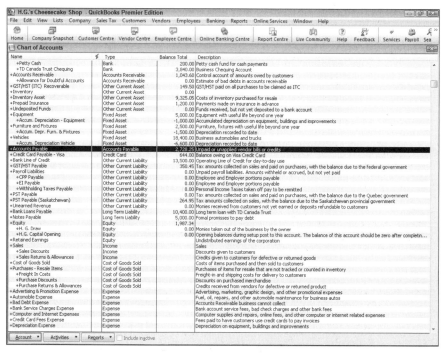

Figure 4-9: A Chart of Accounts as it appears in QuickBooks.

Figure 4-10:
Peek
inside the
Accounts
Payable
account in
QuickBooks.

If you need to make an adjustment to a payment that appears in your computerized system, highlight the transaction, right-click, and then click Edit, Delete, or Void, and make the necessary changes.

While you navigate the General Ledger created by your computerized book-keeping system, you can see how easily someone can make changes that alter your financial transactions and possibly cause serious harm to your business. For example, someone may reduce or alter your bills to customers, or change the amount due to a vendor or supplier. Be sure that you can trust whoever has access to your computerized system and that you have set up secure password access. Also, establish a series of checks and balances for managing your business's cash and accounts. Chapter 7 covers safety and security measures in greater detail.

Other computerized accounting programs allow you to view transactions right on the screen, too. We use QuickBooks for examples throughout the book because this product is one of the most popular computerized accounting systems.

Chapter 5

Keeping Journals

. . . .

. . . .

*W*hen it comes to doing your books, you must start somewhere. You could take a shortcut and just list every transaction in the affected accounts, but after recording hundreds and maybe thousands of transactions in just one month, imagine what a nightmare you'd face if your books didn't balance and you had to find the error. It would be like looking for a needle in a haystack — a haystack of numbers!

Because you enter every transaction in two places — as a debit in one account and a credit in another account — in a double-entry bookkeeping system, you need to have a place where you can easily match or balance those debits and credits. (For more on the double-entry system, flip to Chapter 2.)

Long ago, bookkeepers developed a system of journals to give businesses a starting point for each transaction. In this chapter, we introduce you to the process of journalizing your transactions; we tell you how to set up and use journals, how to post in the General Ledger the transactions to accounts affected by those transactions, and how to simplify this entire process by using a computerized bookkeeping program.

Establishing a Transaction's Point of Entry

In most businesses that don't use computerized bookkeeping programs, a transaction's original point of entry into the bookkeeping system is through a system of journals.

Each transaction goes in the appropriate journal in chronological order. The entry should include information about the date of the transaction, the accounts to which the transaction was posted, and the source material used for developing the transaction.

If, at some point in the future, you need to track how a credit or debit ended up in a particular account, you can find the necessary detail in the journal where you first recorded the transaction. (Before you post each transaction to various accounts in the bookkeeping system, you give it a reference number to help you backtrack to the original entry point.) For example, suppose a customer calls you and wants to know why her account has a $500 charge. To find the answer, you go to the posting in the customer's account; track the charge back to its original point of entry in the Sales journal; use that information to locate the source for the charge; make a copy of the source (most likely a sales invoice or some sort of receipt if you shipped some goods or you delivered some services); and mail, fax, or e-mail the evidence to the customer.

If you've filed everything properly, you'll have no trouble finding the original source material and settling any issue that arises regarding any transaction. For more on what papers you need to keep and how to file them, see Chapter 7.

Keeping one General Journal for all your transactions is perfectly acceptable, but you may find one big journal very hard to manage because you'll likely have thousands of entries in that journal by the end of the year. Instead, most businesses use a system of journals that includes a Cash Receipts journal for incoming cash and a Cash Disbursements journal, sometimes called the Cash Payments journal, for outgoing cash. Not all transactions involve cash and cheques, however, so the two most common non-cash journals are the Sales journal and the Purchases journal. We show you how to set up and use each of these journals in the sections that follow.

When Cash Changes Hands

Businesses deal with cash transactions every day, and you definitely want to know where every penny in your business is going. The best way to get a quick daily summary of cash transactions is by reviewing the entries in your Cash Receipts journal and Cash Disbursements journal. A lot of businesses also review their business bank account transactions online.

If you monitor cash transactions by checking your business's bank account activity via the Internet, watch out. Banks are bound to have delays in processing cheques that your business issues to its vendors and suppliers, so the bank account balance looks higher than it really is. We discuss recording transactions in your business bank account in Chapter 7.

Keeping track of incoming cash

You first record cash received by your business in the Cash Receipts journal. The majority of cash received each day comes from daily sales; other possible sources of cash include deposits of capital from the business's owners, customer bill payments from previous sales, new loan proceeds, collection of rents, and interest earned from savings accounts.

Each entry in the Cash Receipts journal must not only indicate how the business received the cash but also designate the account into which you plan to deposit the cash. Remember, in double-entry bookkeeping, every transaction is entered twice — once as a debit and once as a credit. For example, you credit cash taken in for sales to the Sales account and debit it to the Cash account. In this case, both accounts increase in value. (For more about debits and credits, flip back to Chapter 2.)

In the Cash Receipts journal, the Cash account is always the debit because it's where you initially deposit your money. The credits vary, depending on the source of the funds. Figure 5-1 shows you what a series of transactions looks like in a Cash Receipts journal.

H.G.'s Cheesecake Shop
Cash Receipts Journal
June 2013

CR-17

Date		Account Credited	PR	General Credit	Accounts Receivable Credit	Sales Credit	Cash Debit
June	1	Sales				800.00	800.00
	5	Sales				250.00	250.00
	7	Sandra Smith Ch. 1420	√		200.00		200.00
	9	H.G. Capital		1,500.00			1,500.00
	9	Sales				120.00	120.00
	10	Jack Jones Ch. 141	√		150.00		150.00
	10	Patricia Perry Ch. 310	√		180.00		180.00
	10	Sales				60.00	60.00

Figure 5-1: The first point of entry for incoming cash is the Cash Receipts journal.

You record most of your incoming cash daily because it's cash received by the cashier, called *cash register sales* or simply *sales* in the journal. When you record cheques received from customers, you list the customer's cheque number and name, as well as the amount. In Figure 5-1, the only other cash received is a cash deposit from the owner, H.G., as an investment.

The Cash Receipts journal in Figure 5-1 has seven columns of information:

- ✔ **Date:** The date of the transaction.

- ✔ **Account Credited:** The name of the account credited.

- ✔ **PR (posting reference):** This is a space to insert a check mark to indicate that you have updated your customer's account for each payment received. You probably decided to do this during the month to keep on top of your customer accounts. You enter a check mark at the end of the month when you do the posting to the General Ledger accounts for the transactions listed in the General Credit column. If you choose to use account numbers in your Chart of Accounts, the account number is entered instead of a check mark in the PR column.

- ✔ **General Credit:** Transactions that don't have their own columns. These transactions are entered individually into the General Ledger accounts affected at the end of the month.

  For example, according to Figure 5-1, the owner, H.G., deposited $1,500 of his own money into the H.G. Capital account on June 9 in order to pay bills. The bookkeeper posts the credit shown there to the H.G. Capital account at the end of the month because the H.G. Capital account tracks all information about investments of assets that H.G. makes into the business.

- ✔ **Accounts Receivable Credit:** Any transactions that are posted to the Accounts Receivable account (which tracks information about customers who buy products on account).

- ✔ **Sales Credit:** Credits for the Sales account.

- ✔ **Cash Debit:** Anything that you add to the Cash account.

You can see in Figure 5-6 appearing later in this chapter an illustration of the Cash Receipts journal once you have summarized and posted the totals to the General Ledger at the end of the month.

You can set up your Cash Receipts journal with more columns if you have accounts with frequent cash receipts. The big advantage to having individual columns for active accounts is that, when you total the columns at the end of the month, the total for the active accounts is the only thing you have to post to the General Ledger accounts. This approach requires a lot less work than entering every Sales transaction individually in the General Ledger account and saves a lot of time posting to accounts that involve multiple transactions every month. You need to enter each individual transaction listed in the General Credits column into the affected accounts separately, which takes a lot more time than just entering a column total.

Following outgoing cash

Cash going out of the business to pay bills, salaries, rents, and other necessities has its own journal, called the Cash Disbursements journal. This journal is the point of original entry for all business cash paid out to others.

No businessperson likes to see money go out the door, but imagine what creditors, vendors, and others would think if they didn't get the money that your business owes them. Put yourself in their shoes: Would you be able to buy needed supplies if other businesses didn't pay what they owed you? Not a chance.

You need to track your outgoing cash just as carefully as you track incoming cash (refer to the preceding section). Each entry in the Cash Disbursements journal must not only indicate how much cash the business paid out but also designate which account you decrease in value because of the cash payment. For example, you credit cash paid to cover bills to the Cash account (which goes down in amount) and debit it to the account from which the business pays the bill or loan, such as Accounts Payable. The debit decreases the amount still owed in the Accounts Payable account.

In the Cash Disbursements journal, the Cash account is always the credit, and the debits vary, depending on the outstanding debt or expense the business is paying. Figure 5-2 shows you a series of transactions in a Cash Disbursements journal.

Figure 5-2:
The first point of entry for outgoing cash is the Cash Disbursements journal.

										CD-12
H.G.'s Cheesecake Shop										
Cash Disbursements Journal										
June 2013										
Date		Account Debited	Cheque Number	PR	General Debit	Accounts Payable Debit	Salaries Debit	Cash Credit
June	1	Rent Expense - Cohen	951		1,000.00			1,000.00
	3	Acc. Pay. Henry's B.S.	952	√		500.00		500.00
	4	Acct. Pay Helen's P.G.	953	√		220.00		220.00
	5	Employee Name	954				350.00	350.00
	10	Visa	955		270.00			270.00

The Cash Disbursements journal in Figure 5-2 has eight columns of information:

✔ **Date:** The date of the transaction.

✔ **Account Debited:** The name of the account debited, as well as any detail about the reason for the debit.

✔ **Cheque Number:** The number of the cheque used to pay the debt.

✔ **PR (posting reference):** This is a space to insert a check mark to indicate that you have updated your vendor's account for each payment you have made. You probably decided to do this during the month to keep on top of your vendors' accounts. You enter a check mark at the end of the month when you do the posting to the General Ledger accounts for the transactions listed in the General Debit column. If choose to use account numbers in your Chart of Accounts, the account number is entered instead of a check mark in the PR column.

✔ **General Debit:** Any transactions that don't have their own columns. These transactions are entered individually at the end of the month into the accounts that they affect.

For example, according to Figure 5-2, the business paid rent on June 1, and the bookkeeper will indicate that payment by adding a debit in the Rent Expense account.

✔ **Accounts Payable Debit:** Any transactions that you post to the Accounts Payable account (which tracks bills due).

✔ **Salaries Debit:** Debits to the Salaries Expense account, which increase the amount of salary expenses paid in a particular month.

✔ **Cash Credit:** Anything that the business deducts from the Cash account.

You can set up your Cash Disbursements journal with more columns if you have accounts with frequent cash disbursals. For example, in Figure 5-2, the bookkeeper for this fictional business added one column each for Accounts Payable and Salaries because the business disburses cash for both accounts multiple times during the month. Instead of having to list each disbursement in the Accounts Payable and Salaries accounts, she can just total each journal column at the end of the month and add totals to the appropriate accounts. This approach sure saves a lot of time when you're working with your most active accounts.

You likely have to add another column to your Cash Disbursements journal if your business has to pay goods and services tax or harmonized sales tax (GST/HST). In this column, you enter the amount of GST/HST that your business pays on any and all purchases. You post these amounts to the GST/HST Recoverable account in the General Ledger. Look at the section "Dealing with Sales Taxes," later in this chapter, for more information on your GST/HST responsibilities.

Managing Sales like a Pro

Not all sales involve the immediate collection of cash; many stores allow customers to buy products on account by using a store credit card. (We're not talking about purchases customers make by using a bank-issued credit card; in that case, the bank — not the store or business making the sale — has to worry about collecting from the customer.)

Sales on account come into play when a customer is allowed to take a store's products without paying immediately because she has an account that's billed monthly. The business can use a store-issued credit card or some other method to track credit purchases by customers, such as having the customer sign a sales receipt indicating that the business should charge the amount to the customer's account.

Sales made on account don't involve cash until the customer pays her bill. (In contrast, with credit card sales, the store gets a payment in cash from the card-issuing bank before the customer even pays the credit card bill.) If your business sells on account, the total sales value of the products bought on any particular day, plus any applicable sales taxes, becomes an item for the Accounts Receivable account, which tracks all money due from customers. We talk more about managing Accounts Receivable in Chapter 9.

Before allowing customers to buy on account, your business should require customers to apply for credit in advance so that you can check their credit references.

When something's sold on account, usually the cashier drafts an invoice for the customer to sign when she picks up the product. The invoice lists the items purchased and the total amount due. After getting the customer's signature, you track the invoice in both the Accounts Receivable account and the customer's individual account.

Transactions for sales made on account first enter your books in the Sales journal. Each entry in the Sales journal must indicate the date, the customer's name, the invoice number, and the amount charged.

In the Sales journal, you debit the Accounts Receivable account, which increases in amount. You must also remember to make an entry to the customer's account records because the customer hasn't yet paid for the item, so the business needs to bill her for it. The transaction also increases the amount in the Sales account, which you credit.

Figure 5-3 shows a few days' worth of transactions related to sales on account.

H.G.'s Cheesecake Shop						
Sales Journal						
June 2013						**S - 20**
Date		Customer Account Debited	PR	Invoice Number	Accounts Receivable Debit	Sales Credit
June	1	Sandra Smith	√	443	236.00	236.00
	4	Charlie's Garage	√	444	140.00	140.00
	4	Patricia Perry	√	445	320.00	320.00
	7	Jack Jones	√	446	190.00	190.00

Figure 5-3: The first point of entry for sales made on account is the Sales journal.

The Sales journal in Figure 5-3 has six columns of information:

✔ **Date:** The date of the transaction.

✔ **Customer Account Debited:** The name of the customer whose account you will debit.

✔ **PR (posting reference):** This is a space to insert a check mark when the sales entry has been posted to the individual customer's account. You probably decided to do this during the month to keep on top of your customers' accounts.

✔ **Invoice Number:** The invoice number issued by your business for the customer's purchase.

✔ **Accounts Receivable Debit:** Increases to the Accounts Receivable account.

✔ **Sales Credit:** Increases to the Sales account.

At the end of the month, the bookkeeper can just total the Accounts Receivable and Sales columns shown in Figure 5-3 and post the totals to those General Ledger accounts. He doesn't need to post all the detail because he can always refer back to the Sales journal. However, he must carefully record each invoice noted in the Sales journal in each customer's account. Otherwise, he doesn't know who and how much to bill.

Refer to Figure 4-2 of Chapter 4 for an illustration of the Sales journal once it has been summarized and the totals posted to the General Ledger at the end of the month. The Sales journal also needs to accommodate the GST/HST and provincial sales tax and retail sales tax (PST/RST) that the business must charge on each sale. Have a look at the section "Dealing with Sales Taxes," later in this chapter, for more information on your tax billing responsibilities.

Keeping Track of Purchases

Purchasing products that you plan to sell to customers at a later date is a key type of non-cash transaction. All businesses must have something to sell, whether they manufacture it themselves or buy a finished product from some other business, as is the case for wholesalers. Businesses usually make these purchases on credit from the business that makes the product. In this case, the business becomes the customer of another business.

Transactions for purchases bought on credit first enter your books in the Purchases journal. Each entry in the Purchases journal must indicate the vendor or supplier from whom your business made the purchase, the vendor's invoice number, and the amount charged.

In the Purchases journal, you credit the Accounts Payable account and debit the Purchases account, meaning both accounts increase in value. The Accounts Payable account increases because the business now owes more money to creditors, and the Purchases account increases because the amount spent on goods to be sold goes up.

Figure 5-4 shows some purchase transactions as they appear in the business's Purchases journal.

Figure 5-4:
The first point of entry for purchases bought on credit is the Purchases journal.

		H.G.'s Cheesecake Shop			
		Purchases Journal			
		June 2013			
					P - 19
Date		Vendor Account Debited	PR	Invoice Number	Purchases Debit	Accounts Payable Credit
June	1	Henry's Bakery Supplies	√	H - 492	750.00	750.00
	6	Plates Unlimited	√	10-140	100.00	100.00
	8	Helen's Paper Goods	√	1497	75.00	75.00

The Purchases journal in Figure 5-4 has six columns of information:

✔ **Date:** The date of the transaction.

✔ **Vendor Account Credited:** The name of the vendor from whom the business made the purchases.

✔ **PR (posting reference):** This is a space to insert a check mark when the entry has been posted to the individual vendor's Accounts Payable account. You probably decided to do this during the month to keep on top of your vendors' accounts.

✔ **Invoice Number:** Insert the supplier's invoice number here to make it easier later on when communicating which invoices you are paying.

✔ **Purchases Debit:** Increases to the Purchases account.

✔ **Accounts Payable Credit:** Increases to the Accounts Payable account.

At the end of the month, you can just total the Purchases and Accounts Payable columns, and post the totals to the corresponding General Ledger accounts. You can refer back to the Purchases journal for details, if necessary. However, you should carefully record each invoice in each vendor's account more frequently than just at the end of the month. This practice allows you to have a running total of outstanding bills for each vendor. Otherwise, you don't know how much the business owes, or to whom. And not knowing what you owe can lead to very serious problems, such as the loss of the business's excellent credit rating for paying bills on time.

Refer to Figure 4-3 of Chapter 4 for an illustration of the Purchases journal once it has been summarized and the totals posted to the General Ledger at the end of the month.

If your business purchases merchandise for resale, your business can buy the goods PST/RST exempt but can't avoid paying GST/HST. We discuss tax details in the section "Dealing with Sales Taxes," later in this chapter.

Dealing with Transactions that Don't Fit

Not all your transactions fit in one of the four main journals (Cash Receipts, Cash Disbursements, Sales, and Purchases). If you need to establish other special journals as the original points of entry for transactions, go ahead. The sky's the limit!

If you keep your books the old-fashioned way — on paper — be aware that paper is vulnerable to being mistakenly lost or destroyed. You don't get any electronic backup systems for paper! You may want to consider keeping the number of journals you maintain to a minimum.

For transactions that don't fit in the "big four" journals but don't necessarily warrant the creation of their own journals, consider keeping a General Journal for miscellaneous transactions. The format used is similar to what you use for the other four journals. You need to create the following columns:

✔ **Date:** The date of the transaction.

✔ **Account:** The account affected by the transaction. You need to include more detail here than you do in the other journals because the General Journal affects so many different accounts with so many different types of transactions. For example, you find only sales transactions in the Sales journal and purchase transactions in the Purchase journal; you may find any type of transaction in the General Journal, affecting many less-active accounts.

✔ **PR (posting reference):** This is a space to insert a check mark to indicate that you have updated your customers' and vendors' individual accounts. You probably decided to do this during the month to keep on top of your customers' and vendors' accounts. You enter a check mark in this space when at the end of the month an entry is posted to the individual General Ledger. If the transaction entered is to Accounts Receivable, another check mark is inserted. If the transaction entered is to Accounts Payable, another check mark is inserted.

✔ **General Debit:** Contains debits.

✔ **General Credit:** Contains credits.

All the transactions in this General Journal are non-cash transactions. Cash transactions go into one of the two cash journals: Cash Receipts (refer to the section "Keeping track of incoming cash," earlier in this chapter) and Cash Disbursements (refer to the section "Following outgoing cash," earlier in this chapter).

In a General Journal, you need to enter transactions on multiple lines because each transaction affects at least two accounts (and sometimes more than two). For example, in the General Journal shown in Figure 5-5, the first transaction listed is the return of a cheesecake by S. Smith on June 5. The bookkeeper must post this return of products sold to the customer's Accounts Receivable as a credit. Also, she has to debit the Sales Return account, where the business tracks all products returned by the customer.

June 9 — Return a portion of purchase from Henry's Bakery Supplies, $200, Debit memo No. 346. When a business returns a product purchased, the business tracks the amount in the Purchase Return account, which the business credits. The bookkeeper must also make a debit to the vendor's Accounts Payable account because the vendor now owes less money. Cash doesn't change hands with this transaction.

June 10 — H.G. transfers his car with a fair market value of $10,000 into his business. The bookkeeper posts this transaction to the Vehicle asset account and the H.G. Capital account in Owner's Equity. Rather than deposit cash into the business, H.G. made his personal vehicle a business asset.

Transactions between an owner and his business must be recorded at the asset's *fair value,* which is the value of the asset at the time of the transaction, not the value of the asset at the time of its original purchase. For vehicles, a number of good websites can help you determine an asset's current fair value. (We recommend Auto Trader at www.autotrader.com and Kelley Blue Book at www.kbb.com.) Print the page when you find the fair value that you use to record the investment of the vehicle. The Canada Revenue Agency (CRA) may want to have a look at your research later on when they pay you a visit.

When you record entries in the General Journal, you indent the account name for all the accounts that will be credited, as shown in Figure 5-5. This practice makes reading the entry easier for whoever is reviewing or approving the journal. The explanation that follows can be in as much detail as you think is necessary to answer any questions later on.

Notice that the General Journal has no total columns. Each individual entry has to be posted to the General Ledger.

Refer to Figure 4-4 of Chapter 4 for an illustration of the General Journal once you have completed posting to the General Ledger at the end of the month and you have entered all the check marks in the posting reference column.

Figure 5-5: The point of entry for miscellaneous transactions is the General Journal.

H.G.'s Cheesecake Shop **General Journal** **June 2013**					**GJ 16**
Date		Account Title and Explanation	PR	General Debit	General Credit
June	5	Sales Return		60.00	
		Account Receivable - S.Smith	√		60.00
		Credit memo No. 123			
	9	Accounts Payable - Henry's Bakery Supplies	√	200.00	
		Purchase Returns			200.00
		Debit memo No. 346			
	10	Vehicles		10,000.00	
		H.G. Capital			10,000.00
		H.G. Invests car into the business			

Posting Journal Information to Accounts

When you update your books at the end of the month, you summarize all the journals — that is, you total the columns and post the information to update all the accounts involved.

Posting journal pages is a four-step process:

1. **Number each journal page at the top, if it isn't already numbered.**

2. **Total any column that's not titled General Debit or General Credit.**

   You need to record any transactions in the General Debit or General Credit columns in the individual General Ledger accounts.

3. **Post the entries to the General Ledger accounts.**

   You must post each transaction in the General Credit or General Debit column separately and insert a check mark in the PR column. You need to post just totals to the General Ledger for the other columns in which you enter transactions for more active accounts in the General Journal. List the date and journal page number, as well as the amount of the debit or credit, so that you can quickly find the entry for the original transaction if you need more details.

   The General Ledger account shows only debit or credit (whichever is appropriate to the transaction). Only the journals have both sides of a transaction. (We show you how to work with General Ledger accounts in Chapter 4.)

4. **Use the PR column of the journal to record information about where the entry is posted.**

   If you summarize and total the entry that you plan to post to the accounts at the bottom of the page, you can just put a check mark below the total amount. For transactions listed in the General Credit or General Debit columns, insert a check mark in the PR column. If you have chosen to use account numbers in your chart of accounts, enter instead the account number of the account into which you post the transaction. This process helps you confirm that you've posted all journal entries in the General Ledger.

When you finish posting from one journal, make sure that all the column totals and entries in the General columns have check marks. By making sure that you've recorded everything, you can avoid any problems balancing your General Ledger later on.

You post to the General Ledger at the end of an accounting period as part of the process to complete a reporting cycle. We cover this process in greater detail in Chapter 15.

Figure 5-6 shows a summarized journal page — specifically, the Cash Receipts journal. The bookkeeper has placed a check mark below the totals of the Accounts Receivable Credit, Sales Credit and Cash Debit columns to indicate that the total amounts have been posted to the General Ledger. For the entry of June 9, she posted to the General Ledger the transaction entered in the General Credit column, and placed a check mark in the PR column. If she had chosen to use account numbers in the chart of accounts, she would enter instead the account number of the account into which she posted the transaction. Although this example doesn't list all the transactions for the month (which would, of course, be a much longer list), it does show how you summarize the journal at the end of the month.

As you can see in Figure 5-6, after summarizing the Cash Receipts journal, the bookkeeper has to post entries to only four General Ledger accounts (H.G. Capital, Accounts Receivable Credit, Sales Credit, and Cash Debit) and three customer accounts (S. Smith, J. Jones, and P. Perry). Even better, the entries balance as shown in the table below: $3,260 in debits and $3,260 in credits! (The customer accounts total $530, which is good news because the books credit Accounts Receivable the same amount. The bookkeeper decreased the Accounts Receivable account by $530 because the business received pay-ments, and she also decreased the amount due from the individual customer accounts.)

Figure 5-6:
Summary of Cash Receipts journal entries after the first ten days.

						H.G.'s Cheesecake Shop			
						Cash Receipts Journal			
						June 2013			
									CR-17

Date		Accounts Credited	PR	General Credit	Accounts Receivable Credit	Sales Credit	Cash Debit
June	1	Sales				800.00	800.00
	5	Sales				250.00	250.00
	7	Sandra Smith Ch. 1420	√		200.00		200.00
	9	H.G. Capital	√	1,500.00			1,500.00
	9	Sales				120.00	120.00
	10	Jack Jones Ch. 141	√		150.00		150.00
	10	Patricia Perry Ch. 310	√		180.00		180.00
	10	Sales				60.00	60.00
					530.00	1,230.00	3,260.00
					√	√	√

Debits		*Credits*	
Cash	$3,260	H.G. Capital	$1,500
		Accounts Receivable	$530
		Sales	$1,230
Total debits	$3,260	Total credits	$3,260

Simplifying Your Journaling with Computerized Accounting

You can find the process of recording first to the journals, and then post-ing to the General Ledger and individual customer or vendor accounts, very time-consuming. Luckily, most businesses today use computerized account-ing software, so you don't need to enter the same information so many times. The computer does the work for you.

If you're working with a computerized accounting software package (which we discuss in Chapter 6), you have to enter a transaction only once. The soft-ware automatically posts all the detail that you need to enter into the pen-and-paper journal pages, General Ledger accounts, and customer, vendor, and other accounts. Voila!

The method by which you initially enter your transaction varies, depending on the type of transaction. To show you what's involved in making entries into a computerized accounting system, the following figures show one entry each from the Cash Receipts journal (see Figure 5-7 for a customer payment), the Cash Disbursements journal (see Figure 5-8 for a list of bills to be paid), and the Sales journal (see Figure 5-9 for an invoice). (The screenshots are all from QuickBooks, a popular computerized bookkeeping system.)

As you can see in Figure 5-7, to enter the payment made by Patricia Perry, you need only click the arrow on the Received From drop-down menu to find and select Patricia Perry as a customer. All outstanding invoices then appear. You can put a check mark to the left of the invoices that the customer has paid, indicate the payment method (in this case, a cheque), enter the custom-er's cheque number (if applicable), and click the Save & Close button.

When you use a software package to track your cash receipts, the software automatically updates the following accounts:

✔ The Cash account is debited the appropriate amount.

✔ The Accounts Receivable account is credited the appropriate amount.

✔ The corresponding customer account is credited the appropriate amount.

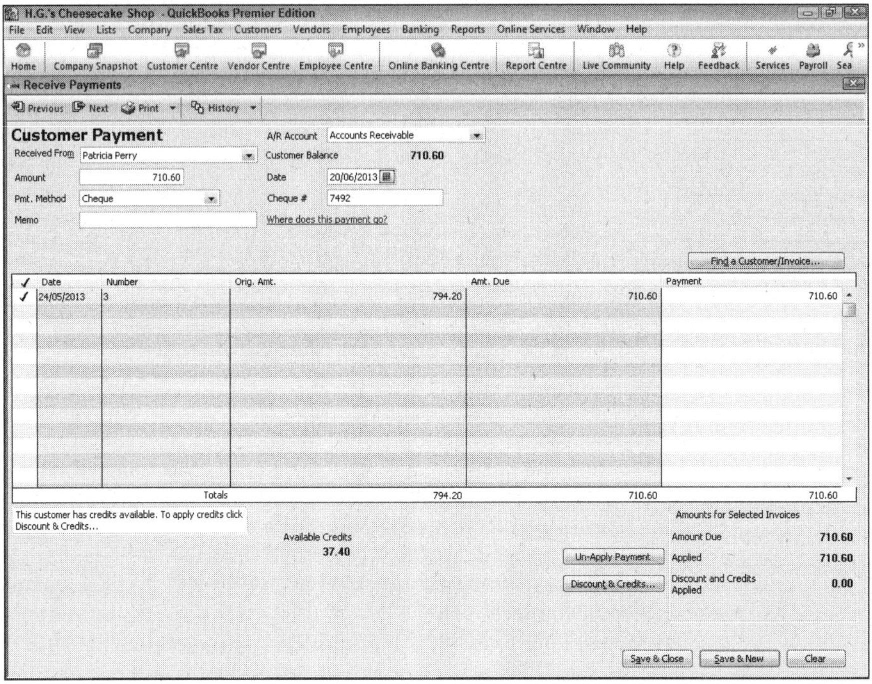

Figure 5-7:
Payment by
customer
Patricia
Perry.

That process is much simpler for you, the bookkeeper, than adding the transaction to the Cash Receipts journal, closing out the journal at the end of the month, adding the transactions to the accounts affected by the cash receipts, and then (finally!) posting to the books.

You can work with cash disbursements even more easily than cash receipts when you have a computerized system on your side. For example, when paying bills (see Figure 5-8), you simply need to go to the Pay Bills screen for QuickBooks. In this example, QuickBooks lists all the May and June bills, so you just select the bills that you want to pay, and the system automatically sets the payments in motion.

The bill-paying perks of this system include

✔ The software package can automatically print cheques.

✔ Each of the vendor accounts updates to show that your business has made the payment.

✔ The Accounts Payable account is debited the appropriate amount for your transaction, which decreases the amount due to vendors.

✔ The Cash account is credited the appropriate amount for your transaction, which decreases the amount of cash available (because the software has designated that cash for use to pay the bills).

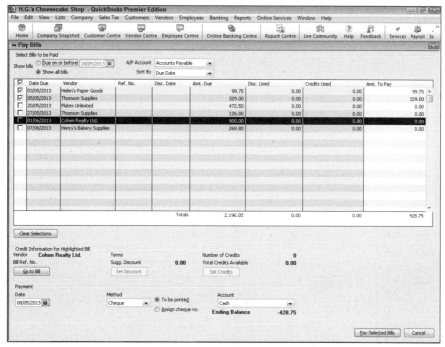

Figure 5-8:
Paying bills
due in May
and June.

While you make the necessary entries into your computerized accounting
system for the information that you find in a pen-and-paper Sales journal
(for example, when a customer purchases your product on account), you
automatically create an invoice for the purchase. Figure 5-9 shows what that
invoice looks like when QuickBooks generates it. When you add the customer
name in the Customer text box, the software automatically fills in all the
necessary customer information. The date appears automatically, and the
system assigns a customer invoice number. You add the quantity and select
the type of product bought in the Item Code section, and the software calculates the rest of the invoice automatically. When you finish filling out the
invoice, you can print it and send it off to the customer.

Figure 5-9 shows sales tax automatically calculated by QuickBooks based on
the S code (which stands for Standard) that appears under the tax column for
the item sold, which means you must charge both GST and PST.

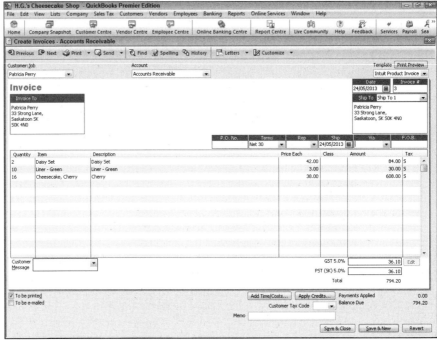

Figure 5-9:
A customer
invoice for
Patricia
Perry's
purchase.

Filling out the invoice in the accounting system also updates all the affected
accounts. The software

✔ Debits the Accounts Receivable account by the appropriate amount
  ($794.20, in our example), which increases the amount due from custom-
  ers by that amount

✔ Credits the Sales account by the appropriate amount ($722.00, in this
  example), which increases the revenue earned by that amount

✔ Credits (increases) the GST Payable account by the appropriate amount
  ($36.10, in our case) for the amount charged for GST

✔ Credits (increases) the PST Payable account by the appropriate amount
  ($36.10, in our example) for the amount charged for PST

✔ Adds the invoice to the customer's outstanding bills so that when the
  customer makes a payment, the outstanding invoice appears on the payment screen

Dealing with Sales Taxes

Don't worry, we won't get into too much taxing detail at this point, but we do need to mention taxes. Although we wish we all had a choice in the matter, you can't opt out of charging taxes.

We admit; we've spared you so far in this chapter — the journals and ledgers actually should have additional columns that show the part of each transaction that belongs to the government. Yes, you have silent partners — the provincial and federal governments. They make you their agent to collect their taxes on your sales transactions. As their agent, you need to follow their rules very carefully.

In the following sections, we cover some general tax rules to keep your silent partner happy.

Goods and services tax or harmonized sales tax (GST/HST)

If you bring in more than $30,000 for goods or services rendered, you have to become a registrant and charge the GST/HST tax. (Even if you don't have revenues of $30,000 a year, you may want to register — we discuss why in the following section.) The federal government wants you to charge 5 percent on practically all goods and services you sell, excluding items such as basic food, medicine, dental work, and bank services. Check out the CRA website (www.cra-arc.gc.ca) for more details concerning what qualifies for GST/HST exemption. After you click the English or French button (depending on what language you speak), the home page appears with two sections for key links: one for individuals and one for businesses. Click the GST/HST link on list of links for businesses. The search tool on the site can help narrow down the large amount of technical detail on this topic.

Registering to charge GST/HST

Before you can register to charge GST/HST, you must have a business number (BN), which we discuss in Chapter 1. If you already have a BN, you may have created your GST/HST remittance account at the same time that you applied for your BN. If you already have a BN but don't have a remittance account, the CRA website offers instructions that show you how to become a registrant.

You have to let your customers know if you charge GST/HST on your sales. You can do that by writing on your invoice or your cash register receipt that the total amount charged includes GST/HST. Or, show the specific amount of GST/HST charged along with any provincial sales tax with the applicable tax rates. If your sale amount exceeds $30, you also have to provide your business number. On the other hand, if your sale amount is below $30, you need only show your business name, invoice date, and total amount paid. Your invoices and business receipts must always show your business or trading name, no matter the size of the sale. If your customer is a business, it needs the GST/HST information. Just like you, your customer wants to claim input tax credits (ITCs), which we discuss in the following section.

You need to charge and collect GST/HST on items other than your sales you record in the Sales and the Cash Receipts journals. When recording your payroll, you may have to add any GST/HST you are required to charge on fringe benefits you give your employees. We discuss this further in Chapter 10. When you charge yourself — or in this case, your employees — any sort of taxes, this is called *self-assessment*. You will discover that the government expects business owners to self-assess in a lot of situations, both personally and in their businesses. You won't be able to save yourself by claiming that you are ignorant of the rules when the tax auditors come pay you a visit.

Even if you don't have revenues in excess of $30,000, you may want to consider voluntarily registering to collect the GST/HST. By becoming a registrant, you can get back the GST/HST your business pays for goods and services. If your customers are registrants themselves, they shouldn't care if you charge them GST/HST. After all, they can claim back all the GST/HST they pay when they buy from you, anyhow!

Recording GST/HST input tax credits

Here's how you keep track of GST/HST credits, which are more formally known as *input tax credits* (ITCs):

- ✔ When you pay GST/HST on purchases, record the amount that you pay as a debit (an increase) in a GST/HST Receivable account. (Some businesses simply call the General Ledger account GST/HST — ITC, or GST/HST Recoverable.)

  You can also use the Simplified Method provided by the CRA to claim ITCs for your business, in which case you do not have to show the GST/HST separately in your records. You need to watch for what GST/HST was charged to your business if the purchase was made from a different province, and then calculate the ITCs accordingly.

  The CRA doesn't notify you if you miss out on some GST/HST credits. You have the responsibility to keep track of the amount you paid to make sure that you get the most money back from the government.

✔ When you charge GST/HST to one of your customers by adding it on your invoice, as in Figure 5-9, you also record an increase in a liability with a credit to the GST/HST Payable account.

In any given month, you probably (hopefully!) charge more GST/HST than you pay. So, by the end of that month, you end up owing the net amount of money (the amount you charged minus the amount you paid) to the government.

✔ At the end of your reporting period (the length of which depends mainly on your business's annual sales — search for General Information for GST/HST Registrants on www.cra-arc.gc.ca for more detailed information), fill out a Goods and Services Tax/Harmonized Sales Tax Return for Registrants (GST/HST) form GST34 and send in the stub portion with a cheque payable to the Receiver General for the amount of the difference between the GST/HST that your business collected and the GST/HST that it paid.

In Chapter 21, we discuss how to fill out the GST34 form and also indicate the different ways that you can file the return.

Provincial sales tax or retail sales tax (PST/RST)

Provincial requirements for charging provincial sales taxes (PST) vary. Alberta has no provincial sales tax at all! In most provinces, the sales tax is grouped with the GST and called the harmonized sales tax (HST). Although governments are attempting to make charging taxes more consistent across Canada, subtle differences still exist, so consult with your business's accountant to ensure that your business is charging and recording the proper tax rate.

You need to be particularly careful if you deliver goods sold to customers located in other provinces or territories. Say, for example, you operate in the province of Ontario and you sell and deliver goods to a customer in the province of Manitoba. You have to charge and remit PST on those sales to the government of Manitoba.

For those provinces that have a combined harmonized tax with the federal government, you need only the CRA GST/HST account for remitting any money that your business owes the government minus any GST/HST your business paid. If, however, you're in a province where the PST and GST are separate, you need to register in order to remit the provincial sales tax according to that particular province's rules, and you need to keep track of the amounts of PST/RST charged in a separate column of your Sales journal.

(Check out your province's website for a link to the PST/RST rules.) Track totals in a General Ledger account called Provincial Sales Taxes Payable.

The provincial government doesn't refund you for any PST/RST your business pays. The PST/RST you pay gets added to the invoice cost of the truck or the supplies, for example, when you first make the entry in any of the journals.

Provinces don't charge PST on all purchases of merchandise. PST registrants — who are retailers — buy merchandise intended for resale without having to pay PST because they charge their customers PST on that merchandise. The provincial government doesn't intend to tax the goods two or three times. It wants the consumers of the goods to pay the PST at the end of the distribution channel — and on the highest price paid.

Chapter 6

Computer Options for Your Bookkeeping

A very few small-business owners who have been around awhile still do things the old-fashioned way — keep their books in paper journals and ledgers. However, in this age of technology and instant information, the vast majority of today's businesses computerize their books.

Not only is computerized bookkeeping easier than the pen-and-paper method, but it also minimizes the chance of errors because most of the work that you do to a computerized system's ledgers and journals involves inputting data for transactions on forms that even someone without training in accounting or bookkeeping can understand. (Refer to Chapters 4 and 5, respectively, for the lowdown on ledgers and journals.) The person entering the information doesn't need to know whether something is a debit or credit (refer to Chapter 2 for an explanation of the difference), because the computerized system takes care of everything.

In this chapter, we explore the two top accounting software packages for small businesses, discuss the basics of setting up your own computerized books, talk about how you can customize a program for your business, and give you some pointers on converting your manual bookkeeping system to a computerized one.

Surveying Your Software Options

More than 50 different types of accounting software programs are on the market, and all are designed to computerize your bookkeeping. The more sophisticated ones target specific industry needs, such as construction, food services, or utilities, and they can cost thousands of dollars. A quick Internet search unearths the options available to you. Several sites offer demos of their software packages.

Luckily, as a small-business owner, you probably don't need all the bells and whistles offered by the top-of-the-line programs. Instead, two software programs that we review in this chapter can meet the needs of most small businesses. Using one of the two systems we recommend, you can get started with an initial investment of as little as $200. It may not be fancy, but basic computerized accounting software can do a fine job of helping you keep your books. And you can always upgrade to a more expensive program, if needed, while your business grows.

The two programs that meet any small business's basic bookkeeping needs are Simply Accounting Pro by Sage and QuickBooks Pro by Intuit. Each of these packages has an affordable (and practically identical) price. These software companies also offer simple systems that can take care of billing and cash transactions, but neither has full General Ledger capabilities — Sage has Simply Accounting First Step, and QuickBooks has EasyStart. Either of these two software packages can get you started for as little as $80. But if you can afford it, we recommend that you step at least one notch above the basic levels to QuickBooks Pro or Simply Accounting Pro. These software packages offer a General Ledger module, which allows you to prepare a full trial balance and financial statements.

Accounting software packages are updated almost every year because tax laws and laws involving many other aspects of operating a business, such as payroll, change so often. In addition, computer software companies are always improving their products to make computerized accounting programs more user-friendly, so be sure that you always buy the most current version of an accounting software package.

Simply Accounting Pro

Simply Accounting Pro is a cost-effective choice for bookkeeping software if you're just starting up and don't have sophisticated bookkeeping or accounting needs. This program caters to the bookkeeping novice and even provides an option that lets you avoid accounting jargon by using words such as "purchase" and "vendor" in the icon list, rather than "accounts payable," when you want to record a purchase of goods from a vendor. The program includes several accounting templates for documents such as sales orders, quotes, receipts, and other basic needs for a variety of industries, including medical/dental, real estate, property management, and retail firms.

Simply Accounting Pro has an integrated feature that allows you to do Employee Direct Deposit or electronic funds transfers (EFTs) for payroll. QuickBooks does not have this feature. On the other hand, you can file your GST/HST return online using QuickBooks but not with Simply Accounting Pro.

If you're working with another software system to manage your business data and want to switch to Simply Accounting Pro, you may be able to import that data directly into Simply Accounting. (You can find information about how to import data included with the program.) You can import data from software such as Microsoft Excel (a spreadsheet program) or Access (a database program). If you're converting from QuickBooks or another accounting software program called MYOB, you can easily import your data to Simply Accounting.

QuickBooks Pro

QuickBooks Pro offers the best of both worlds: an easy user interface (for the novice) and extensive bookkeeping and accounting features (for the experienced bookkeeper or accountant). We chose to use QuickBooks to demonstrate various bookkeeping functions throughout this book because it is so user-friendly. Yes, it's our favourite bookkeeping software, but we're not alone — more small-business owners today use QuickBooks than any other small-business accounting software package. For additional information on this software, check out *QuickBooks 2012 All-in-One For Dummies*, by Stephen L. Nelson (Wiley).

Most people have a love/hate relationship with Intuit support (Intuit's the company that makes QuickBooks). We've had good support experiences not only with QuickBooks but also with its other popular software packages, such as TurboTax and Quicken. But we also know others who have complained loudly about support problems.

QuickBooks Easy Start, priced around $80, can meet most of your bookkeeping and accounting needs. If you want to track inventory, download your online banking info, or integrate your bookkeeping with a point-of-sale package, which integrates cash-register sales, you need to get QuickBooks Pro, which sells for around $200 and allows up to five simultaneous users. You'll need to upgrade even further if you want to create sales orders, track back orders, and forecast sales and expenses. Determining what version of QuickBooks is best for you really depends on what your specific business needs are.

Add-ons and fees

The accounting programs that we recommend in the section "Surveying Your Software Options," in this chapter, offer add-ons and features that you're likely to need, such as

✔ **Tax updates:** If you have employees and want up-to-date tax information and forms to do your payroll by using your accounting software, you need to buy an update each year. The software suppliers or their distributors may instead charge you a monthly fee for the package, which gives you access to the updates when you need them.

✔ **Direct credit card and debit card payment processing:** If you want the capabilities to perform these tasks, you have to pay

additional fees. In fact, QuickBooks advertises its add-ons in these areas, such as Enterprise Solutions, throughout its system; you can see the advertisements pop up on a number of screens.

✔ **Point-of-sale software:** This add-on helps you integrate your sales at the cash register with your accounting software. A more sophisticated version of the software helps you manage inventory at several locations.

Before you sign on for one of the add-ons, make sure you understand what fees you have to pay. Usually, the software supplier or a distributor advises you of the additional costs whenever you try to do anything that incurs extra fees.

QuickBooks is the most versatile software if you plan to use other software packages along with it. QuickBooks can share data with countless popular business software applications. You can easily share sales, customer, and financial data, too, so you don't have to enter that information twice. To find out if QuickBooks can share data with the business software applications you're currently using or plan to use, contact Intuit directly (www.intuit.ca).

Setting Up Your Computerized Books

After you pick your software, the hard work is done; actually setting up the package probably takes you less time than researching your options and picking your software. Both packages we discuss in this chapter (refer to the section "Surveying Your Software Options," earlier in this chapter) have good start-up tutorials to help you set up the books. QuickBooks even has an interactive interview that asks questions about all aspects of how you want to run your business and then sets up what you need based on your answers.

Simply Accounting Pro and QuickBooks Pro both produce a number of sample Charts of Accounts (refer to Chapter 3) that you can use as starting points to save time. Start with one of the charts offered by the software. You can then tweak the sample chart by adding and deleting accounts to suit your business's needs. If you want to, you can start from scratch.

You use QuickBooks EasyStep Interview to start creating your company file. To access this function, click the File command in the top menu bar. After you follow the interview and have entered all the basic information, a basic Chart of Accounts is created automatically. You can view the results of your entries on the Company Information screen by choosing the Company command on the top menu bar. Figure 6-1 shows you the QuickBooks Company Information for H.G.'s Cheesecake Shop.

Figure 6-1:
As part of the initial interview in QuickBooks, the system helps you record your basic company information.

Both Simply Accounting Pro and QuickBooks Pro ask you to enter a company name, address, and business number (BN) to get started. You then select an accounting period (see Figure 6-1). If the calendar year is your accounting period, you don't have to change anything. But if your business is incorporated, which means it can have a fiscal year other than the calendar year (such as September 1 to August 31), you must enter that information. After you enter this information, the software recognizes the fiscal year for the part of the accounting cycle that involves closing the books. We discuss how the software is involved in closing the books in Chapter 22.

WARNING!

If you don't change your accounting period to match your fiscal year when you first record your company's information in your accounting software, you'll have to delete the business from the system and start over.

You are asked during the QuickBooks EasyStep Interview to select the industry in which your business operates. Your choice guides QuickBooks to create a preliminary Chart of Accounts for your business that saves you a lot of work.

Figure 6-2 shows you the QuickBooks screen for adding accounts to your Chart of Accounts, where we enter an expense account as an example. Note the Other Account Types drop-down list, which allows you to choose which group of accounts your new expense account will be grouped in for your financial reports. You can access this screen by right-clicking in the Chart of Accounts listing. (Refer to Chapter 3 for our discussion of the Chart of Accounts.)

Choose your fiscal year

Many retail businesses don't close their books at the end of December because the holiday season isn't a good time for those businesses to close out for the year. Each year, because of gift cards and other new ways to give gifts, retail businesses can see very active purchases after the holidays. Therefore, many retail businesses operate on a fiscal year of February 1 to January 31 so that they can close the books well after the holiday season ends.

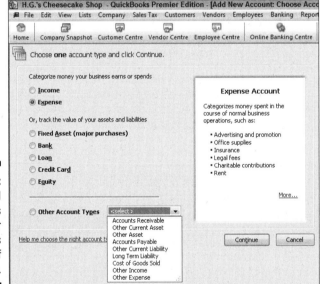

Figure 6-2:
Add accounts in your QuickBooks Chart of Accounts.

Customizing software to match your operations

After you set up the basics (refer to the preceding section), you can customize the software to fit your business's operations. For example, you can pick the type of invoices and other business forms that you want to use.

You can also input information about your bank accounts and other key financial data. Then, you can add opening balances to accounts for customers and vendors so that you can track future cash transactions. Make your main business bank account the first account listed in your software program, labelled as either Cash in Chequing or just Cash.

After you enter your bank and other financial information, you can enter data unique to your business. If you want to use the program's budgeting features, you enter your budget information before entering other data. (We show you how to enter budget information in Chapter 23.) Then, you add your vendor and customer accounts so that when you start entering transactions, you already have the vendor or customer information in the system. If you don't have any outstanding bills or customer payments due, you can wait and enter vendor and customer information when the need arises.

If you have payments that you need to make or money that you need to collect from customers, be sure to input that information so that your system is ready when it comes time to pay the bills or input a customer payment on account. Also, you don't want to forget to pay a bill or collect from a customer!

You may be able to import data about your customers, vendors, and employees from the software package that you're currently using, such as Microsoft Excel or Access. Full instructions for importing data come with the software program you choose.

Don't panic about entering everything into your computerized system right away. All programs make it very easy to add customers, vendors, and employees at any time.

You need to enter information about whether you collect GST/HST and provincial sales taxes from your customers and, if you do, the sales tax rates. We discuss when and how you charge these taxes in Chapter 5. Your software also lets you pick a format for your invoices, set up payroll data, and make arrangements for how you want to pay bills.

Converting your manual bookkeeping to a computerized system

If you're converting a manual bookkeeping system to a computerized system, your conversion takes a bit more time than just starting fresh because you need to be sure that your new system starts with information that matches your current books. The process for entering your initial data varies, depending on the software you choose, so we don't go into detail about that process here. To ensure that you properly convert your bookkeeping system, use the information that comes with your software — read through the manual, review the start-up suggestions that the software makes while you set up the system, and pick the methods that best match your style of operating.

The best time to convert your pen-and-paper books to computerized versions is at the end of an accounting period. That way, you don't have to do a lot of extra work adding transactions that already occurred during a period. For example, if you decide to computerize your accounting system on March 15, you have to add all the transactions that occurred between March 1 and March 15 into your new system. You may even have to go back to the beginning of the fiscal year. You can make the process much easier by waiting until April 1 to get started, even if you buy the software on March 15. Although you can convert to a computerized accounting system at the end of a month, the best time to do the conversion is at the end of a calendar or fiscal year. Otherwise, you have to input data for all the months of the year that have passed.

Whenever you decide to start your computerized bookkeeping, use the data from the trial balance that you used to close the books at the end of the last fiscal year. (We explain how to prepare a trial balance in Chapter 16.) In the computerized system, enter the balances in your trial balance for each of the accounts. Asset, Liability, and Equity accounts should have carry-over balances, but Revenue and Expense accounts should have zero balances.

Of course, if you're starting a new business, you don't have a previous trial balance. In that case, you just enter any balances you may have in your Cash accounts, any assets your business may own when it starts up, and any liabilities that your business may already owe relating to start-up expenses. You also add any contributions that owners made to get the business started in the Equity accounts.

After you enter all the appropriate data, run a series of financial reports, such as an income statement (called Profit and Loss in QuickBooks) and balance sheet, to be sure you entered the data correctly and the software formats that data the way you want. If, for example, you need subtotals in financial statements, you can add that feature to your computerized financial statements or reports right away.

You need to be sure that you've entered the right numbers, so verify that the new accounting system's financial reports match what you created manually. If the numbers are different, now's the time to figure out why. Otherwise, the reports you do at the end of the accounting period will have the wrong information. If the numbers don't match, don't assume that the error can be only in the data entered. You may find that you made an error in the reports you developed manually. Of course, check your entries first, but if the income statement and balance sheet still don't look right, double-check your old trial balances, as well.

Chapter 7

Controlling Your Books, Your Records, and Your Money

● ●

In This Chapter

▶ Protecting your business's cash

▶ Maintaining proper paperwork and electronic backups

▶ Dividing employee responsibilities

▶ Insuring your cash handlers

● ●

*E*very business takes in cash in some form. Whether in the form of dollar bills, cheques, credit cards, debit cards, or electronic payments, it's all eventually deposited as cash into the business's accounts. Before you take in that first penny, controlling that cash and making sure none of it walks out the door improperly should be your first concern as a businessperson.

You have to deal with the monumental task of finding the right level of cash control, while at the same time allowing your employees the flexibility to sell your products or services, and provide ongoing customer service. If you don't have enough controls, you risk theft or embezzlement. Yet, if you have too many controls, employees may cause your business to miss out on sales or anger your customers.

In this chapter, we explain the basic protections that you need to put in place to be sure all cash coming into or going out of your business is clearly documented and controlled. We also review the type of paperwork or electronic files you need to keep so that you can document the use of cash and other business assets. Finally, we tell you how to organize your staff to properly control access to your assets and insure yourself against possible misappropriation of those assets.

Putting Controls on Your Business's Cash

Think about how careful you are with your personal cash. You find various ways to protect how you carry it around, you dole it out carefully to your family members, and you may even hide cash in a safe place in the house just in case you need it for unexpected purposes. You've probably switched from using cash to using debit or credit cards for a vast majority of your personal purchases, just to avoid the risk of losing your cash.

If you're that protective of your cash when you're the only one who handles it, consider the vulnerability of business cash. After all, you aren't the only one handling the cash for your business. You have some employees encountering incoming cash at cash registers and others opening the mail to find cheques to purchase your products or pay your accounts receivable, as well as cheques from other sources. And don't forget that employees may need petty cash to pay for mail or courier deliveries sent COD (cash on delivery) or to pay for other unexpected, low-cost needs.

If you were around to watch every transaction in which cash enters your business, you wouldn't have time to do the things you need to do to grow your business. If your business is small enough, you can maintain control of cash going out by signing all cheques, but as soon as the business grows, you may not have time for that.

You can drive yourself crazy with worry about all this cash flow, but the truth is that just putting in place the proper controls for your cash can help protect your business's family jewels. Cash flows through your business in four key ways:

- Deposits, transfers, and payments into and out of your chequing accounts
- Deposits, transfers, and payments into and out of your savings accounts, if you have any
- Petty cash funds in critical locations where the business may need fast cash for small payments
- Transactions made through your cash registers

The following sections cover some key controls for each of these cash flow points.

Chequing accounts

Almost every dime that comes into your business flows through your business's chequing account (or at least that's what *should* happen). Whether you have cash collected at your cash registers, payments received in the mail, electronic funds transfers (EFTs), cash used to fill the cash registers with floats, petty cash accounts, payments sent out to pay business obligations to creditors, or any other cash need, this cash enters and exits your chequing account. So, you use your chequing account as your main tool to protect your cash flow.

Choosing the right bank

You need to find the right bank to help you set up your chequing account and the controls that limit access to that account. When evaluating your banking options, ask yourself the following questions:

- ✔ Does this bank have a branch that's conveniently located in relation to my business?
- ✔ Does this bank operate at times when I need it most?
- ✔ Does this bank offer a full range of Internet banking options?
- ✔ Does this bank offer secure ways to deposit cash, even when the bank is closed?

  Most banks have secure drop boxes for cash so that you can deposit receipts as quickly as possible at the end of the business day, rather than your having to secure the cash overnight.

Visit local bank branches yourself and check out the type of business services each bank offers. Pay particular attention to

- ✔ The type of personal attention you receive
- ✔ How the bank representatives handle questions
- ✔ What type of charges the bank may tack on for special services such as providing coins for floats.

Some banks require business-account holders to call a centralized line for assistance, rather than depend on local branches. Some banks are even adding charges if you use a teller, rather than an ATM (automatic teller machine). Other banks charge for every transaction, whether it's a deposit, withdrawal, debit card transaction, or cheque. Many banks have charges that differ for business accounts, and most charge your business for printing cheques. If you're planning to accept credit cards and debit cards, compare the services offered for those transactions, as well.

Deciding on types of cheques

After you choose your bank, you need to consider what type of cheques you want to use in your business. For example, you need different cheques, depending on whether you handwrite each cheque or print cheques from your computerized accounting system, or perhaps even both.

If you plan to write your cheques, you most likely use a business cheque that has a stub attached to the left of the cheque. The cheque-and-stub format provides the best control for manual cheques because each cheque and corresponding stub is pre-numbered. When you write a cheque, you also fill out the stub with details about the date, the cheque's recipient (usually referred to as the *payee*), and the purpose of the cheque. The stub also has a space to keep a running total of the balance in your bank account. An alternative to the stub is a format of cheques that provides you with a control duplicate that is retained in your chequebook. You don't keep a running balance when you use duplicate cheques, but using this technique means you can get away with less writing.

If you plan to print cheques and deposit slips (which we discuss in the following section) from your computerized accounting system, you need to order business forms that match your system's programming. Each computer software program has a unique template for printing cheques and deposit slips.

Rules administered by the Canadian Payments Association (CPA) dictate the format of cheques. These rules are set up to protect banks and account holders against fraud.

If you use QuickBooks, the format of cheques you select depends on the type of printer you intend to use. You can select different styles of cheques, but we recommend a format that leaves the best paper trail. On each page, rather than a stub, two additional blank spaces follow the detachable cheque that already has your key business information pre-printed. In the first blank space, at the bottom of the cheque voucher, QuickBooks prints out the detail you'd expect to find on a manual voucher or stub — the date, name of the recipient, cheque number, and purpose of the cheque. You detach and keep this section in your records as a control to document what was paid for with the cheque that you've just used. You can decide to staple this portion of the voucher to the supporting invoice from your vendor, or you can keep these vouchers in numerical order for future reference. In the remaining middle section of the form, your system prints the information that the recipient of the cheque needs. For example, if you're creating a cheque to pay an outstanding invoice, you include all information that the vendor needs to properly credit that invoice, such as the amount, the invoice number, and your customer account number. If you're preparing a payroll cheque, one of the blank sections should contain all the required payroll information, including the amount of gross earnings, details of all the deductions and the amount of net cheque for the current payment, and possibly year-to-date totals. Send the cheque and the portion that includes the detail to your vendor, employee, or other recipient.

Initially, when the business is small, you can keep control of the outflow of money by signing each cheque. But when the business grows, you probably find that you need to delegate cheque-signing responsibilities to someone you trust, especially if your business requires you to travel frequently. Many small-business owners set up with the bank cheque-signing procedures that allow one or two of their staff to sign cheques up to a designated amount, such as $1,000. Any cheques for more than that designated amount require the owner's signature, or the signature of an employee and a second designated person, such as an officer of the business.

Of course, you don't just withdraw from your business's chequing account at the ATM. You'll be happy to know business bank accounts don't allow that to happen, because too much opportunity exists for undocumented withdrawals of cash.

Arranging deposits to the chequing account

You also need to deposit money into the businesses chequing account, and you want to be sure your deposit slips contain all the needed detail, as well as documentation to back up the deposit information. Most banks provide printed deposit slips that have all the necessary detail so that you can be sure the bank deposits the money in the appropriate account. Along with a cheque order, printing companies dealing through banks usually offer to provide you a For Deposit Only stamp. The stamp includes the name of your business and the chequing account number, which you can use on the back of the cheques. (If you don't get that stamp through the bank, be sure to have one made as soon as possible at a stationery store.)

Instruct whoever opens your business mail to use your For Deposit Only stamp immediately on the back of any cheque the business receives in the mail. Stamping "For Deposit Only" on the back of a cheque makes it a lot harder for anyone to use that cheque for anything other than its intended business purposes. Also make sure that the employee in charge of opening the mail and handling cheques for deposit is not also responsible for making deposits at your bank. (We talk more about controls for incoming cash in the "Dividing staff responsibilities" section, later in this chapter.) If you get both personal and business cheques sent to the same address, set up some instructions for the person opening the mail regarding how to differentiate the types of cheques and how to handle each type of cheque to best protect your incoming cash, whether for business or personal purposes.

To secure incoming cash even more carefully, some businesses set up lockbox services with a bank. Customers or others who send cheques to the business mail cheques to a post office box number that goes directly to the bank, and a bank employee opens and deposits the cheques right into the business's account. Businesses sometimes use this method of collection if the money they receive comes from a customer in another country or is in a foreign currency. Providing this option to customers makes it easier to make collections and often speeds up the process.

You can also offer your customers the option of paying you with an electronic funds transfer (EFT). EFTs offer you a secure and fast way of getting payments into your business account.

You may think that making bank deposits is as easy as one, two, three, but when it comes to business deposits involving multiple cheques, things get a bit more complicated. To properly make deposits to your business's chequing account, follow these steps:

1. **Record on the deposit slip the amounts of all cheques you're depositing, as well as the total cash you're depositing.**

2. **Make photocopies of all cheques that you deposit so that you have a record, in case something gets lost or misplaced at the bank.**

3. **After you make the deposit, attach the copies of all the cheques to the deposit receipt and add any detail regarding the source of the deposited cash; file everything in your daily bank folder.**

   We talk more about filing in the section "Keeping the Right Paperwork," later in this chapter.

Savings accounts

Some businesses find that they have more cash than they need to meet their immediate needs. Rather than keep that extra cash in a non-interest-bearing account, many businesses open a savings account to store the extra cash stash. Some businesses choose to open a trading account that gives the business access to a money market fund that pays interest. Transactions in and out of savings or trading accounts are mostly done electronically.

If you're a small-business owner who has few employees, you probably control the flow of money into and out of your savings or trading account. While you grow and find that you need to delegate the responsibility for the business's savings, be sure to think carefully about who gets access and how you want to document the flow of funds into and out of the savings or trading account. Your bank can suggest some ways to add some password access controls.

Petty cash accounts

Every business needs to make small cash payments on a regular basis. Whether it's money used to pay the mail carrier or courier delivery person when he brings a letter or package COD, or money for some office supplies that you need to buy before the next bulk supply delivery, businesses need to keep some cash on hand, called *petty cash,* for unexpected expenses. Having to prepare a cheque for these small amounts is not practical and takes too much time, and each cheque incurs bank fees.

You certainly don't want to have a lot of cash sitting around in the office, but you should keep $100 to $200 in a petty cash box. If you're faced with cash expenses more or less often than you initially expected, you can adjust the amount kept in petty cash accordingly.

No matter how much you keep in petty cash, be sure you set up a good control system that requires anyone who uses the cash to write a voucher that specifies how much he used and why. Whenever possible, the person who initially spends the money should also attach a cash receipt (from the store or post office, for example) to the voucher in order to justify the cash withdrawal. In most cases, a staff person buys something for the business and then gets reimbursed for that expense. If the expense is small enough, you can reimburse that person by using the petty cash fund. If the expense is more than a few dollars, you may want to ask the person to fill out an expense account form and get reimbursed by cheque. You usually use petty cash for minor expenses.

You can best control petty cash by picking one person in the office or store to manage the use of petty cash. Before giving that person more cash and replenishing the petty cash fund, she should be able to prove how the cash was used and why it was used.

Whenever someone in your business spends petty cash, insist on obtaining receipts. In Chapter 5, we discuss why you want to account for the GST/HST paid on all purchases, and payments made from the petty cash fund are no exception. Cash register receipts and other types of sales slips show the amount of GST/HST paid on petty cash transactions, and you don't want to miss out on getting reimbursed this tax.

Cash registers

Have you ever gone into a business and tried to pay with a large bill only to find out the cashier can't make change? It's frustrating, but it happens in many businesses, especially when they don't carefully monitor the money in their cash registers. Most businesses empty cash registers each night and put any cash that they don't deposit in the bank that night into a locked safe. However, many businesses instruct their cashiers to periodically deposit their cash in a business safe throughout the day and get a paper voucher to show the cash deposited. These daytime deposits minimize the cash held in the cash register drawer, in case the store is the victim of a robbery.

All these types of controls are necessary parts of modern business operations, but they can have consequences that make customers angry. Most customers just walk out the door and don't come back if they can't buy what they want by using the bills that they have on hand.

At the beginning of the day, cashiers usually start out with a set amount of cash in the register drawer. This amount is called a *float*. While they collect money and give out change, the register records the transactions. At the end of the day, the cashier must count out the amount of money left in the register, print out a summary total of all transactions that passed through that register, and total the cash collected. Then, the cashier must prove that the amount of cash remaining in the register totals the amount of cash the register started with, plus the amount of cash sales collected during the day. (We give you an illustration of a cash-out form that is filled out by the cashier in Chapter 9.) After the cashier balances the register, the staff person in charge of cash deposits (usually the store manager or someone on the accounting or bookkeeping staff) takes all the cash out, except the amount for the next day's float, and deposits it in the bank. You should also assign to the same person in charge of checking that the cashier properly balances the cash the job of checking that credit and debit card sales balance to the amounts reported in the cash register summary totals. (We talk more about the separation of staff duties in the section "Dividing staff responsibilities," later in this chapter.)

In addition to having the proper amount of cash in the register so that your business can give customers the change they need, you also must make sure that your cashiers are giving the right amount of change and actually recording all sales through their cash registers. Keeping an eye on cashier activities is good business practice, and you can protect against cash theft by your employees. The cashiers can pocket some extra cash in three ways:

> ✔ **They don't record the sale in the cash register and instead pocket the cash.** You can rely on some electronic controls to help you prevent this fraud. Most cash registers use a scanner to read the Universal Product Code (UPC barcode) off a product. The UPC allows the computer system to access your computer records and come up with the correct selling price the cash register then uses to process the sale. Your computerized inventory records get immediately updated with the sale. Scanning

products causes a beep sound to occur, and your supervisor has a good chance of noticing when goods get passed by the register without a sound. The best deterrent to this type of theft is supervision. You can also install cameras to keep a watch on your cashiers.

✔ **They don't provide a sales slip or receipt and instead pocket the cash.** In this scenario, the cashier neglects to give a sales receipt to one customer in line. The cashier gives the next customer the unused sales receipt but doesn't actually record the second transaction in the cash register. Instead, he just pockets the cash from the second transaction. In the business's books, the second sale never took place. The customer whose sale wasn't recorded has a valid receipt, though it may not match exactly what she bought, so she likely doesn't notice any problem unless she wants to return something later. Your best defence against this type of deception is to post a sign reminding all customers that they should get a receipt for all purchases and that they need the receipt to get a refund or exchange. Providing numbered sales receipts that appear in duplicate on the master copy of the cash register tape can also help prevent this problem; cashiers need to balance the day's cash to the total amount the cash register master tape indicates has passed through their registers.

✔ **They record a false credit voucher and keep the cash for themselves.** In this case, the cashier writes up a credit voucher for a nonexistent customer and then pockets the cash himself. Most stores control this problem by using a numbered credit voucher system for sales returns, so the business can carefully monitor each credit with some hard evidence that proves it's based on a previous customer purchase, such as a cash register receipt. Also, stores usually require that a manager or head cashier reviews the reason for the credit voucher, whether a return or exchange, and approves the transaction before the cashier can give cash or credit. When the bookkeeper records the sales return in the books, she records the number for the credit voucher with the transaction so that she can easily find the detail about that credit voucher if someone raises a question later about the transaction.

Some cash registers require a key to let the cashier record a credit transaction. Only the head cashier, supervisor, or manager of the store can use the key. A store may also have customers fill out their name, address, and phone number on the credit voucher or separate refund slip. Later on in the day, the manager calls a sample of customers to verify that they actually made a return at the store.

Even if cashiers don't deliberately pocket cash, they can do so inadvertently by giving the wrong change. If you run a retail outlet, training and supervising your cashiers is a critical task that you must either handle yourself or hand over to a trusted employee.

Keeping the Right Paperwork

When it comes to handling cash — whether you're talking about the cash register, deposits into your chequing accounts, or petty cash withdrawals — a lot of paper changes hands. In order to properly control the movement of cash into and out of your business, careful documentation is key. And don't forget about organization; you need to be able to find that documentation if questions about cash flow arise later.

Monitoring cash flow isn't the only reason you need to keep loads of paperwork. In order to prepare your income tax return and write off business expenses, you need to have receipts for those expenses. You also need details about the money you paid to employees and the taxes collected for your employees so that you can file the proper reports with government departments. (We discuss taxes in Chapter 21, and dealing with the government when it comes to employee matters in Chapter 11.) Any small-business owner needs to set up a good filing system and know what to keep and for how long to keep it.

Creating a filing system

To get started setting up your filing system, you need some supplies:

- **Filing cabinets:** This one's pretty self-explanatory — it's hard to have a filing system if you don't have anything to keep the files in.

- **File folders:** Use these folders to set up separate files for each of your vendors, employees, and customers who buy merchandise or services on account, as well as files for backup information about each of your transactions. Many bookkeepers file transaction information chronologically, which in turn corresponds to the order in which the transactions are recorded in the journals. If a transaction relates to a customer, vendor, or employee, the bookkeeper adds a duplicate copy of the transaction to the individual file, as well.

  Even if you have a computerized accounting system, you need to file paperwork related to the transactions that you enter into your computer system. You should still maintain employee, vendor, and customer files in hard copy, just in case something goes wrong, such as your computer system crashing. In that case, you need the originals to restore the data. Of course, you should prevent that type of crisis at all costs by backing up your computerized accounting system's data regularly. Daily backups are best; one backup per week is the longest you should ever go.

✔ **Three-ring binders:** These binders are great for things such as your Chart of Accounts (refer to Chapter 3), your General Ledger (refer to Chapter 4), and your system of journals (refer to Chapter 5) because you add to these documents regularly, and the binders make it easy to add additional pages. Be sure to number the pages when you add them to the binder so that you can quickly spot a missing page. How many binders you need depends on how many financial transactions you have each accounting period. You can keep everything in one binder, or you may want to set up a binder for the Chart of Accounts and General Ledger, and then a separate binder for each of your active journals. Decide based on what makes your job as bookkeeper easier.

✔ **Expandable files:** Sometimes referred to as *accordion files* because of their pleated sides, you can use these files to keep track of current vendor activity and any bills that your business owes. Make sure that you have an

- **Alphabetical file:** Use this file to track all the outstanding purchase orders you have sent to each vendor. After you fill the order, you can file all details about that order in the vendor's individual file, in case questions about the order arise later.

- **Twelve-month file:** Use this file to keep track of bills that you need to pay. Simply place the bill in the slot for the month in which it's due. Many businesses also use a 30-day expandable file. At the beginning of the month, the bookkeeper places the bills in the 30-day expandable file based on the dates that the business needs to pay them. This approach provides a quick and organized visual reminder for when bills are due.

If you're using a computerized accounting system, you likely don't need the second expandable file by date because your accounting system can remind you when bills are due (as long as you add the information to the system when the bill arrives).

✔ **External hard drives or other storage media:** Use these media to back up your computerized system on a weekly or, better yet, daily basis. Keep the devices in a fire safe or someplace that won't be affected if the business is destroyed by a fire. (A fire safe is a must for any business; it's the best way to keep critical financial data safe.) If you can afford it, have two electronic storage devices that you can alternate for backups. Fresh backups are brought offsite from your business location, and outdated backups are brought back from that location for the next backup.

Figuring out what to keep and for how long

As you can probably imagine, the pile of paperwork you need to hold on to can get very large very quickly. When they see their files getting thicker and thicker, most businesspeople wonder what they can toss, what they really need to keep, and how long they need to keep it.

Generally, you should keep most transaction-related paperwork for as long as the taxman can come and audit your books. The CRA requires you to keep your records for six years from the date of the last taxation year. This policy applies to electronic records as well as hard-copy books and records. If you fail to file tax returns or file taxes fraudulently (and we hope this isn't the case for you), the CRA may question you at any time. Prior year tax reassessments have no limit when the CRA can prove that you're guilty of tax evasion.

You must keep indefinitely records and supporting documents concerning long-term acquisitions and disposal of property, the share register of an incorporated business, and other historical information that can have an impact on the sale, liquidation, or wind-up of the business. We strongly recommend that you keep your General Ledger indefinitely.

If you find that a certain type of record takes up a lot of storage space, you may destroy those records at an earlier time than we recommend in this section if you receive written permission from the CRA. Retailers, for example, may not want to hang on to the cash register master tapes for longer than a couple of years. Check the CRA's website (www.cra-arc.gc.ca) to download the form you need to fill out to obtain permission to destroy some records early. Enter the form number T137 – Request for Destruction of Records in the search engine. Be ready to describe in full detail the particular documents that you want permission to destroy.

The taxman isn't the only reason to keep records around longer than one year. You may need proof-of-purchase information for your insurance company if an asset is lost, stolen, or destroyed by fire or other accident. Also, you need to hang on to information regarding any business loan until you pay it off, just in case the bank or finance company questions how much you've paid. After you pay off the loan, be sure to keep proof of payment indefinitely, in case a question about the loan ever arises. Also, keep information about real estate and other assets held as investments.

Keep the current year's files easily accessible in a designated filing area, and keep the most recent past year's files in accessible filing cabinets if you have room. Box up records when they hit the 2-year-old mark and put them in offsite storage. Be sure to date your boxed records with information about what each box contains, when you put them into storage, and when you can destroy them. So many people forget to include information about when they can destroy the boxes, so those boxes just pile up until the business runs out of room to store them and total desperation sets in. Then, someone must take the time to sort through the boxes and figure out what the business needs to keep and what it can destroy, and that's not a fun job.

Protecting Your Business against Internal Fraud

Many businesspeople start their operations by carefully hiring people they can trust, thinking, "We're like family — they'll never steal from me." Unfortunately, the businesspeople who put too much trust in just one employee discover the truth.

Too often, a business owner finds out too late that even the most loyal employee may steal from the business if the opportunity arises and the temptation becomes too great — or if the employee finds herself caught up in a serious personal financial dilemma and needs fast cash. Some thieves rationalize their behaviour by taking the stance that they are underpaid, that the business can afford to take the loss, or that the loss is insured.

After introducing you to the various ways people can steal from a business, we talk about steps you can take to prevent it.

Facing the reality of financial fraud

The four basic types of financial fraud are

- ✔ **Embezzlement:** Also called *larceny,* the illegal use of funds by a person who controls those funds. For example, a bookkeeper may use the business's money for his own personal needs. Many times, embezzlement stories don't make it into the paper because businesspeople are so embarrassed that they choose to keep the affair quiet. They usually settle privately with the embezzler and try to get restitution, rather than face public scrutiny. We don't recommend this approach. The embezzler can just move on to another business and get away with the crime all over again. We recommend you get the police involved.

- ✔ **Internal theft or pilferage:** When employees steal business assets, for example, taking office supplies or products that the business sells without paying for them. Internal theft is often the culprit behind inventory shrinkage.

✔ **Payoffs and kickbacks:** Situations in which employees accept cash or other benefits in exchange for access to the business. This type of situation often creates a scenario in which the business that the employee works for pays more for the goods or products than necessary. That extra money finds its way into the pocket of the employee who helped facilitate the access. For example, say Business A wants to sell its products to Business B. An employee in Business B helps Business A get in the door. Business A prices its product a bit higher and gives the employee of Business B that extra profit in return for helping it out. A *payoff* is given before the sale is made, essentially saying, "Please." A *kickback* is paid after the sale is made, essentially saying, "Thank you." In reality, payoffs and kickbacks are a form of bribery, but few businesses report or litigate this problem (although businesses often fire employees when those businesses uncover such deals).

✔ **Skimming:** Occurs when employees take money from receipts and don't record the revenue on the books. Restaurants and bars have long had a bad reputation for this type of fraud.

Although any of these financial crimes can happen in a small business, the one that hits small businesses the hardest is embezzlement. Embezzlement happens most frequently in small businesses when only one person has access to or control over most of the business's financial activities. For example, a bookkeeper may write cheques, make deposits, and balance the monthly bank statement — talk about having your fingers in a very big cookie jar.

Caught with fingers in the cookie jar

Alice is a bookkeeper who's been with Business A for a long time. She gets promoted to office manager after she's been with the business for 20 years. She's like a family member to the business owner, who trusts her implicitly. Because he's so busy with other aspects of running the business, the owner gives her control of the daily grind of cash flow. The beloved office manager handles or supervises all incoming and outgoing cash, reconciles the bank account, handles payroll, signs all the cheques, and files the business's tax returns.

All that control gives her the opportunity, credibility, and access to embezzle a lot of money. At first, the owner's trust is well-founded, and Alice handles her new responsibilities very well. But after about three years in the role as office manager, she develops a gambling problem she can't control.

Alice decides to pay herself more money. She adds her husband or other family members to the payroll and documents the cheques paid to them as consulting expenses. She draws large cash cheques to buy nonexistent office supplies and equipment, and then — the worst of all — she files the business's tax returns and pockets the money that should go to paying the taxes due. The business owner doesn't find out about the problem until the CRA comes calling, and by then, the office manager has retired and moved away.

Sound far-fetched? Well, it's not. You may not hear this exact scenario, but you're likely to see stories in your local newspaper about similar embezzlement schemes.

Dividing staff responsibilities

Your primary protection against financial crime is properly separating staff responsibilities that involve the flow of business cash. Ideally, you should never have one person handle more than one of the following tasks:

- **Bookkeeping:** The bookkeeper reviews and enters all transactions into the business's books. The bookkeeper also makes sure that transactions are accurate, valid, appropriate, and have the proper authorization. For example, if a transaction requires paying a vendor, the bookkeeper makes sure the charges are accurate and that someone with proper authority has approved the payment. The bookkeeper can review documentation of cash receipts and the overnight deposits taken to the bank, but she shouldn't be the person who actually handles the cash or makes the deposit. Also, if the bookkeeper is responsible for handling collections received from external parties, such as customers or vendors, she shouldn't be the one to enter those transactions in the books.

- **Authorizing:** One or more managers are delegated to authorize expenditures for their departments. You may decide that transactions over a certain amount must have two or more authorizations before the business can send a cheque to pay a bill. Your business should clearly spell out authorization levels, and everyone needs to follow those levels, even the owner or president of the corporation. (Remember, as owner, you set the tone for how the rest of the office operates; if you take shortcuts, you set a bad example and undermine the system you put in place. Your employees watch what you do and are prone to imitate your habits — good or bad.)

- **Money handling:** Someone must have direct contact with incoming cash or revenue, whether it's by cheque, credit card, EFT, or credit transaction, as well as outgoing cash flow. The person who handles money directly, such as a cashier, shouldn't be the one who prepares and makes bank deposits. Likewise, the person writing cheques to pay the business's bills shouldn't be authorized to sign those cheques. To be safe, one person should prepare the cheques based on authorized documentation, and a second person should sign those cheques after reviewing the authorized documentation that supports the payment.

When setting up your cash-handling systems, try to think like an embezzler to figure out ways someone may take advantage of a system.

- **Preparing and analyzing the financial statements and reports:** Someone who's not involved in the day-to-day entering of transactions in the books should prepare the financial statements and reports. For most small businesses, the bookkeeper turns over the raw reports from the computerized accounting system to an outside accountant, who reviews the materials and prepares the financial statements. In addition, he does a financial analysis of the business activity results for the previous accounting period. This analysis is designed to uncover errors or omissions so that they can be corrected before the financial statements are sent to the various interested parties.

Here's the bottom line: Don't give an employee access to cash and the books at the same time. If you do, that employee may feel very tempted to take your cash and cover her tracks by cooking the books.

We realize that you may be just starting up a small business and therefore don't have enough staff to separate all these duties. Until you do have that capability, be sure to stay heavily involved in the inflow and outflow of cash in your business. Here are some ways you can stay heavily involved:

- ✔ **Pick up directly at your bank's location, open the mail for your business's bank statements every month, or sign in to online banking and keep a close watch on the transactions.** You can give someone else the responsibility to prove out the statement and reconcile the bank account, but you should still keep an eye on the transactions listed. You can do this during the month by viewing the business's bank account online. You can spot unusual activity immediately and get the problem resolved before it gets out of hand.

- ✔ **Periodically look at your business cheque voucher system and verify their numerical sequence to be sure there aren't any cheques missing.** A bookkeeper who knows that you periodically check the books is less likely to find an opportunity for theft or embezzlement. If a cheque or page of cheques goes missing, act quickly to find out whether someone in your business used the cheques legitimately. If you can't find the answer, call your bank and try to put a stop payment on the missing cheque numbers.

- ✔ **Periodically observe cash handling by your cashiers and managers to be sure they're following the rules you established.** This process is known as *management by walking around* — the more often you're out there, the less likely you are to be a victim of employee theft and fraud. Break your routine once in a while. Your presence in any situation should be unpredictable.

- ✔ **Get to know your employees so that you can more easily detect signs of financial or other personal problems.** Build up a rapport so that they feel free to discuss such issues with you in confidence.

- ✔ **Examine all invoices and supporting data before you sign cheques, if you're the signing authority on the chequing account.** Make sure that the business actually received all the merchandise or services and that the price charged seems reasonable.

- ✔ **Don't sign blank cheques.** Don't leave a supply of signed blank cheques when you go on vacation.

> ✔ **Make it a habit to make the business's daily bank deposit.** Try to do this deposit yourself as often as you can. This procedure will give you added opportunities to detect unusual transactions, events, or employee behaviour.

Balancing control costs

As a small-business owner, you're always trying to balance the cost of protecting your cash and assets with the cost of adequately separating cash-related duties. Don't put in too many controls that end up costing you money. For example, you may put in inventory controls that require salespeople to contact one particular person who has the key to your product display case or warehouse. This kind of control may prevent employee theft, but it also may result in lost sales because salespeople can't find the key-holder when they're dealing with an interested customer. In the end, the customer gets mad, and you lose the sale.

When you put internal controls in place, talk to your staff both before and after instituting the controls to see how those controls are working and to check for any unforeseen problems. Be willing and able to adjust your controls to balance the business needs of selling your products, managing the cash flow, and keeping your eye on making a profit.

Generally, when you make rules for your internal controls, be sure that the cost of protecting an asset is no more than what the asset you're trying to protect is worth. For example, don't go overboard to protect office supplies by forcing your staff to sit around idle, waiting for hours to access more printer paper while you and a manager are away from the office.

Ask yourself these four questions when you design your internal controls:

> ✔ What exactly do I want to prevent or detect — errors, sloppiness, theft, fraud, or embezzlement?
>
> ✔ Do I face the problem frequently?
>
> ✔ What do I estimate the loss to be?
>
> ✔ What will implementing the change in procedures to prevent or detect the problem cost me?

You can't answer these questions all by yourself, so consult with your managers and the staff whom the changes will affect. Get their answers to these questions and listen to their feedback.

When you finish putting together the new internal control rule, be sure to document why you decided to implement the rule and the information you collected in developing it. Communicate clearly to your employees what you expect from them. After you've had the rule in place for awhile, test your assumptions. Be sure that you're actually detecting the errors, theft, fraud, or embezzlement that you expected to detect. Check the costs of keeping the rule in place by looking at cash outlay, employee time and morale, and the impact on customer service. When in doubt, consider consulting an expert. If you find any problems with your internal controls, take the time to fix them and change the rule, again documenting the process. If you have detailed documentation, two or three years down the road when employees question why you have them doing something, you'll have the answer. You can determine whether the problem is still a valid one and whether you still need the rule — or whether you need to change it.

Protecting Your Cash through Employee Bonding

If you have employees who handle a lot of cash, you absolutely must insure your business against theft. This insurance, called *fidelity bond,* helps you protect yourself against theft and reduces your risk of loss. Employee bonding is a common part of an overall business insurance package. Explain to your employees that getting this insurance coverage is a matter of policy, rather than any feeling of mistrust on your part.

If you carry a fidelity bond on your cash handlers, you're covered for losses sustained by any employee who's bonded. You also have coverage if an employee's act causes losses to a client of your business. For example, if you're a financial consultant and your bookkeeper embezzles a client's cash, you're protected for the loss.

You can buy fidelity bond insurance through the company that handles your business insurance policies. The cost varies greatly, depending on the type of business you operate and the amount of cash or other assets that the employees you want to bond handle. If an employee steals from you or one of your customers, the insurance covers the loss.

Employers bond employees who handle cash, as well as employees who may be in a position to steal something other than cash. For example, a janitorial service bonds its workers in case a worker steals something from one of its customers. If a customer reports something missing, the insurance company that bonded the employee covers the loss. Without a bond, the employer must pay back the customer for any loss.

Part III

Tracking Day-to-Day Business Operations with Your Books

The 5th Wave   By Rich Tennant

BOOKKEEPING

"I think if you subtract the figure in the 'Days I Go Home Early' column from the figure in the 'Snippy Attitude' column you'll reach a zero-sum figure."

In this part . . .

Do you want to know every single financial transaction that happens in your business each and every day? You should. Tracking every transaction is the only way that you can put all the pieces together and see how well your business is doing financially.

This part shows you how to track your day-to-day business operations by recording sales and purchases, as well as any discounts, returns, and allowances. We discuss how you deal with service revenue and any related accrued or unearned revenue. Also, because you can't run a business without paying your employees, we guide you through the basics of setting up and managing employee payroll — and all the government paperwork you must do after you hire your workforce.

Chapter 8

Buying and Tracking Your Purchases

*I*n order to make money, your business must have something to sell. Whether you sell products or offer services, you have to deal with costs directly related to the goods or services that you sell. Those costs primarily come from the purchase or manufacturing of the products you plan to sell or the materials you need in order to provide the services.

All businesses must keep careful watch over the cost of the products that they plan to sell or services they plan to offer. Ultimately, your business's profits depend on how well you manage those costs because, in most cases, costs increase over time with inflation, rather than decrease. How often do you find a reduction in the price of needed items? You know that a reduction doesn't happen often (except with technology-related products). If costs increase but the price to the customer remains unchanged, you make a smaller profit on each sale.

In addition to the costs to produce goods or services, every business has additional expenses associated with purchasing supplies needed to run the business. The bookkeeper has primary responsibility for monitoring all these costs and expenses when she pays invoices, as well as alerting business owners or managers when vendors increase prices. This chapter covers how to track purchases and their costs, manage inventory, buy and manage supplies, and pay the bills for the items your business buys.

Keeping Track of Inventory

Products that your business plans to sell are called *merchandise inventory,* or just plain *inventory.* As a bookkeeper, you use two accounts to track inventory:

- **Purchases:** Where you record the actual cost from the purchase of goods that the business plans to sell. You need to add to the cost of purchases what you pay for any freight to bring in the inventory to your place of business. As well, you need to deduct any purchase returns and allowances and purchase discounts. (We provide a description of all of these accounts in Chapter 3). All of these accounts are used to calculate the *Cost of Goods Sold,* which is an item on the income statement (see Chapter 19 for more on the income statement).

- **Inventory:** Where you track the book value of inventory on hand. This value appears on the balance sheet as an asset in a line item called *Inventory* (see Chapter 18 for more on the balance sheet).

Businesses track physical inventory on hand by using one of two methods:

- **Periodic inventory:** Conducting a physical count of the inventory in the stores and in the warehouse. You can do this count daily, monthly, yearly, or for any other period that best meets your business needs, depending on how quickly the inventory is turned over and sold. (Many stores close for all or part of a day when they must count inventory.)

- **Perpetual inventory:** Adjusting inventory counts each time the business makes a sale. In order to use this method, you must manage your inventory by using a computerized accounting system that's tied into your point of sale (usually cash registers or scanners).

Even if you use a perpetual inventory method, you still need to do a periodical physical count of inventory to be sure those numbers match what's in your computer system. Because theft, damage, and loss of inventory aren't automatically entered in your computer system, the losses don't show up until you do a physical count of the inventory you have on hand in your business.

Many businesses implement a policy to do a comparison of the physical inventory on hand to the records for certain categories of inventory on a rotating basis. Doing so is less disruptive to the business and is more cost-effective than counting the entire inventory, because you use less staff resources.

Your business derives additional benefits from finding errors early on. Updating the inventory record and making it accurate throughout the year helps you ensure that you're not relying on inventory that you don't have.

You can avoid having customers become upset with you when they've been told you have stock of a particular item, only to later find that their purchase orders can't be filled. Finding a big shortfall in inventory relatively early in the year also gives you a heads up if you're having problems with employee pilferage. We discuss employee pilferage in Chapter 7.

Taking a physical count

Your computerized bookkeeping system can make the task of taking a physical inventory count of the goods on hand a little easier. Figure 8-1 shows H.G.'s Cheesecake Shop's Physical Inventory Worksheet. From the Reports command taken from the top menu bar in QuickBooks, select Inventory and click Physical Inventory Worksheet to generate this report. This printout lists all inventory items on hand and provides space to manually insert the number of items counted at the physical count.

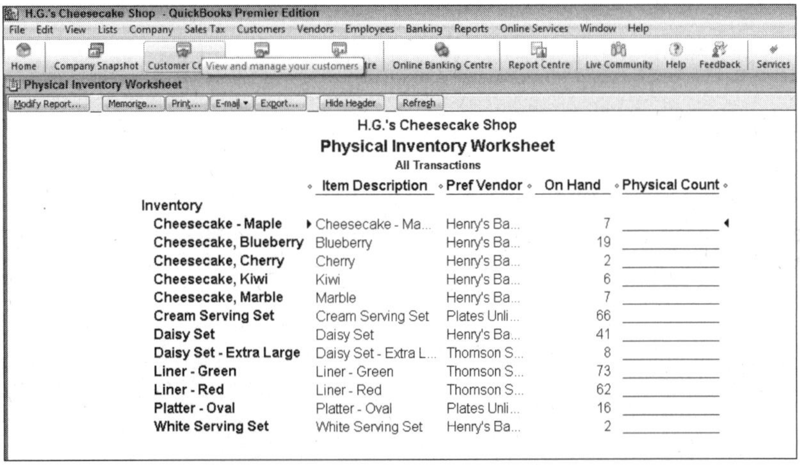

	Item Description	Pref Vendor	On Hand	Physical Count
Inventory				
Cheesecake - Maple	Cheesecake - Ma...	Henry's Ba...	7	
Cheesecake, Blueberry	Blueberry	Henry's Ba...	19	
Cheesecake, Cherry	Cherry	Henry's Ba...	2	
Cheesecake, Kiwi	Kiwi	Henry's Ba...	6	
Cheesecake, Marble	Marble	Henry's Ba...	7	
Cream Serving Set	Cream Serving Set	Plates Unli...	66	
Daisy Set	Daisy Set	Henry's Ba...	41	
Daisy Set - Extra Large	Daisy Set - Extra L...	Thomson S...	8	
Liner - Green	Liner - Green	Thomson S...	73	
Liner - Red	Liner - Red	Thomson S...	62	
Platter - Oval	Platter - Oval	Plates Unli...	16	
White Serving Set	White Serving Set	Henry's Ba...	2	

Figure 8-1: Physical Inventory Worksheet printed from QuickBooks inventory records.

After you have taken the physical inventory count, you can follow up on any discrepancies and correct the bookkeeping records.

Calculating the cost of goods sold

When preparing your income statement at the end of an accounting period (whether that period is for a month, a quarter, or a year), you need to calculate the cost of goods sold in order to calculate the profit made.

When you want to calculate the cost of goods sold, you must first find out how many items of inventory your business sold. You start with the amount of inventory on hand at the beginning of the month (called *beginning inventory*), as recorded in the Inventory account, and add the amount of purchases, less purchase returns as recorded in the Purchases and Purchase Returns accounts, to arrive at the goods available for sale. Then, you subtract the inventory on hand at the end of the month, which you determine by counting the remaining inventory.

Here's how you calculate the number of goods sold:

> Beginning inventory + Net purchases = Goods available for sale – Ending inventory = Items sold

If you are unable to track purchases and sales item by item but can calculate transactions in dollar values, the preceding equation still holds true, but you would do the calculations in dollar values, as follows:

> Cost of beginning inventory + Cost of net purchases = Goods available for sale – Ending value of inventory = Cost of goods sold

Keep in mind that the cost of net purchases includes the cost of freight-in charges and is reduced by the dollar value of any purchase discounts, returns, or allowances.

Assuming you are able to keep track of your inventory item by item, after you determine the number of goods sold, you compare that number to the actual number of items sold by the business during that accounting period, which you base on sales figures collected throughout the month. If the numbers don't match, you have a problem. The mistake may be in the inventory count, or items may be unaccounted for because they've been misplaced or damaged and discarded. In the worst-case scenario, you may have a problem with theft by customers or employees. The term used to describe this loss of inventory is *inventory shrinkage*.

Entering the initial cost

When your business first receives inventory, you enter the initial cost of that inventory into the bookkeeping system based on the shipment's invoice. In some cases, invoices are sent separately and the goods received come with only a packing slip. If that's the case, you should still record the receipt of the goods because the business incurs the cost from the day it receives and takes possession of the goods, so you must be sure that it has the money to pay for the goods when the invoice arrives and the bill comes due. (You track outstanding bills in the Accounts Payable account.)

The receipt of inventory is a relatively easy entry in the bookkeeping system. For example, if your business buys on account $1,000 of inventory that you plan to sell, you make the following record in the books:

	Debit	*Credit*
Purchases	$1,000	
— Accounts Payable		$1,000

The Purchases account increases by $1,000 to reflect the additional costs, and the Accounts Payable account increases by the same amount to reflect the amount of the bill that your business needs to pay in the future.

When inventory enters your business, in addition to recording the actual costs, you need more detail about what the business bought, how much of each item it bought, and what each item cost. You also need to track

✔ How much inventory you have on hand

✔ The book value (the cost, generally) of the inventory you have on hand

✔ When you need to order more inventory

You may find tracking these details for each type of product that your business buys a nightmare, especially if you're trying to keep the books for a retail store, because you need to set up a special Inventory journal with pages detailing purchase and sale information for every item you carry. (Refer to Chapter 5 for the scoop on journals.)

However, computerized accounting simplifies this process of tracking inventory. You can enter details about inventory initially into your computer accounting system in several ways:

✔ If you pay by cheque or credit card when you receive the inventory, you can enter the details about each item on the cheque or credit card form.

✔ If you use purchase orders, you can enter the detail about each item on the purchase order, record receipt of the items when they arrive, and update the computer record when you receive the bill.

✔ If you don't use purchase orders, you can enter the detail about the items when you receive the merchandise and update the computer record when you receive the bill.

To give you an idea of how a computerized accounting software program collects this information, Figure 8-2 shows how H.G.'s Cheesecake Shop prepares and sends out a purchase order to a vendor, Henry's Bakery Supplies, to buy more inventory.

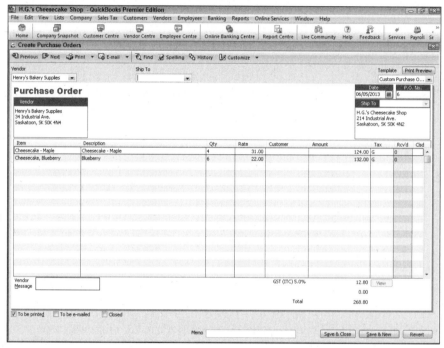

Figure 8-2: Recording a purchase order for goods for resale using QuickBooks.

Figure 8-3 shows you the next step in recording the purchase, when the goods arrive with an invoice from Henry's Bakery Supplies, and how to enter the details in QuickBooks. This particular form is for the receipt of inventory that includes a bill, but the software collects similar information on its cheque, credit card, and purchase order forms.

On the form in Figure 8-3, in addition to recording the name of the vendor, date received, and payment amount, you also record details about the items bought, including the quantity and cost. When you load each item into the computerized accounting system, you can easily track cost detail over time.

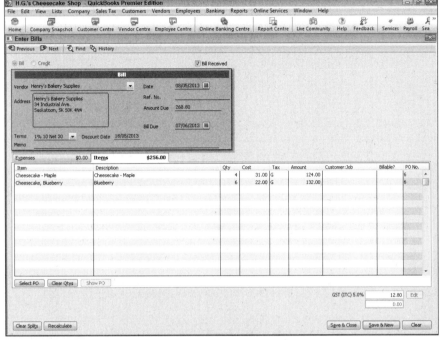

Figure 8-3:
Recording
the receipt
of inven-
tory that
includes a
bill by using
QuickBooks.

Figure 8-4 shows how you initially set up an inventory item in the computerized accounting system. In addition to the item name, you add two descriptions to the system: One is an abbreviated version that you can use on purchase transactions, and the other is a longer description that appears on customer invoices (sales transactions). You can input a cost and sales price if you want, or you can leave them at zero and enter the cost and sales prices with each transaction.

If you have a set contract purchase price or sales price on an inventory item, you can save time by entering it on this QuickBooks item form, shown in Figure 8-4, so that you don't have to enter the price each time you record a transaction. But, if the prices change frequently, you may want to leave the space blank so that you don't forget to enter the updated price when you enter a transaction.

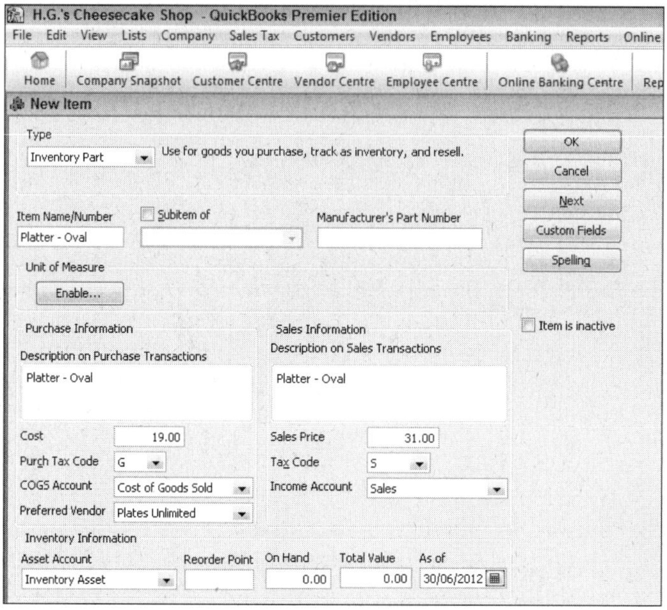

Figure 8-4:
Setting up an inventory item by using QuickBooks.

As shown in Figure 8-4, you can track information about inventory on hand and when you need to reorder inventory by using this form. To be sure your store shelves are never empty, you can enter a number that indicates at what point you want to reorder inventory for each item. As shown in Figure 8-4, you can indicate the Reorder Point in the section called Inventory Information, and then QuickBooks will give you an inventory reminder when your inventory reaches the reorder point.

After you complete and save the form that records the receipt of inventory in QuickBooks, the software automatically

 ✔ Adjusts the quantity of inventory that you have in stock

 ✔ Increases the asset account called Inventory

 ✔ Lowers the quantity of items on order (if you initially entered the information as a purchase order)

 ✔ Averages the cost of inventory on hand

 ✔ Increases the Accounts Payable account

Managing inventory and its book value

After you record the receipt of inventory, you have the responsibility of managing the inventory that you have on hand. You also must know the book value of that inventory. You may think that as long as you know what you paid for the items, you can easily calculate the value. Well, accountants can't let it be that simple, so they actually have three different cost formulas for inventory:

- **FIFO (First In, First Out):** You assume that the business sells the first items put on the shelves (the oldest items) first. Stores that sell perishable goods, such as grocery stores, use this inventory cost formula most often. For example, when fresh cartons of milk arrive at a store, the person stocking the shelves unloads the older milk cartons, puts the fresher milk at the back of the shelf, and then puts the older milk in front. Each carton of milk (or other perishable item) has a best-before date indicating the last day it can be sold, so food stores always try to sell the oldest stuff first, while it's still sellable. (They try, but how many times have you reached to the back of a food shelf to find items with the longest shelf life?)

- **Averaging:** You average the cost of goods received, so you don't need to worry about which items the business sells first or last. A retail or services environment uses this cost formula most often because prices are constantly fluctuating, sometimes simply because of the quantities purchased, so an average cost works best for managing the cost of goods sold.

- **Specific Identification:** You maintain cost figures for each inventory item individually. Retail outlets that sell big-ticket items, such as cars, use this type of inventory cost formula. In order to use this cost formula, the items that you sell must have unique identifying features so that you can tell which one you're selling. In the case of cars, for example, each car has a unique serial number.

Cost formulas are based on assumptions. As best you can, try to pick a formula of costing inventory that matches up with the physical movement of the inventory that you sell. However, if you have a bucket of nails and want to use FIFO, you don't actually have to worry about emptying the bucket, adding your new shipment of nails, and then replacing the old nails on top. The customer doesn't need to purchase the first nail you stocked.

No matter what cost formula you choose, by the time you need to report the value of your inventory on your balance sheet, you have to subject that inventory to a *valuation test,* which ensures that your business will at least recoup its costs when it sells the inventory. You can't leave the book value of inventory on your balance sheet at an amount higher than the value you expect from selling it. The technical term for this test of valuation is the *lower of cost and net realizable value*. You may think of this adjustment as an impairment adjustment. We discuss the impairment of fixed assets in Chapter 12.

In the case of inventory, you determine the net realizable value of an item by taking your selling price and deducting what it'll cost you to sell that item. This test isn't designed to postpone a loss by hanging on to bad, outdated, or overvalued inventory. If inventory has suffered a loss in value, such as some sort of deterioration or technological obsolescence, you must reflect that loss in the book value of the inventory right away.

Does anyone remember pet rocks? If you don't remember or don't know what we're talking about, years ago, a salesman in California sold rocks as pets. Yes, people paid good money to buy rocks. Soon, that fad changed, and nobody wanted to buy the inventory. The rocks in inventory became worthless. Businesses that sell trendy items or inventory that can be affected by fashion fads often take large hits to their profit because of their fickle customers.

After you choose an inventory cost formula, you need to use the same formula each year on your financial reports and when you file your business's income tax return. If you decide to change the cost formula that you use, you or your accountant need to follow very strict accounting rules to make that change happen. First, you have to justify that the new cost formula is better for your business. You need to explain the reasons for the change to both the CRA and to your financial backers. If you're running a business that's incorporated and has sold shares, you need to explain the change to your shareholders. You likely also have to show how the change in inventory cost formula affects your prior financial statements and adjust your profit margins in previous years to reflect the new inventory cost formula's effect on your long-term profit history.

If you think changing cost formulas is a big deal, you're absolutely right. A change attracts a lot of attention to your business from investors or from the CRA, because they may think you are trying to manipulate the profit by changing the cost of goods sold. Do yourself a favour and give a lot of thought to this choice of cost formulas before you start tracking the cost of inventory.

You don't necessarily need to avoid changes, however. Sometimes, you have to make them — for example, if a corporation buys out your business, you need to adopt the same cost formula that the parent company uses.

Figuring out the best cost formula for you

We're sure you're wondering why it matters so much which inventory cost formula you use. The key to the choice is the effect on your bottom line, as well as the income taxes that your business has to pay.

FIFO, because it assumes that your business sells the oldest (and, most likely, the lowest priced) items first, results in a low cost-of-goods-sold number. Because you subtract cost of goods sold from sales to determine profit, a low cost-of-goods-sold number produces a high profit. For more on cost of goods sold, refer to the section "Calculating the cost of goods sold," earlier in this chapter.

The Averaging cost formula gives a business the fairest picture of what's happening, on average, with inventory costs and trends. Using this cost formula brings the least amount of bias to the results. If you're operating a business in which inventory prices are constantly going up and down, you likely want to choose this cost formula.

QuickBooks uses the Averaging cost formula to calculate Cost of Goods Sold and Inventory line items on its financial reports, so if you choose this cost formula, you can use QuickBooks and the financial reports it generates. However, if you choose to use one of the other two inventory cost formulas, you can't use the QuickBooks financial report numbers. Instead, you have to print out a report of purchases, freight-in charges, purchase returns and allowances, and purchase discounts and then calculate the accurate numbers to use on your financial reports for the Cost of Goods Sold and Inventory accounts.

If your inventory items aren't unique, you can't implement the Specific Identification cost formula. Also, don't use this formula if the individual costs of your inventory items are so low that it doesn't make sense to put in the extra effort required to track the cost of each item individually.

Check with your accountant to see which inventory cost formula works best in the type of business you're operating.

Comparing the cost formulas

To show you how much of an effect inventory cost formulas can have on profit margin, in this section we compare two of the most common cost formulas: FIFO and Averaging. In this example, we assume Business A bought the inventory in question at different prices in three different purchases. In our illustration that follows, the Beginning Inventory is valued at $500 (that's 50 items at $10 each).

Here's the calculation for determining the number of items sold (refer to the section "Calculating the cost of goods sold," earlier in this chapter):

Beginning inventory + Net purchases = Goods available for sale – Ending inventory = Items sold

50 + 500 = 550 – 75 = 475

Here's what the business paid to purchase the inventory:

Date	Quantity	Unit Price
April 1	150	$10
April 15	150	$25
April 30	200	$30

Table 8-1 illustrates how you calculate the cost of goods sold and ending inventory by using the Averaging cost formula.

Table 8-1	Averaging Cost Formula Calculation of Cost of Goods Sold and Ending Inventory					
	Cost		**Quantity**		**Book Value**	
Beginning inventory	$10	@	50	=	$500	
Purchases	$10	@	150	=	$1,500	
	$25	@	150	=	$3,750	
	$30	@	200	=	$6,000	
Total inventory			550		$11,750	
Average inventory	$11,750	÷	550	=	$21.36	
Cost of goods sold	$21.36	×	475	=	$10,146	
Ending inventory	$21.36	×	75	=	$1,602	

Remember, the cost-of-goods-sold number appears on the income statement, and you subtract it from sales. The ending-inventory number shows up as an asset on the balance sheet. For all three inventory cost formulas, the cost of goods sold goes into the income statement and the ending inventory goes into the balance sheet.

Table 8-2 offers an example of how you calculate the cost of goods sold by using the FIFO cost formula. We use the same information from Table 8-1. With this formula, you assume that the business first sells the first items that it receives, and because the first items it receives appear in the beginning inventory, we start with them.

Table 8-2	FIFO Cost Formula Calculation of Cost of Goods Sold and Ending Inventory				
	Quantity		*Cost*		*Book Value*
Beginning inventory	50	@	$10	=	$500
Next in — April 1	150	@	$10	=	$1,500
Then — April 15	150	@	$25	=	$3,750
Then — April 30	125	@	$30	=	$3,750
Cost of goods sold	475				$9,500
Ending inventory	75	×	$30	=	$2,250

Note: The FIFO cost formula uses only 125 of the 200 units purchased on April 30. Because this formula assumes that the first items into inventory are the first items sold (or taken out of inventory), the business first uses the 50 items in the beginning inventory balance. Then it uses the items from April 1. Then, it uses the April 15 items, and finally takes the remaining needed items from those bought on April 30. Because the business bought 200 on April 30 but needed only 125, 75 of the items bought on April 30 are left in ending inventory.

The business sells these items to the customers for $40 per unit, which means total sales of $19,000 for the month (that's $40 × 475 units sold). In this example, we look at the *gross profit,* which is the profit from sales before considering expenses incurred for operating the business. We talk more about the different profit types and what they mean in Chapter 19. You calculate gross profit by using the following equation:

Sales – Cost of goods sold = Gross profit

Table 8-3 shows a comparison of gross profit for the two cost formulas used in this example scenario.

Table 8-3	Comparison of Gross Profit Based on Inventory Cost Formulas	
Income Statement Line Item	*FIFO*	*Averaging*
Sales	$19,000	$19,000
Cost of Goods Sold	$9,500	$10,146
Gross Profit	$9,500	$8,854

Looking at the comparisons of gross profit, you can see that inventory valuation can have a major effect on your bottom line. FIFO likely gives you the highest profit because, due to the effects of inflation, the first items you buy are usually the cheapest.

Buying and Monitoring Supplies

In addition to inventory, a business must buy supplies that it uses to operate the business, such as paper, toner, pens, and paper clips. Supplies that a business doesn't use in direct relationship to the manufacturing or purchasing of goods or services for sale fall into the category of *expenses.*

When it comes to monitoring the supplies you use, just how closely you want to watch things depends on your business needs. You can make the Expense categories that you establish as broad as Office Supplies and Store Supplies, or you may want to set up accounts for each type of supply that your business uses. Each additional account just gives you one more thing that you need to manage and monitor in the accounting system, so determine whether keeping a very detailed record of supplies is worth your time.

Your best bet is to carefully track supplies that make a big dent in your budget with an individual account. For example, if you anticipate that your business will use a lot of paper, monitor that usage with a separate account called Paper Expenses.

Many businesses don't use their bookkeeping system to manage their supplies. Instead, they designate one or two people as office managers or supply managers so that they can keep the number of General Ledger accounts used for supplies to a minimum. Other businesses decide that they want to monitor supplies by department or division, and they set up a supply account for each one. That arrangement puts the burden of monitoring supplies in the hands of the department or division managers.

Staying on Top of Your Bills

Eventually, you have to pay for both the inventory and the supplies you purchase for your business. In most cases, you post the bills to the Accounts Payable account when they arrive, and you pay them when they're due. A large chunk of the cash that you pay out of your Cash account (refer to Chapters 5 and 7 for more information on the Cash account and handling cash) takes the form of the cheques that you send out to pay bills due in

Accounts Payable, so you need to have careful controls over the five key functions of Accounts Payable:

- ✔ Entering the bills that the business needs to pay into the accounting system
- ✔ Preparing cheques to pay the bills
- ✔ Signing cheques to pay the bills
- ✔ Sending out payment cheques to vendors
- ✔ Reconciling the chequing account

In your business, the person who enters the bills that the business needs to pay into the system probably also prepares the payment cheques, but someone else should do the other tasks. Never allow the person who prepares the cheques to also review the bills that the business needs to pay and sign the cheques — unless, of course, that person's you, the business owner. The person signing the cheques should carefully review what bills (with related shipping documents) the cheques pay, verify that the paperwork shows proper management approvals for the payments, and confirm the accuracy of the cheques' amounts. Also, separate responsibilities so that you can be sure the person who reconciles your chequing account doesn't also receive merchandise inventory or prepare or sign cheques. (We talk more about cash control and the importance of separating duties in Chapter 7.)

Properly managing Accounts Payable can save your business a lot of money by preventing late fees or interest charges, and by taking advantage of purchase discounts offered for paying early. If you're using a computerized accounting system, enter the bill due date and any discount information at the time you receive the inventory or supplies (refer to Figure 8-3 for how to record this information).

If you're working with a paper system, rather than a computerized accounting system, you need to set up some way to be sure you don't miss bill due dates. Many companies use two accordion files: one that's set up by the month, and another that's set up by the day. When a bill first comes in, you put it into the first accordion file, according to the month in which it's due. On the first day of that month, the Accounts Payable clerk pulls all the bills due that month and puts them in the daily accordion file based on the date the bill is due. The Accounts Payable clerk then mails payment cheques in time to arrive in the vendor's office by the due date.

In some cases, businesses offer a purchase discount if your business pays its bills early. For example, in Figure 8-3 the terms for discount from Henry's Bakery Supplies are 1% 10 Net 30. This means that if H.G.'s Cheesecake Shop pays the bill in 10 days from the date of the bill, it can take a 1 percent discount; otherwise, it must pay the amount due in full in 30 days. In addition, many businesses state that they charge interest or late fees if you don't pay a bill in 30 days.

The total amount due for the bill shown in Figure 8-3 is $268.80. If the business pays the bill in ten days it can take a 1 percent discount, or $2.69. This amount may not seem like much, but if your business buys $100,000 of inventory and supplies in a month, and each vendor offers a similar purchase discount, you can save $1,000 each month. Over the course of a year, discounts on purchases can save your business a significant amount of money and improve your profits.

Chapter 9

Counting Your Sales

. . . .

In This Chapter

▶ Taking in cash

▶ Discovering the ins and outs of selling on credit

▶ Keeping track of money coming into your business

▶ Offering volume discounts

▶ Speeding up collections

▶ Staying on top of sales returns and allowances

▶ Recognizing when and how to record service revenue

▶ Finding out who owes you money

▶ Dealing with bad debts

▶ Recovering taxes from the government

. . . .

*E*very business loves to take in money — and that means you, the book-keeper, have a lot to do to make sure sales are properly tracked and recorded in the books. In addition to recording the sales themselves, you must track customer accounts, sales discounts offered to customers, and customer sales returns and allowances.

If the business sells goods or services on account, you have to carefully monitor customer accounts in Accounts Receivable, including monitoring whether customers pay on time and alerting the sales team if customers are behind on their bills (meaning the business needs to deny those custom-ers future sales on credit). Some customers never pay, and in that case, you must adjust the books to reflect nonpayment as a bad debt.

This chapter reviews the basic responsibilities that fall to a business's book-keeping and accounting staff for tracking sales, making adjustments to those sales, monitoring customer accounts, and alerting management to slow-paying customers.

Collecting on Cash Sales

Most businesses collect some form of cash as payment for the goods or services they sell. Cash receipts include more than just bills and coins; cheques, electronic fund transfers (EFTs), debit cards, and credit cards also are considered cash sales for the purpose of bookkeeping. In fact, with electronic transaction processing (that's when a customer swipes his debit or credit card through a machine), the bank usually makes a deposit to the business's chequing account the same day.

The only type of payment that doesn't fall under the umbrella of a cash payment is a sale made on account. And by *on account,* we mean credit offered to customers directly by your business, rather than through a third party, such as a bank credit card or loan. We talk more about this type of sale in the section "Selling on Credit," later in this chapter.

Discovering the value of sales receipts

Modern businesses generate sales slips in one of three ways: by the cash register, by the credit card machine, or by hand (written out by the salesperson, often in the case of large-ticket items like vehicles). Whichever of these three methods you choose to handle your sales transactions, the sales receipt serves two purposes:

- ✔ It gives the customer proof that she purchased the item and took possession of it on a particular day at a particular price in your store, in case she needs to exchange or return the merchandise.

- ✔ It gives the store a receipt that it can use at a later time to enter the transaction into the business's books. At the end of the day, the head cashier or manager also uses the receipts to prove out the cash register and ensure that the cashier has taken in the right amount of cash based on the sales he made. (In Chapter 7, we talk more about how you can use cash receipts as an internal control tool to manage your cash.)

You're probably familiar with cash receipts, but just to show you how much usable information a cash sales receipt can offer to the bookkeeper, Table 9-1 shows a sample receipt from a cash sale at a bakery.

Table 9-1 — Cash Sales Receipt 7/25/2012

Item	Quantity	Price	Total
White Serving Set	1	$40	$40
Cheesecake, Marble	1	$20	$20
Cheesecake, Blueberry	1	$20	$20
Subtotal			$80
GST @ 5%			$4
Total			$84
Cash paid			$85
Change			$1

You've probably never thought about how much bookkeeping information a sales receipt contains. Receipts offer a wealth of information that you can use for your business's accounting system. A look at a receipt tells you the amount of cash collected, the type of products sold, the quantity of products sold, and how much GST was charged and collected.

Unless your business uses some type of computerized system at the point of sale (which is usually the cash register) that's integrated into the business's accounting system, the cash register collects sales information throughout the day and prints that information out in a summary form at the end of the day. At that point, you enter the details of the day's sales in the books.

If you don't use your computerized system to monitor inventory, you use the data collected by the cash register to simply enter into the books the cash received, total sales, and sales tax billed and collected. Although in actuality, you'd have many more sales and much higher numbers at the end of the day, here's what an entry in the Cash Receipts journal would look like for the receipt and daily deposit to the bank account:

Account	Debit	Credit
Cash	$84	
—Sales		$80
—GST Payable		$4

Cash sales for July 25, 2012.

In this example entry, Cash is an Asset account shown on the balance sheet (see Chapter 18 for more about balance sheets), and its balance increases with the debit. The Sales account is a Revenue account on the income statement (see Chapter 19 for more about income statements), and its balance increases with a credit, showing additional revenue. (We talk more about debits and credits in Chapter 2.) In the GST Payable account, the business records the goods and services tax that it collects for the Canada Revenue Agency (CRA). (We discuss your responsibility to charge this tax in Chapter 5.) The GST/HST Payable account is a Liability account that appears on the balance sheet, and its balance increases with this credit transaction.

Businesses may also have to charge their customers provincial sales tax (PST) on cash sales slips and invoices. If your business needs to charge PST, you need to add a second charge to the sales slip for this tax. In some provinces, the GST and PST are combined as harmonized sales tax (HST). You credit a PST Payable account at the time of sale for the liability that the business owes to the provincial government. We discuss when you need to charge PST in Chapter 5. You can make payments for these taxes either monthly or quarterly, depending on rules set by the province in which your business operates. We talk more about tax reporting and payment in Chapter 21.

Recording cash transactions in the books

If you're using a computerized accounting system, you can enter more detail about the day's transactions, such as refunds from the day's receipts, and track inventory sold, as well. Most of the computerized accounting systems include the ability to track the sale of inventory. Figure 9-1 shows you the QuickBooks Sales Receipt form that you can use to input cash sales.

In addition to the information included in the Cash Receipts journal, QuickBooks also collects information about the items sold in each transaction. QuickBooks then automatically updates inventory information, reducing the amount of inventory on hand. When the inventory number falls below the reorder number you set (refer to Chapter 8), QuickBooks alerts you that the business needs to purchase more inventory.

If the sales receipt in Figure 9-1 is for an individual customer, you can enter her name and address in the Sold To field.

If your business accepts credit cards, expect the fees that the business has to pay to credit card companies or to your bank to reduce your profit. Usually, you face monthly fees, as well as fees per transaction; however, each business sets up individual arrangements with its bank regarding these fees. You pay similar fees for debit card transactions. Sales volume affects how much you pay in fees, so when researching bank services, be sure to compare debit and credit card transaction fees to find a good deal.

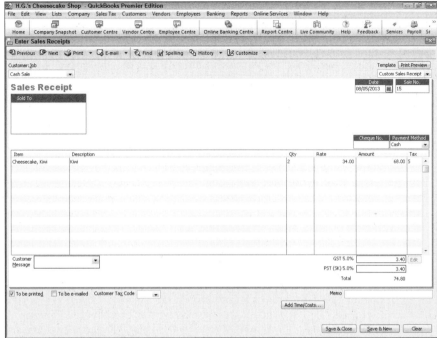

Figure 9-1:
An example
of a cash
sales
receipt in
QuickBooks.

Selling on Credit

Many businesses decide to sell to customers on direct credit (commonly referred to as *on account*), meaning the business offers the credit, not a bank or credit card provider. This approach offers more flexibility in the type of terms that you can offer your customers, and you don't have to pay bank fees. However, it involves more work for you, the bookkeeper, and more risk if a customer doesn't pay what he owes.

If you accept a customer's bank-issued credit card for a sale and the customer doesn't pay the bill, you still get your money — the bank has to collect from the customer, and it takes the loss if she doesn't pay. But if you decide to offer credit to your customers directly, your business takes the loss when a customer doesn't pay.

Deciding whether to offer credit

The decision to offer credit depends on what your competition is doing and, to some extent, on what you can afford to offer. For example, if you run an office supply store and all other office supply stores allow their customers to purchase on account so that their customers can more easily get supplies, you probably need to offer credit to stay competitive.

If you want to allow your customers to buy on account, you first need to set up some ground rules. You have to decide

- ✔ How you plan to check a customer's credit history
- ✔ The minimum customer income level that your business will accept for a customer to become approved for credit
- ✔ How long the customer has to pay the bill before you charge him interest or late fees
- ✔ What balances, if any, you allow your customers to carry forward from month to month
- ✔ What discount terms you may consider offering to some of your key customers

The harder you make it to get credit and the stricter you make the bill-paying rules, the less chance you have of a taking a loss. However, you may lose customers to a competitor that has lighter credit rules. For example, you may require a minimum income level of $50,000 and make customers pay in 30 days if they want to avoid late fees or interest charges. Your sales staff reports that these rules are too rigid because your direct competitor down the street allows credit on a minimum income level of $30,000 and gives customers 60 days to pay before late fees and interest charges. Now, you have to decide whether you want to change your credit rules to match those of your competition. But, if you do lower your credit standards to match your competitor, you may end up with more customers who can't pay on time or at all because you qualify customers for credit at lower income levels and give them more time to pay. If you loosen your qualification criteria and bill-paying requirements, you have to carefully monitor your customer accounts to be sure they're not falling behind.

The key risk you face is selling products for which you never receive payment. For example, if you allow customers 30 days to pay and cut them off from buying goods if their accounts fall more than 30 days behind, then the most you can lose is the amount sold over a two-month period (60 days). But if you give customers more leniencies, such as allowing them 60 days to pay and cutting them off after payments are 30 days late, you're faced with three months (90 days) of sales for which you may never receive payment.

At the other end of the spectrum, you may consider giving your credit customers a chance at a price reduction if they pay you very quickly. You may consider this particularly worthwhile if cash is tight. For example, you may offer key customers a 2 percent sales discount on their purchases if they pay their bill in 10 days, rather than waiting until the end of the 30-day payment term originally negotiated. (See "Recording Sales Discounts," later in this chapter, for more info.)

Recording sales-on-account transactions in the books

When your business makes sales on credit, you have to enter specific information into the accounting system. In addition to inputting information regarding cash receipts (see the section "Collecting on Cash Sales," earlier in this chapter), you update the customer accounts to be sure your business bills each customer and collects the money. You debit the Accounts Receivable account, an Asset account shown on the balance sheet (see Chapter 18), which shows money due from customers.

Here's how a journal entry of a sale made on account looks:

Account	Debit	Credit
Accounts Receivable	$84	
—Sales		$80
—GST Payable		$4

Sales on account to S. Smith for July 25, 2012.

In addition to making this journal entry, you enter the information into the customer's account so that your business can send out invoices. When the customer pays the bill, you update the individual customer's record to show that your business has received payment and enter the following into the bookkeeping records:

Account	Debit	Credit
Cash	$84	
—Accounts Receivable		$84

Collection on account from S. Smith on invoice 123.

If you're using QuickBooks, you enter purchases on account by using an invoice form like the one in Figure 9-2. Most of the information on the invoice form is similar to the sales receipt form (see the section "Collecting on Cash

Sales," earlier in this chapter), but the invoice form also has space to enter a different address for shipping (the Ship To field) and includes payment terms (the Terms field). On the sample invoice form shown in Figure 9-2, you can see that payment is due in 30 days.

QuickBooks uses the information on the invoice to update the following accounts:

- ✔ Accounts Receivable
- ✔ Inventory
- ✔ The customer's account
- ✔ GST/HST and PST Charged

Based on this data, when it comes time to remind the customer of what she owes you at the end of the month, with a little prompting from you (see Figure 9-3), QuickBooks generates statements for all customers who have outstanding invoices. You can easily generate statements for specific customers or for all customers on the books. By the way, some people refer to these statements as *monthly reminder statements*.

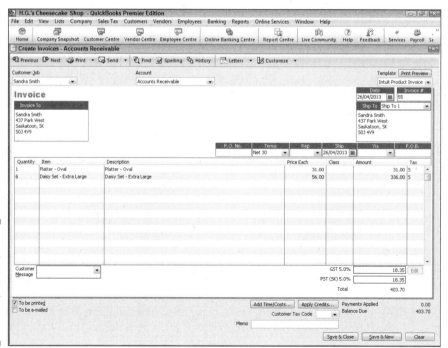

Figure 9-2:
A QuickBooks sales invoice for sales made on account.

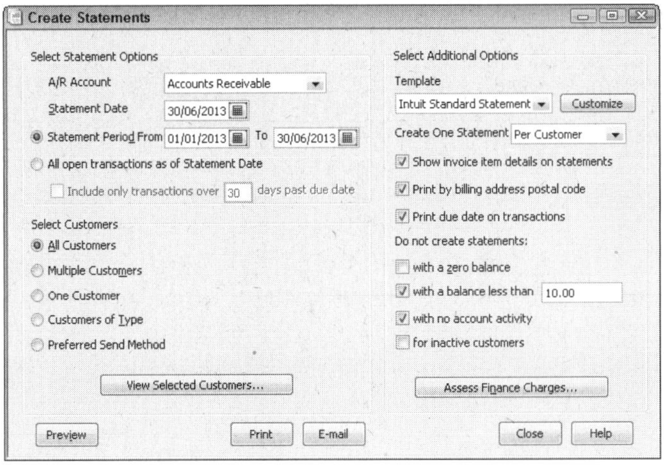

Figure 9-3:
Generating
statements
for custom-
ers by using
QuickBooks.

When you receive payment from a customer, follow these steps:

1. **Enter the customer's name on the customer payment form (shown in Figure 9-4) or select the customer's name using the drop-down menu beside the Received From field.**

   QuickBooks automatically lists all outstanding invoices.

2. **Select the check box next to the invoice or invoices paid.**

   QuickBooks updates the Accounts Receivable account, the Cash account, and the customer's individual account to show that your business has received payment.

If your business uses a point-of-sale program that's integrated into the computerized accounting system, you can really easily record sales on account transactions. Sales details feed into the system when your business makes each sale, so you don't have to enter the detail at the end of the day. These point-of-sale programs save a lot of time, but they can get very expensive. You or the business's accountant should figure out whether your business can justify the cost.

Even if customers don't buy on account, point-of-sale programs provide businesses with an incredible amount of information about their customers and what those customers like to buy. Your business can use this data in the future for direct marketing and special sales so that you can increase the likelihood of repeat business.

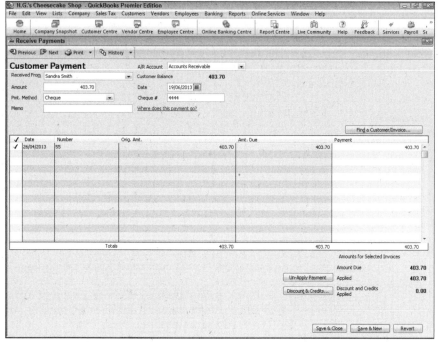

Figure 9-4:
In QuickBooks, recording collections from customers who buy on credit starts with the customer payment form.

Proving Out the Cash Register

To ensure that cashiers don't pocket a business's cash, at the end of each day, cashiers must *prove out* (show that they have the right amount of cash in the register based on the sales transactions during the day) the amount of cash, cheques, and debit card and credit card charges, as well as bills for sales on account that they took in during the day.

This process of proving out a cash register actually starts at the end of the previous day, when cashier John Doe and his manager agree to the amount of cash left in John's register drawer as a float to be used for making change. You record cash sitting in cash registers or cash drawers as part of the Cash on Hand account. We discuss the handling of floats in Chapter 7.

When John comes to work the next morning, he starts out with the amount of cash left in the drawer as a float. At the end of the business day, either he or his manager runs a summary of activity on the cash register for the day to produce a report of the total sales taken in by the cashier. John counts the amount of cash in his register, as well as totalling the cheques, debit card receipts, credit card receipts, and sales-on-account charges. He then completes a cash-out form that looks something like Table 9-2.

Table 9-2	Cash Register: John Doe 7/25/2012		
Receipts	*Sales*	*Credit*	*Cash*
Beginning cash float			$100
Cash sales	$400		$400
Credit card sales	$800	$800	
Debit card sales	$300	$300	
Sales on account	$400	$400	
Totals	$1,900	$1,500	
Total cash in register			$500

A store manager reviews John Doe's cash register summary (produced by the actual register) and compares it to the cash-out form. If John's *ending cash* (the amount of cash remaining in the register) doesn't match the cash-out form, he and the manager try to pinpoint the mistake. If they can't find a mistake, they fill out a cash-overage or cash-shortage form.

The store manager decides how much cash to leave in the cash drawer or register as a float (usually the same amount every day) for the next day and deposits the remainder. She does this task for each of her cashiers and then deposits all the cash and cheques from the day in a night deposit box at the bank. She sends a report that includes details of the deposit to the book-keeper so that the data makes it into the accounting system. The bookkeeper enters the data on the cash Sales Receipts form (refer to Figure 9-1) if the business uses a computerized accounting system or into the Cash Receipts journal if the business keeps the books manually (refer to Chapter 5).

Tracking Volume Discounts

Businesses offer volume discounts at some point in time to generate more sales or remain competitive. Volume discounts are usually in the form of a sale with 10 percent, 20 percent, or an even higher percentage off purchases, depending on the relationship with the customer or the size of the order.

When you offer volume discounts to customers, track the amount of your volume discounts in a separate account so that you can keep an eye on how much you discount sales in each month. If you find you're losing more and more money to discounting, look closely at your pricing structure and competition to find out why your business needs to frequently lower your prices in order to make sales. You can track volume discount information very easily by using the data found on a standard sales register receipt. The receipt from a bakery shown in Table 9-3 includes volume discount details.

Table 9-3	Cash Sales Receipt 7/25/2012		
Item	*Quantity*	*Price*	*Total*
White Serving Set	1	$40	$40.00
Cheesecake, Marble	1	$20	$20.00
Cheesecake, Blueberry	1	$20	$20.00
Subtotal			$80.00
Volume discount @ 10%			$(8.00)
Subtotal after discount			$72.00
GST @ 5%			$3.60
Total			$75.60
Cash paid			$85.00
Change			$9.40

From this example, you can see clearly that the store takes in less cash when it offers volume discounts. When recording the sale in the Cash Receipts journal, you record the volume discount as a debit. This debit increases the Volume Discount account, which you subtract from the Sales account to calculate the net sales. (We walk you through all these steps and calculations when we discuss preparing the income statement in Chapter 19.) Here's what the bakery's entry for this particular sale looks like in the Cash Receipts journal:

Account	*Debit*	*Credit*
Cash	$75.60	
Volume Discount	$8.00	
—Sales		$80.00
—GST Payable @ 5%		$3.60

Cash receipts for July 25, 2012.

If you use a computerized accounting system, add the volume discount as a line item on the sales receipt or invoice; the system automatically adjusts the sales figures and updates your Volume Discount account. Many software packages apply volume discounts on invoices to come up with the final selling price, but the amount of discount is not tracked in the books.

Recording Sales Discounts

Similar to your being offered purchase discounts from your vendor for quick payment (which we discuss in Chapters 3 and 8), you can offer sales discounts to your customers for prompt collection. The idea is to speed up collections by giving your customer a small discount in return for getting your money practically immediately.

After you negotiate them, the discount terms you offer your customer appear in the terms box on the sales invoice. The clock starts ticking on the invoice date to arrive at the due date. When your customer takes advantage of the discount, the amount is entered and tracked in a separate account in the books.

 Watch for those situations where you have offered a generous sales discount but your customer fails to take advantage of the reduction in the amount owing for early payment. This is a red flag that indicates that your customer is in financial difficulty. Monitor the situation, and consider suspending sales until you receive cash for the amount already owed.

Keep in mind when considering offering sales discounts what the current interest rates are at the bank. Offering a 2 percent discount to a customer to speed up collection (your customer pays you after 10 days instead of in 30 days) doesn't make sense if you can borrow money at the bank at an annual rate of 5 percent.

Recording Sales Returns and Allowances

Most stores deal with *sales returns* on a regular basis. Customers often return items that they've purchased because the item is defective, they change their minds, or for any other reason. Instituting a no-return policy is guaranteed to produce very unhappy customers, so to maintain good customer relations, you should allow sales returns.

Sales allowances are very similar to sales returns. When you issue a customer a credit note for a sales allowance, you're giving the customer a reduction in the price because of some defect or damage that the product suffered, possibly during shipping. Instead of having damaged goods returned to your store or warehouse, you may decide to let the customer keep the product at a reduced price. Businesses often take this measure to settle with a customer because those businesses really don't want to resell defective inventory. Imagine a nice, big scratch on a fine piece of wood furniture. You get the picture.

Many businesses have begun to use sales incentive programs. You have to record the sale of a gift card in the books differently than a sale of inventory. A gift card that your business sells is actually a liability for the business because the business receives cash but hasn't yet given any merchandise or service in exchange. For that reason, you enter gift card sales in a Gift Card Liability account. When a customer makes a purchase at a later date and uses the gift card, you reduce the Gift Card Liability account by the sale amount plus any sales taxes that your business charges on the sale. Monitoring the Gift Card Liability account allows a business to keep track of how much the business still owes in merchandise or services.

You may find accepting sales returns a more complicated process than accepting sales allowances — at least, from an internal control point of view. Usually, a business posts in its store a set of rules for returns that may include the following:

- Returns are allowed only within 30 days of purchase.
- You must have a receipt or invoice to return an item.
- If you return an item without a receipt, you can obtain only store credit available for a future sale, similar to a gift card.

You can set up whatever rules you want for returns. For internal control purposes, the key to returns is monitoring how your staff handles them. In most cases, you should require a manager's approval on returns and allowances. Also, be sure your staff pays close attention to how the customer originally paid for the item he returns. You certainly don't want to give your customer cash if he charged the sale on account — that's just handing over your money! After the manager approves a return, the cashier returns the amount paid by cash or credit card. Customers who bought the items on account don't get any money back. Instead of providing a refund, the cashier fills out a form so that the business can subtract, with a credit, the amount of the original purchase from the customer's account.

You use the information collected by the cashier who handled the return to input the sales return data into the books. For example, if a customer returns a $40 item that she purchased with cash, you record the cash refund in the General Journal or the Cash Disbursements Journal like this:

Account	*Debit*	*Credit*
Sales Returns	$40	
GST Payable @ 5%	$2	
—Cash		$42

To record return of purchase, 7/30/2012.

If the customer bought the item with a volume discount, you also calculate the amount of the discount in the sales return and reduce the price to show that discount.

In this journal entry

- ✓ The Sales Returns account increases. This account normally carries a debit balance, and you subtract it from Sales when you prepare the income statement, thereby reducing revenue.

- ✓ The debit to the GST Payable account reduces the amount in that account because your business no longer owes GST on the sale. If the sale had any PST charged, the PST Payable account is also reduced with a debit in your entry.

- ✓ The credit to the Cash account reduces the amount of cash in that account.

If you are using QuickBooks to record a credit memo issued to your customer, you access the Create Credit Memos/Refunds input screen via the Customer link on the top menu bar.

Figure 9-5 shows H.G.'s Cheesecake Shop issuing a credit memo to Patricia Perry, a customer, because she returned an item for credit.

QuickBooks uses the information on the credit memo to update the following accounts for a sales return:

- ✓ Sales (reduced with a debit)

- ✓ Accounts Receivable (reduced with a credit)

- ✓ Inventory (increased with a debit)

- ✓ Cost of Goods Sold (reduced with a credit)

- ✓ The customer's account (reduced with a credit)

- ✓ GST/HST and PST Payable (reduced with a debit)

Note that instead of recording transactions in the Sales Returns and Allowances account set up in your Chart of Accounts, QuickBooks is programmed instead to reduce the Sales account. You can use the Report function in QuickBooks to give you the details of all credit memo entries to sales, and make a summary adjusting journal entry to Sales Returns and Allowances (debit) and credit Sales.

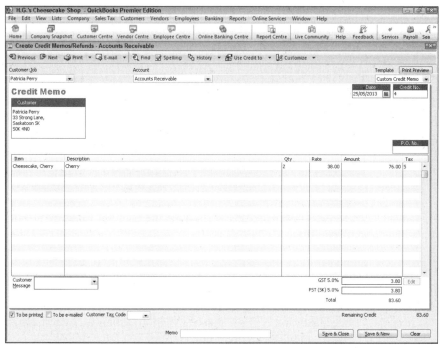

Figure 9-5: Recording and issuing a credit memo in QuickBooks for goods returned or a sales allowance granted to a customer.

We describe how to move amounts between General Ledger accounts in Chapter 17.

Recording Service Revenue

Unlike the merchandising business where you simply sell inventory, the service business creates a few more dilemmas. You have to ask yourself when exactly you need to record a sale of services to increase your profits. When you sell merchandise, the exact point in time when you reduce your inventory asset and when you record a sale is clear: The accounting rules state that you record a sale when the customer takes legal possession of the inventory. But when it comes to providing a service, the lines become blurred.

The basic accounting rule states that service revenue is recorded when it is earned. The next question you will likely ask is, When do I earn my revenue? Basically, revenue is earned when you have provided the service to your customer and not necessarily when you send a bill or collect the cash from your customer. So what does this mean? You can increase your revenues in your accounts with a credit and increase your profit as you do work and earn revenue. Take, for example, the case of an architect who negotiates an assignment with his customer involving the drafting of a set of plans for the construction of a warehouse. The architect's price is $1,000 for his work, and he will bill the customer when the work is complete.

Accrued revenue

If the architect in our example can deliver the service very quickly and bill his customer before the end of the month, no bookkeeping issue exists. If, on the other hand, the work takes several months because of some approval delays, some of the revenue may be counted in the months that the architect does his work.

At the end of the month of May, say, when the job is half done, it is fair for the architect to accrue half of the revenue. This way, his income statement gets the increase from the revenue that rightly should be included for the month of May. The timing of the collection of the cash is not the determining factor.

Based on this example, $500 of accrued revenue is recorded at the end of May using the following entry:

Account	*Debit*	*Credit*
Accounts Receivable	$500	
—Service Revenue		$500

To record the accrual of revenue for the month of May.

We discuss in more detail how to estimate and record accrued revenue using an adjusting journal entry at the end of the month or at the end of the year in Chapter 17.

Unearned revenue

What if the timing of collecting the cash from the architect's customer is completely different, you ask? Good question. Suppose the architect decides that he needs to protect himself against the risk that his customer won't pay her bill at the end of the job. In this case, he insists that half of the total price, or $500, be collected as a deposit before any of the work gets done. When he collects the $500, say, at the beginning of May, he really has done nothing to deserve this money. For now, he can record the collection of the cash as a liability to his customer. He has to either deliver the work or give his customer a refund of the $500. This logic is the same logic applied to the sale of gift cards, which we discuss earlier in this chapter.

The architect records the collection of the cash as follows:

Account	Debit	Credit
Cash	$500	
—Unearned Revenue		$500

> To record the unearned revenue from the collection of a deposit from a customer in May.

Cash, which goes on the balance sheet, increases by $500 with a debit, and Unearned Revenue, a liability account that also appears on the balance sheet, increases with a credit. So far, the architect cannot recognize an increase to the income statement because no work has been done and no revenue has been earned.

How and when does the unearned revenue become revenue, you ask? Another great question! Based on the accounting rule we mention earlier, the architect is allowed to record some revenue if some of the work is done. He doesn't have to wait until the whole job has been completed to recognize revenue. In a situation like this, you can and should recognize revenue the same way you recognize accrued revenue. You estimate how much of the whole job is done and record your estimated amount as revenue.

If the job begins and ends in the following month, which in our example is the month of June, the architect has no bookkeeping issues. He can send out a bill that will trigger the recording of all of the revenue as follows:

Account	Debit	Credit
Accounts Receivable	$500	
Unearned Revenue	$500	
—Service Revenue		$1,000

> To record an invoice of $1,000 sent to a customer at the completion of an assignment in June.

Keep in mind when preparing your invoice that you need to take into account the cash deposit you received and previously recorded to the Unearned Revenue account; in this case, the architect accounts for a $500 deposit.

If, on the other hand, the work takes several months to complete because of some approval delays, some of the revenue is counted in the months in which the architect does his work (refer to the preceding section).

Suppose that half of the unearned revenue becomes earned by the end of June. In this case, the architect needs to recognize an increase in his Service Revenue account with a credit on the income statement. Think of this adjustment from the perspective of the liability account: The architect reduces his obligation to the customer, and so reduces the Unearned Revenue liability account, with a debit for the amount of work that has been done so far, which he estimates to be worth $250. He then records the following at the end of June:

Account	Debit	Credit
Unearned Revenue	$250	
—Service Revenue		$250

To record revenue earned during the month of June.

We discuss in more detail in Chapter 17 how you can estimate and record adjustments to Unearned Revenue when preparing financial statements at the end of the month or at the end of the year.

Monitoring Accounts Receivable

Making sure customers pay their bills is a crucial responsibility of the book-keeper. Before sending out the monthly statements, you should prepare an *Aging Summary report,* which lists all customers who owe money to the business and how old each debt is. If you keep the books manually, you collect the necessary information from each customer account. If you keep the books in a computerized accounting system, you can generate this report automatically. Either way, your Aging Summary report should look similar to the example report from a bakery that we show you in Table 9-4.

Table 9-4	Aging Summary Report — As of Aug. 1, 2012			
Customer	*Current*	*31–60 Days*	*60–90 Days*	*> 90 Days*
S. Smith	$84.00	$46.15	$0.00	$0.00
J. Doe	$0.00	$0.00	$65.78	$0.00
H. Harris	$89.64	$0.00	$0.00	$0.00
M. Man	$0.00	$0.00	$0.00	$125.35
Totals	$173.64	$46.15	$65.78	$125.35

The aging summary quickly tells you which customers are behind in their bills. In this example, customers are cut off from future purchases when their payments are more than 60 days late, so J. Doe and M. Man can't buy on account until they pay their bills in full.

 Give a copy of your aging summary to the sales manager so that he can alert staff to problem customers. He can also arrange for the appropriate collections procedures. Each business sets up its own collections process, but usually it starts with a phone call or e-mail, followed by letters, and possibly even legal action, if necessary.

Accepting and Expecting Your Losses

You may encounter a situation in which your business never gets paid by a customer, even after your business goes through an aggressive collections process. In this case, you have no choice but to write off the accounts receivable as a bad debt and accept the loss.

Because you can't predict which accounts will go bad, you need to estimate what amount you think is likely to go bad. Based on this estimate, you make an entry to create and later on increase with a credit an account called Allowance for Doubtful Accounts. This account, which appears on the balance sheet along with the Accounts Receivable account, has two purposes:

- ✔ It reduces the book value of the Accounts Receivable down to a more realistic value for this asset.
- ✔ It keeps track of the specific customer account receivable that you write off. To recognize the expected losses, you increase an Expense account called Bad Debt Expense. We discuss how to record bad debt expenses and increases to the Allowance for Doubtful Accounts account in Chapter 17.

Most businesses review their Aging Summary reports every three to six months and decide which accounts they need to write off as bad debt. When you write off a customer's account, the Allowance for Doubtful Accounts account decreases because it normally has a credit balance, and the Accounts Receivable account decreases.

To give you an idea of how you write off an account, assume that one of your customers never pays $40 that's due. Here's what your journal entry looks like for the writeoff of this bad debt, assuming that you didn't charge taxes:

Account	Debit	Credit
Allowance for Doubtful Accounts	$40	
—Accounts Receivable		$40

In a computerized accounting system, you record this entry by using the General journal. We show you how to use the General journal in Chapter 17.

Recovering GST/HST

When you write off an account receivable, remember to recover any GST/HST that you charged on the sale from the CRA. The amount that you originally recorded on the sale increased the GST/HST Payable account (we show you how to charge GST/HST on a sale in Chapter 5). After you record the amount charged for GST/HST to the GST/HST Payable account, you're obligated to remit the tax to the CRA by the deadline date, whether the customer has paid you or not.

Because you're not expecting to collect the account when you write it off, not getting back from the CRA the money that your business paid for the GST/HST charged on the transaction would simply add insult to injury. Everyone, the CRA included, agrees that fairness must prevail and that the CRA must share in your losses.

Here's how to recover that GST/HST tax. We use the same example that we do in the preceding section, except that, in this case, the business charged 5 percent GST on the original sale.

Account	Debit	Credit
Allowance for Doubtful Accounts	$40	
GST Payable @ 5%	$2	
—Accounts Receivable		$42

You can't reduce the liability for GST/HST simply by estimating and increasing your Allowance for Doubtful Accounts account. According to the CRA, you have to record an actual writeoff of the accounts receivable on your books before your business can record a reduction to your GST/HST Payable account. Unfortunately, if you charged PST/RST, you can't recover that tax on the account receivable that you couldn't collect.

Chapter 10

Employee Payroll and Benefits

. . . .

In This Chapter

▶ Hiring employees

▶ Withholding employee taxes

▶ Figuring out each employee's net pay

▶ Making voluntary deductions

▶ Knowing the difference between tax-exempt and taxable benefits

▶ Calculating employees' paycheques

▶ Preparing and recording payroll

▶ Dealing with payroll responsibilities

. . . .

*U*nless your business has only one worker (you, the owner), you most likely have employees — and that means you have to pay them, offer benefits, and manage a payroll.

Responsibilities for hiring and paying employees usually are shared between the human resources staff and the bookkeeping staff. As the bookkeeper, you must complete all government tax-related forms and handle all payroll responsibilities, including paying employees, withholding and remitting employee payroll taxes, collecting and managing employee benefit contributions, and paying benefit providers. This chapter examines the various employee staffing issues that bookkeepers need to be able to manage.

Staffing Your Business

After you decide that you want to hire employees for your business, you must be ready to deal with a lot of government paperwork. In addition to paperwork, you're faced with many decisions about how the business will pay employees and who must maintain the paperwork required by provincial and federal government entities.

You not only have to know what your business needs to do to satisfy government bureaucracies before your business hires the first person but also must decide how frequently you plan to pay employees, as well as what type of wage and salary scales you want to set up.

Although you may have a written agreement or contract with an individual who is working for your business as a self-employed contractor, the Canada Revenue Agency keeps a close eye on these types of relationships. If the CRA finds evidence that an employer-employee relationship exists, it will consider this individual your employee for the purpose of payroll deduction rules, and you will also have the added responsibilities associated with treating this person as an employee.

Remembering two critical numbers

Before you can start paying employees, your business needs to ensure that it has two vital numbers:

- ✔ **Your payroll business number (BN):** As we discuss in Chapter 1, you can't get a payroll account without getting a business number (BN) with the CRA. Your BN is the basis for your payroll remittance account with the federal government.

  If you didn't open a payroll account in the past because you didn't expect to hire employees, you have to register for the account before the first remittance due date. Your first remittance due date is generally the 15th day of the month following the month in which you began withholding deductions from your employees' pay.

- ✔ **Your employees' Social Insurance Numbers (SINs):** Before you hire an employee, you first must be sure that he's eligible for employment in Canada. Asking for a person's Social Insurance Number (SIN) is the simplest way to determine his eligibility for employment. You need to know a person's SIN whenever you reference that person in government documents. You, as the employer, communicate transactions concerning your employee — including the amount of money you pay him, as well as any taxes and benefits your business collects and pays on his behalf — to the various government agencies that use this unique number.

Filling out TD1 – Personal Tax Credits Return

Every person you hire must fill out a TD1 form called the Personal Tax Credits Return. You've probably filled out a TD1 at least once in your life, if you've ever worked for someone else in Canada. You can download the form from the Canada Revenue Agency (CRA) website: www.cra-arc.gc.ca. (Just enter the form number into the site's search engine.) You don't have to file this form with the government; you, the employer, should keep it in your payroll records. The TD1 provides evidence of your employees' eligibility for the amount of tax that your business will withhold from their paycheques.

The TD1 form, shown in Figure 10-1, tells you (the employer) how much you need to take out of your employees' gross pay in income taxes. Employees indicate whether they have additional dependents or deductions, such as tuition fees, which reduce their tax bills when they file their personal income tax returns. The amount of income taxes you need to take out of each employee's paycheque depends on the total claim amount taken from Item 13 of Page 1 of the TD1.

On Page 2 of the TD1, the employee has the option to have additional taxes deducted from her paycheque. Your employee may choose this option to force herself to save money that she will recoup when filing her annual tax return in the following year. Your employee may have other income — perhaps from a rental property — that she knows will end up costing extra income taxes by the time she files her personal income tax return. This option then becomes a way for the employee to make an instalment payment towards that additional tax liability.

You don't need to verify the accuracy of what your employee tells you about such entries as the number of dependents, for example. At the bottom of page 2 of the TD1, the employee certifies the accuracy and completeness of her statements.

If you know that the information an employee provides on Form TD1 is false, you should confront the employee with this knowledge and ask him to make the necessary changes to his form. The CRA considers it a serious offence to knowingly accept a Form TD1 that contains false or deceptive statements. If you're not sure whether you need to follow up or not, contact your tax services office of the CRA for advice.

Canada Revenue Agency / Agence du revenu du Canada

2012 PERSONAL TAX CREDITS RETURN TD1

Your employer or payer will use this form to determine the amount of your tax deductions.
Read the back before completing this form. Complete this form based on the best estimate of your circumstances.

Last name	First name and initial(s)	Date of birth (YYYY/MM/DD)	Employee number

Address including postal code	For non-residents only – Country of permanent residence	Social insurance number

1. Basic personal amount – Every resident of Canada can claim this amount. If you will have more than one employer or payer at the same time in 2012, see "More than one employer or payer at the same time" on the next page. If you are a non-resident, see "Non-residents" on the next page.   **10,822**

2. Child amount – Either parent (but not both), may claim $2,191 for each child born in 1995 or later, that resides with both parents throughout the year. If the child is **infirm, add $2,000** to the claim for that child. Any unused portion can be transferred to that parent's spouse or common-law partner. If the child does not reside with both parents throughout the year, the parent who is entitled to claim the "Amount for an eligible dependant" on line 8 may also claim the child amount for that same child.

3. Age amount – If you will be 65 or older on December 31, 2012, and your net income for the year from all sources will be $33,884 or less, enter $6,720. If your net income for the year will be between $33,884 and $78,684 and you want to calculate a partial claim, get the TD1-WS, *Worksheet for the 2012 Personal Tax Credits Return*, and complete the appropriate section.

4. Pension income amount – If you will receive regular pension payments from a pension plan or fund (excluding Canada Pension Plan, Quebec Pension Plan, Old Age Security, or Guaranteed Income Supplement payments), enter $2,000 or your estimated annual pension income, whichever is less.

5. Tuition, education, and textbook amounts (full time and part time) – If you are a student enrolled at a university or college, or an educational institution certified by Human Resources and Skills Development Canada, and you will pay more than $100 per institution in tuition fees, complete this section. If you are enrolled full time, or if you have a mental or physical disability and are enrolled part time, enter the total of the tuition fees you will pay, plus $400 for each month that you will be enrolled, plus $65 per month for textbooks. If you are enrolled part time and do not have a mental or physical disability, enter the total of the tuition fees you will pay, plus $120 for each month that you will be enrolled part time, plus $20 per month for textbooks.

6. Disability amount – If you will claim the disability amount on your income tax return by using Form T2201, *Disability Tax Credit Certificate*, enter $7,546.

7. Spouse or common-law partner amount – If you are supporting your spouse or common-law partner who lives with you, and whose net income for the year will be less than $10,822 ($12,822 if he or she is **infirm**) enter the difference between this amount and his or her estimated net income for the year. If your spouse's or common-law partner's net income for the year will be $10,822 or more ($12,822 or more if he or she is **infirm**), you cannot claim this amount.

8. Amount for an eligible dependant – If you do not have a spouse or common-law partner and you support a dependent relative who lives with you, and whose net income for the year will be less than $10,822 ($12,822 if he or she is **infirm** and you **did not claim the child amount** for this dependant), enter the difference between this amount and his or her estimated net income. If your eligible dependant's net income for the year will be $10,822 or more ($12,822 or more if he or she is **infirm**), you cannot claim this amount.

9. Caregiver amount – If you are taking care of a dependant who lives with you, whose net income for the year will be $15,033 or less, and who is either your or your spouse's or common-law partner's:
- parent or grandparent (aged 65 or older), enter $4,402 ($6,402 if he or she is **infirm**) or
- relative (aged 18 or older) who is dependent on you because of an infirmity, enter $6,402.
If the dependant's net income for the year will be between $15,033 and $19,435 ($15,033 and $21,435 if he or she is **infirm**) and you want to calculate a partial claim, get the TD1-WS, and complete the appropriate section.

10. Amount for infirm dependants age 18 or older – If you support an infirm dependant age 18 or older who is your or your spouse's or common-law partner's relative, who lives in Canada, and whose net income for the year will be $6,420 or less, enter $6,402. You cannot claim an amount for a dependant you claimed on line 9. If the dependant's net income for the year will be between $6,420 and $12,822 and you want to calculate a partial claim, get the TD1-WS, and complete the appropriate section.

11. Amounts transferred from your spouse or common-law partner – If your spouse or common-law partner will not use all of his or her age amount, pension income amount, tuition, education and textbooks amounts, disability amount or child amount on his or her income tax return, enter the unused amount.

12. Amounts transferred from a dependant – If your dependant will not use all of his or her **disability amount** on his or her income tax return, enter the unused amount. If your or your spouse's or common-law partner's dependent child or grandchild will not use all of his or her **tuition, education, and textbook amounts** on his or her income tax return, enter the unused amount.

13. TOTAL CLAIM AMOUNT – Add lines 1 through 12.
Your employer or payer will use this amount to determine the amount of your tax deductions.

Continue on the next page ➤

TD1 E (12)

(Vous pouvez obtenir ce formulaire en français à **www.arc.gc.ca/formulaires** ou au **1-800-959-3376**.)

Canada

© Canada Revenue Agency. Reproduced with permission of the Minister of Public Works and Government Services Canada, 2012

Figure 10-1: All employees should complete CRA Form TD1 when you hire them.

Picking pay periods

You need to decide how frequently you plan to pay employees before you hire staff. Most businesses choose one or more of these four pay periods:

- ✔ **Weekly:** Your business pays employees every week, and you must do payroll 52 times a year.

- ✔ **Biweekly:** Your business pays employees every two weeks, and you must do payroll 26 times a year.

- ✔ **Semi-monthly:** Your business pays employees twice a month (commonly on the 15th and last day of the month), and you must do payroll 24 times a year.

- ✔ **Monthly:** Your business pays employees once a month, and you must do payroll 12 times a year.

You can choose to use any of these pay periods, and you may even decide to use more than one type. For example, some businesses pay *hourly employees* (employees paid by the hour) weekly or biweekly, and pay *salaried employees* (employees paid by a set salary, regardless of how many hours they work) semi-monthly or monthly. Whatever your choice, decide on a consistent pay period policy and be sure to make your policy clear to employees when you hire them.

Besides hourly and salaried pays, you may also pay your employees on commission or for piecework. An example of piecework is the planting of tree seedlings. The tree planter gets paid for each seedling planted.

The decision concerning pay periods may be out of your hands. In some industries, such as the construction industry, the union agreement requires a weekly payroll.

Employees prefer the biweekly pay period. Most employees tie fixed payments, such as preauthorized debits to their bank account for mortgage payments, to your payroll dates.

Keeping time with time sheets

For each employee who's paid hourly, you need to have some sort of time sheet to keep track of work hours. The employees themselves usually complete the time sheets, and their managers approve those time sheets. The managers then send completed and approved time sheets to the bookkeeper, who calculates paycheques based on the exact number of hours worked.

Investigating laws concerning employment

You have a lot of leeway regarding the level of wages and salary you pay your employees, but you still have to follow the rules laid out by the government.

For hourly paid employees, you need to make sure that the hourly rate of pay you offer new employees falls within your province's minimum wage guidelines.

You can find the Canada Labour Code on the Canadian Department of Justice's website at www.justice.gc.ca. This documentation deals with private sector minimum employment standards in Canada. It sets out the federal, provincial, and territorial legislative provisions dealing with the minimum age for employment, maximum hours of work and overtime pay, minimum wages, equal pay for equal work, the weekly rest day, general holidays with pay, annual vacations with pay, parental leave, and individual and group terminations of employment. Along with an overview of the law, you can find specific information concerning the provisions that exist in each Canadian jurisdiction.

Most employees covered by the Employment Standards Act (ESA) — which include full-time, part-time, temporary, and seasonal employees, as well as contract workers and student workers — are eligible for an annual vacation with pay after 12 months of employment. The minimum vacation time under the ESA is two weeks a year. However, job-specific exemptions to the vacation-with-pay part of the ESA mean certain workers aren't eligible.

The employer pays for statutory holidays. The number and length of these holidays vary from province to province.

Collecting Employee Taxes

You, the bookkeeper, must both follow wage and salary guidelines set for your business and know how to calculate the employee taxes that the business must deduct from each employee's paycheque.

Three deductions are mandatory:

- ✔ The Canada Pension Plan (CPP) or, in Québec, the Québec Pension Plan (QPP).
- ✔ Employment Insurance (EI).
- ✔ The combined provincial and federal income taxes. (In the province of Québec, Revenu Québec doesn't combine the federal and provincial portions of personal income taxes.)

Canada and Québec Pension Plans (CPP/QPP)

The employer and employee are equal partners when it comes to contributing into the Canada or Québec Pension Plan. Employees 18 years of age and older, and those less than 70 years of age, have to contribute 4.95 percent of their employment earnings in excess of $3,500 per year. For each pay period, the employer withholds an amount of the CPP contribution from the gross pay earned by the employee. Your employees can opt to start drawing CPP benefits when they reach 60 years of age.

You may find it unfair and inappropriate to force your employees to contribute to the CPP pension plan when they have reached the age of 60 or 65 and are already drawing their CPP retirement pensions. Starting January 1, 2012, an employee who is between the ages of 65 and 70 can give you a completed and signed Form CPT30, Election to Stop Contributing to the Canada Pension Plan, which will allow you to stop deducting CPP from the otherwise pensionable earnings of this employee. You may want to encourage employees who fit into this situation to follow through with this option, since it will save you the amount you have to pay as a contribution to the CPP pension plan.

The money you deduct from your employee's pay belongs to that employee, but you handle it as an agent of the government. You set aside this money, along with an equal amount that your business pays. You must make the payment to the Receiver General by the deadline date, usually by the 15th day of the following month. For the province of Québec, you pay the Québec income tax and QPP to the Québec Minister of Revenue.

You can calculate the CPP/QPP relatively easily. The government collects CPP/QPP only on annual income in excess of $3,500. If you use a biweekly payment schedule, in order to determine the amount of pay that isn't subject to CPP, you divide the $3,500 exemption by 26 pay periods per year, giving you $134.62. Therefore, your employee earns $134.62 each pay period that's not pensionable. So, you withhold 4.95 percent (the rate of CPP) on anything the employee earns over that amount. For the Québec Pension Plan, the rate has changed to 5.025% starting in 2012. The mechanics of the calculation of QPP are the same as that for CPP.

To see CPP/QPP deductions in action, consider Stan, an employee who earns $2,000 in gross pay for two weeks of work. After the bookkeeper deducts $134.62, which the Canada and Québec Pension Acts don't consider pensionable, the remaining amount draws a deduction as follows:

$$(\$2,000.00 - \$134.62) \times 4.95 \text{ percent} = \$92.34$$

The bookkeeper deducts $92.34 from Stan's gross pay, and the employer matches the amount of $92.34, making the amount later remitted for CPP/QPP $184.68.

Because the Canada and Québec plans have a maximum contribution each year, employees who have relatively high gross earnings meet the maximum contribution at a certain point in the calendar year. They experience a holiday from contributing to the CPP/QPP plan from that point forward to the end of the calendar year. The amount of contribution starts back at zero on the first pay period in January of the following calendar year, so the deductions start all over again.

Employment Insurance (EI)

The Employment Insurance program requires that employees pay into the program until their maximum contribution for the year has been reached. No age limit for EI exists. For 2012, the maximum amount of insurable earnings was $45,900, and the premium rate was 1.83 percent of gross pay. The maximum annual contribution for 2012 was therefore $839.97 ($45,900 × 1.83 percent). As in the case of CPP, the Québec rates for EI also differ from those used in all the other provinces.

Here's an example of EI deductions in action. Stan (whom we talk about in the preceding section) earns a gross pay of $2,000 for a two-week period, which amounts to an annual pay of $52,000 ($2,000 × 26 pay periods). Because Stan's annual gross pay is higher than the maximum insurable earnings of $45,900, the bookkeeper makes the following calculation and deducts that amount from each of Stan's paycheques for EI until the maximum is reached:

$2,000.00 × 1.83 percent = $36.60

As opposed to the matching (same amount) requirement for the CPP/QPP, the employer needs to contribute 1.4 times the amount that the bookkeeper deducts from the employee's gross pay. In the case of Stan, his employer has the following additional benefits expense:

$36.60 × 1.4 = $51.24

The employer remits to the Receiver General the combined amount of EI, along with the income taxes withheld and the combined CPP of the employee and employer, on the 15th of the month following the pay-period month. We discuss how to do this payment in Chapter 11.

Combined income tax withheld

Line 13 of your employee's TD1 form (refer to Figure 10-1) provides the employee's total claim amount. To determine the amount of income taxes that you must deduct from the employee's pay, you need to determine your province's claim code for the employee's total claim amount. You can find claim codes in each province's payroll deduction table, which you can find on the CRA website (www.cra-arc.gc.ca). The amount deducted for taxes gets lower the higher the federal claim code number.

Although the government doesn't require businesses to deduct CPP and EI under some specific circumstances, which are too long to list here (like when an employee is over the age of 69 and may stop contributing to CPP, for example), that's not the case with income tax. As long as an employee collects a paycheque, the government collects income tax.

Stan, whose CPP and EI we talk about in the preceding sections, has gross wages of $2,000 for a two-week pay period. Stan's single, he has no dependents, and he lives in the province of Ontario. His claim code is 1, so the government taxes his pay at the highest possible rate.

By looking at the federal and provincial income tax tables (located on the CRA website) for 2012, or using CRA's online calculator at https://apps.cra-arc.gc.ca/ebci/rhpd/, the bookkeeper determines the amount of the combined taxes is $358.29.

In addition to CPP, EI, and combined income taxes, you may have to withhold some pay for income taxes on certain taxable benefits. Later in the chapter we outline some typical taxable benefits on which you have to withhold income taxes.

Each time a federal or provincial government passes into law a fiscal budget, personal income tax rates may change. You need to diligently look up the tables to determine whether the ones you've used in the past still apply. The government reminds you by mail that some changes are coming into effect and highlights dates that you need to remember. If you use computerized payroll software, the provider delivers the necessary software updates for your accounting system.

Determining Net Pay

Net pay is the amount an employee receives in cash after an employer subtracts all tax and benefit deductions. In other words, after the bookkeeper subtracts all deductions from a person's gross pay, that person is left with the net pay.

After you figure out all the necessary CPP, EI, and taxes that you need to withhold from an employee's paycheque, you can calculate the paycheque amount by using this equation:

Gross pay – (CPP + EI + Combined income tax) = Net pay

Stan, whom we talk about in the preceding sections, wants to know his net pay. Here's how you calculate Stan's net pay, subtracting CPP, EI, and combined income tax:

$2,000.00 – ($92.34 + $36.60 + $358.29) = $1,512.77

In the simplest situations, this equation gives you the net pay, so you prepare the employee's cheque or the bank electronic funds transfer to the bank account of your employee for that amount. But you may encounter two major changes to this calculation:

✔ Sometimes, you have to add taxable benefits earned by the employee to the gross pay when you calculate the income subject to income taxes, CPP and EI, meaning that you may have to make large deductions.

✔ You have to change the calculation when the employee makes voluntary deductions, such as a charitable donation to the United Way.

This net pay calculation doesn't factor in any benefits. Many businesses offer their employees health, retirement, and other benefits — but those businesses usually expect the employees to share a portion of the costs. Because some of these benefits are taxable and some aren't, you need to take this distinction into account when you calculate income taxes, CPP, and EI. If an employee agrees to contribute an amount towards his benefits, you deduct that amount for the gross pay to arrive at the employee's net pay.

Considering Voluntary Deductions

Besides the deductions that the government requires employers take from employee gross pay, you can also take optional deductions from an employee's paycheque. Employees must request in writing optional deductions from their gross pay. Here are the most common voluntary deductions:

✔ **Registered Retirement or Education Savings Plans (RRSPs and RESPs), and Tax-Free Savings Account (TFSA) deductions:** Some people find saving money difficult. In order to help an employee save for her retirement or for major purchases, such as a home, an employer may offer assistance in achieving that goal. Several savings schemes are available.

A couple of common plans provide for some of an employee's pay-cheque, usually a fixed amount per pay period, to be deposited directly into her RRSP, RESP, or TFSA.

- **Canada Savings Bonds deductions:** Banks approach employers in October of every year to sell Canada Savings Bonds to their employees through payroll deductions. You need to keep additional paperwork to offer to help your business's employees save money. Usually, the business is not financially involved in the purchase of bonds in any way. It is simply following its employees' written instructions to take additional voluntary deductions off their paycheques in order to purchase the bonds. But your business can also buy the bonds on behalf of your employees. Refer to `www.csb.gc.ca/payroll-savings-program/employers` for more details.

- **Charitable donation deductions:** Many employees agree to the voluntary deduction of a donation to non-profit organizations such as the United Way. An employer obtains a written instruction from the employee permitting the employer to make a fixed deduction from the employee's paycheques for this donation. The employer holds this money until an agreed-upon date, at which point the employer pays the non-profit organization.

Although they're not exactly voluntary, many employees pay union dues, which the employer automatically deducts from the employee's pay.

Whatever voluntary deduction an employee requests, make sure you get the instructions in writing. Your employee should sign and date those instructions. Obtaining such a document not only resolves later disputes but also fulfills the legal requirement to have this document on file. Don't forget whose money you're dealing with, after all.

Surveying Your Benefits Options

Benefits, sometimes called *fringe benefits,* include programs that you provide employees to better their lives, such as health insurance and retirement savings opportunities. Most benefits are tax-exempt, which means that the employee doesn't have to pay taxes on them. However, some benefits are taxable, so the employee has to pay income taxes on the money or the fair value of the benefits received. This section reviews some of the different tax-exempt and taxable benefits you can offer your employees.

Also, the government requires that you add GST/HST to the value of some taxable benefits received. And when you calculate CPP and EI to withhold from an employee's paycheque, you need to include the benefits to determine the pensionable and insurable amount of earnings. We don't go into all the combinations of all potential cash and non-cash benefits — but suffice it to say that the list is quite long. Go to the CRA website (www.cra-arc.gc.ca) and search for the keywords "benefits" and "allowances" to get more details. In the following sections, we discuss the most popular benefits.

Tax-exempt benefits

Several benefits are *tax-exempt,* or not taxed. Retirement benefits are the most common of this type of benefit. In addition, you deduct anything that an employee pays toward the retirement plan from his gross pay when calculating the combined income taxes, so the employee doesn't have to pay taxes on that part of his salary or wages.

For example, an employee may share contributions to a formal retirement pension plan with an employer. If an employee who earns $2,000 in a two-week period voluntarily contributes $100 into her business's retirement plan, you also subtract that $100 from her gross pay before you calculate net pay. In addition, you reduce the amount subject to combined income tax by $100 before you calculate the federal and provincial government's cut. In other words, the employee receives a net pay that's not reduced by the $100, but by the after-tax cost of her contribution to the pension plan.

If an employer doesn't have a formal pension plan, that employer may offer an alternative to encourage employees to save for retirement. Employers offer to take voluntary deductions each pay period, which they deposit into each employee's designated Registered Retirement Saving Plans (RRSPs). A lot of businesses use RRSPs because the RRSP belongs to the employee, and therefore he can keep and continue using the same RRSP when he changes employers. (For more information about RRSPs, refer to "Considering Voluntary Deductions.")

Besides the RRSP or registered pension plan contributions, as an employer you can offer a myriad of other tax-exempt benefits to employees:

- ✔ **Child care expenses:** The government doesn't tax child care if that child care meets all the following conditions:

    - The services are provided at the employer's place of business.

    - The employer directly manages the services.

    - All the employees can receive the services at minimal or no cost.

    - The services aren't available to the general public, only to employees.

✔ **Counselling services:** The government doesn't tax employee counselling services if they relate to any of the following:

- An employee's reemployment

- An employee's retirement

- An employee's mental or physical health (such as counselling for tobacco, drug, or alcohol abuse; stress management; or employee assistance programs), or the health of a relative of an employee

✔ **Insurance plans:** You, as the employer, can offer group sickness, private health care, disability, accident, or income maintenance insurance plans to your employees without those benefits becoming taxable.

✔ **Meals:** The employer can provide overtime meals, or a reasonable allowance for overtime meals, without it becoming a taxable benefit if the employee works two or more hours of overtime right before or right after his scheduled hours of work and the overtime happens infrequently (fewer than three times a week).

If your business provides subsidized meals to an employee (for example, in an employee dining room or cafeteria) and the employee pays a reasonable amount for the meals, the CRA doesn't consider these meals a taxable benefit.

✔ **Moving expenses and relocation benefits:** When your business transfers an employee from one of your places of business to another, the government can't tax the amount that the business pays or reimburses the employee for certain moving expenses. These reimbursements include any amounts the employer pays to move the employee, the employee's family, and their household effects.

✔ **Professional membership dues:** When an employer pays professional membership dues on behalf of an employee and the business is the primary beneficiary of the payment, the CRA doesn't consider this payment a taxable benefit applied to the employee.

✔ **Recreational facilities:** A recreational facility or club doesn't give rise to a taxable benefit to employees if the business provides an in-house facility or pays an organization to provide a recreational facility that's available to all employees free of charge or for a minimal fee. You must demonstrate that the benefit is principally for the advantage of the business rather than your employees.

✔ **Social events:** If a business provides a free party or other social event to all employees and the cost is $100 per person or less, the CRA doesn't consider it a taxable benefit.

✔ **Subsidized school services:** If your business provides free or subsidized school services in remote areas for your employees' children, the CRA doesn't consider that service a taxable benefit.

> ✔ **Tuition fees, scholarships, and bursaries:** When your business pays for employee training that benefits mainly your business, CRA allows the payment without a taxable benefit treatment.
>
> ✔ **Uniforms and special clothing:** An employee doesn't receive a taxable benefit when your business supplies that employee with a distinctive uniform that she has to wear while carrying out her employment duties, or the employer provides an employee with special clothing (including safety footwear) designed to protect her from hazards associated with the employment.

Taxable benefits

We can more easily come up with the list of possible fringe benefits offered to employees that aren't considered taxable than tell you everything that *is* taxable. Some popular taxable benefits include the following:

> ✔ Certain rent-free and low-rent housing
>
> ✔ The value of board and lodging
>
> ✔ Interest-free and low-interest loans
>
> ✔ Personal use of a motor vehicle that the employer owns or leases
>
> ✔ Holiday trips, gifts, subsidized meals, personal use of cellular phones or home Internet services, or any other taxable benefit the business pays for
>
> ✔ Employer-provided parking and transit passes

By far, the CRA considers the majority of employee benefits taxable. The most complicated calculations of taxable benefits concern an employee's use of a business-owned or business-leased vehicle. For the proper calculation of the standby charge, you need to consult the CRA website (www.cra-arc.gc.ca).

Some employers recognize that some of the benefit plans offered to their employees don't represent true value to their employees. For example, when spouses each have a family medical and dental plan, the spouse who has the earliest birthday in the calendar year must make the claims. Therefore, the other spouse somewhat wastes his plan because he can use it only if the first plan doesn't cover 100 percent of the out-of-pocket costs. In this case, the employee with the birthday later in the year would be better off opting out of the medical plan and requesting instead another optional benefit offered by the employer, such as an additional contribution to a retirement plan.

You need to research the status of any of your business's taxable benefits on the CRA website and determine whether you need to include the amount of these benefits in the amount of pensionable, insurable, and/or taxable earnings when you calculate CPP, EI, and combined income tax deductions. You also need to research whether you need to charge GST/HST on some fringe benefits paid to employees. We discuss charging GST/HST in Chapter 5.

Preparing Payroll and Posting It in the Books

After you know the details about your employees' deductions and their benefit costs, you can then calculate the final payroll and post it to the books.

Calculating payroll for hourly employees

When you're ready to prepare payroll for employees, you first need to collect time records from each person that your business pays hourly. Some businesses use time clocks and some use time sheets to produce the required time records. Popular additions to recent computerized systems are scanners that read barcodes or strips from employee ID cards. Whatever method a business uses, the manager of each department usually reviews the time records for each employee she supervises and then sends those time records to you, the bookkeeper.

With time records in hand, you have to calculate gross pay for each employee. For example, if an employee worked 45 hours and your business pays him $12 an hour, here's how you calculate gross pay:

40 regular hours × $12 per hour = $480

5 overtime hours × $12 per hour × 1.5 overtime rate = $90

$480 + $90 = $570

In Manitoba, for example, a business must pay their employees overtime for any hours worked over 40 in a seven-day workweek. This employee worked 5 hours more than the 40 hours allowed, so the business needs to pay him at time plus one-half. In Ontario, on the other hand, the minimum number of hours that an employee has to work in order to get overtime pay is 44 hours per week.

Doling out funds to salaried employees

In addition to employees whom your business pays based on hourly wages, you also must prepare payroll for salaried employees. You can calculate paycheques for salaried employees relatively easily — you just need to know those employees' base salaries and their pay period calculations. For example, if a salaried employee makes $42,900 per year and is paid biweekly (totalling 26 pay periods), that employee's gross pay is $1,650 for each pay period ($42,900 ÷ 26 = $1,650).

Totalling up for commission cheques

Calculating payroll for employees whom your business pays based on commission can involve the most complex calculations. To show you a number of variables, in this section we calculate a commission cheque based on a salesperson who sells $60,000 worth of products during one month.

For a salesperson on a straight commission of 10 percent, you calculate pay by using this formula:

Total amount sold × Commission percentage = Gross pay

$60,000 × 0.10 = $6,000

For a salesperson who has a guaranteed base salary of $2,000, plus an additional 5 percent commission on all products sold, you calculate pay by using this formula:

Base salary + (Total amount sold × Commission percentage) = Gross pay

$2,000 + ($60,000 × 0.05) = $5,000

Although the employee who receives a base salary may be happy that she can count on that salary each month, she actually makes less with a base salary than straight commission because she receives such a lower commission rate. By selling $60,000 worth of products, she made only $3,000 in commission at 5 percent. Without the base pay, she would have made 10 percent on the $60,000 (or $6,000), so she actually got paid $1,000 less with a base pay structure that includes a lower commission pay rate than the straight commission income.

If she has a slow sales month of just $30,000 worth of products sold, she would receive

- ✔ **On straight commission of 10 percent:** $30,000 \times 0.10 = \$3,000$

- ✔ **With 5 percent commission plus base salary:** $30,000 \times 0.05 = \$1,500$ plus $2,000 base salary, totalling $3,500

In a slow month, the salesperson makes more money with the base salary than with the higher commission rate.

You can calculate commissions in many other ways. One common way is to offer higher commissions on higher levels of sales. By using the figures in the preceding example, this type of pay system encourages salespeople to keep their sales levels over $30,000 to get the best commission rate.

If a business uses a graduated commission scale, a salesperson can make a straight commission of 5 percent on his first $10,000 in sales, then 7 percent on his next $20,000, and finally 10 percent on anything over $30,000. Here's what his gross pay calculation looks like by using this commission pay scale:

$$(\$10,000 \times 0.05) + (\$20,000 \times 0.07) + (\$30,000 \times 0.10) = \$4,900 \text{ gross pay}$$

Another type of commission pay scheme involves a base salary, plus tips. Restaurant and bar businesses commonly use this method.

Counting tips and gratuities

Tips fall into two categories: controlled tips and direct tips. *Controlled tips* are gratuities that the employer controls. These tips usually occur when the employer adds a mandatory service charge or percentage to a customer's bill to cover tips. Because the employer collects the tips, the CRA requires the employer to include these amounts in the employee's wages. Consequently, the CRA considers the amounts an employer pays to employees from controlled tips as pensionable, insurable, and taxable. Employees end up receiving their tips as part of their net paycheques.

You, or your accounting software, calculate taxes that you withhold from an employee's gross pay on the base wage plus tips, so the cheque that you prepare for the employee includes the base wage and tips, minus any taxes due.

Direct tips occur when the employer has no control over the tip amount and no control over the tip distribution. The CRA considers that the customer pays the direct tips, not the employer. In these situations, the employer merely acts as a conduit for the tip from the customer to the worker. When a customer pays a bill by using a debit card, she includes an amount for a tip, and the employer returns the tip amount in cash to the employee.

Unlike controlled tips, direct tips aren't subject to CPP contributions or EI premiums. The employee needs to keep track of the amounts that he receives and to declare the total amount on his personal income tax returns. The province of Québec does have an exception. Employees who work in a regulated establishment in the province of Québec must declare their direct tips to their employer, and so the employer adds the amount of these tips to the employee's gross pay, which the bookkeeper uses to calculate QPP, EI, and income taxes.

Preparing and Recording Payroll Cheques

After you obtain all the necessary information about the gross pay, taxable benefits, and voluntary deductions for your employees, you need to go ahead and calculate the paycheques. Although all the gross pay belongs to an employee because she earned her pay, she doesn't get it all in cash. As an employer, you act as an agent of the different governments – and you may possibly act as an agent to the employee when it comes to how she wants to handle her money. After you calculate the payroll, you need to post the transactions to the books. In addition to the Cash account, payroll affects many General Ledger accounts:

✔ **Employee Withholding Taxes Payable:** Record the liability for the amount that you need to send off to the Receiver General for the combined federal and provincial income tax that you deduct from an employee's gross pay. If your business is in Québec, you have to use a separate account for the provincial withholding tax.

✔ **CPP/QPP Payable:** Record the liability for the amount that you need to pay to the Receiver General for the Canada Pension Plan deductions or to the Minister of Revenue of Québec for the Québec Pension Plan.

✔ **EI Payable:** Record the liability for the amount that you need to pay to the Receiver General for the employee's Employment Insurance coverage.

You will probably also need to make entries in additional General Ledger accounts. These accounts include ones for the amounts withheld from gross pay based on the employment agreement that your business has with your employee for such items as medical plan premiums, life insurance premiums, savings plans (such as RRSPs), or voluntary donations (such as to the United Way), as we outlined earlier in this chapter.

When you post the payroll journal entry, you indicate the withdrawal of money from the Cash account, as well as record liabilities for future cash payments that your business must make for withheld income taxes, CPP/QPP, and EI. Just to give you an example of the proper setup for a payroll journal entry, we assume the total payroll is $20,000, with $1,000 set aside each for CPP and EI, and $5,000 for income taxes withholding payable. Here's what your journal entry for posting payroll would look like:

Account	*Debit*	*Credit*
Salaries and Wages Expense	$20,000	
—Withholding Taxes Payable		$5,000
—CPP Payable		$1,000
—EI Payable		$1,000
—Cash		*$13,000*

To record payroll for May 27, 2013.

In this entry, you increase the expense account for salaries and wages, as well as all the accounts in which you record future obligations for withholding taxes and employee portions of CPP/QPP and EI. For this payroll entry, you decrease the amount of the Cash account only for the net pay that the business gives the employees. Later on, you reduce the Cash account for the cash payments that the business makes to the Receiver General for the withholding taxes, CPP/QPP, and EI that your business withheld from the employee's gross pay.

Direct deposits: EFTs

Most employers nowadays insist on paying their employees by using electronic funds transfers (EFTs) through the employees' banks. When enrolling an employee for EFT, obtain a voided cheque or a form from the employee's bank that clearly gives you, the employer, all the transit and branch number details so that you can properly execute the payment as a direct deposit to your employee's bank account.

We recommend the practice of using EFTs for several reasons:

✔ Your employee can't lose his cheque or put his cheque through the clothes washer (it's happened to us!). Replacing a lost or stolen cheque takes a lot of your time and costs a lot of your business's money. A stop-payment on the original lost cheque has to be put into place at a substantial bank fee.

✔ As an employer, you don't have to worry that someone other than your employee can illegally cash your employee's cheque.

✔ EFTs are fast and efficient, and they save your employee the time it takes to go to her local bank to cash or deposit her paycheque. We've heard plenty of stories about employees getting their paycheque at noon on Friday, and then disappearing all afternoon on their way to the bank.

As we mention in the section "Collecting Employee Taxes," earlier in this chapter, both the employer and employee must pay into the Canada or Québec Pension Plan and the Employment Insurance Program. We discuss the task of sending off these combined payments with the appropriate forms to the proper government authorities in Chapter 11.

Outsourcing Payroll and Benefits Work

Because of all that you need to do to prepare payroll, your small business may want to outsource the work of payroll and benefits. We don't disagree with a business making that choice. Many businesses outsource this work because it's such a specialized area and requires extensive software to manage both payroll and benefits.

If you don't want to take on the job of calculating payroll and benefits, you can pay for a monthly payroll service from the software company that provides your accounting software. The QuickBooks payroll features include calculating earnings and deductions, printing cheques or making direct deposits, providing updates to the tax tables, and supplying data that you need to complete all the government forms related to payroll. The advantage of doing payroll in-house is that you can more easily integrate the payroll into the business's books.

Chapter 11

Employer-Paid Benefits and Government Payroll Reporting

. . . .

In This Chapter

▶ Filing and remitting CPP/QPP and EI contributions and withholding taxes

▶ Figuring out workers' compensation

▶ Keeping accurate employee records

. . . .

*Y*ou may think that employees make your job as a business owner easier — we're afraid you're wrong on that one. Having employees really gives you a mixed bag. Although employees help you keep your business operating and enable you to grow, they also add a lot of government paperwork.

After your business hires employees, you need to complete regular reports for the government regarding the withholding income taxes and benefits you must pay toward the employees' Canada or Québec Pension Plan (CPP/QPP) and Employment Insurance (EI). Also, every province and territory requires employers to buy workers' compensation insurance based on employees' salary and wages.

This chapter reviews the federal and provincial government reporting requirements for employers, as well as the records that you, the bookkeeper, must keep in order to complete and file these reports. In Chapter 10, we show you how to calculate the employee side of Canada or Québec Pension Plan and Employment Insurance. This chapter looks at the employer side of these taxes, as well as other employer-paid government benefits.

Paying Employer Portions of CPP/QPP and EI

As we mention in Chapter 10, the employee and employer pay equally for CPP/QPP. You're both on the hook to contribute 4.95 percent of the employee's annual gross pay over $3,500, up to the maximum amount (which was $50,100 in 2012). For the province of Quebec, calculation mechanism is essentially the same, but the rates used for QPP may vary from the federal rate used in other provinces. Be sure to keep an eye on when you reach that maximum, to ensure that the business and the employee don't contribute unnecessarily to the pension plan.

If you ever over-contribute to the CPP/QPP on behalf of an employee, don't expect the Canada Revenue Agency (CRA) to refund the over-contribution to your business. On the other hand, if you deduct too much of an employee's gross pay for CPP/QPP, the CRA refunds any over contribution to the employee when he files his personal tax return in April.

When it comes to the Employment Insurance (EI) program, the employer contributes more than the employee. As the employer, you have to pay 1.4 times — or 140 percent of — what you deduct from your employee's gross pay.

Filing Form PD7A

When you create a payroll account for remittances (which we discuss in Chapter 10), the CRA sends you the Statement of Account for Current Source Deductions form, numbered PD7A. This form allows you to accurately remit the employer and employee shares of CPP/QPP, EI, and withholding taxes deducted from your employees' gross pay. If you operate in the province of Quebec, a similar system is in place. Check the Revenu Québec website for detailed instructions. (See the following section to determine how often you should complete and remit PD7A.)

The CRA personalizes the PD7A form for your business, and this form is divided into two parts: the top portion (the payroll records) and the bottom detachable portion (the Remittance Voucher).

The top of the form contains the following pre-printed information provided by the CRA:

- The date of the employer's PD7A statement of account
- The account number, which is the business number (BN) followed by the payroll account number (RP)
- The name of the employer

✔ Any amounts the employer owes from the previous reporting period

✔ Current balances of amounts paid for the year to date

✔ An explanation of any changes

When the CRA makes any changes to the PD7A, based on the last remittance or assessment, an explanation follows on the body of the form, along with an area to enter the following information (which you also enter on the Remittance Voucher for your reporting period):

✔ **CPP contributions:** Employer and employee portions combined.

✔ **EI premiums:** Employer and employee portions combined.

✔ **Tax deductions:** Combined federal and provincial withholding income taxes.

✔ **Current payment:** The total CPP, EI, and income taxes that you're remitting.

✔ **Gross payroll:** All money that employees earn before you make any deductions, such as income tax. Gross payroll includes regular wages, commissions, overtime pay, paid leave, taxable benefits and allowances, piecework payments, and special payments. You enter the same amount in this box that you do in the monthly total of all amounts on your employees' T4 slips, which appears in Box 14, Employment Income. We discuss T4 slips in Chapter 20.

✔ **Number of employees in last pay period:** This number includes any employee for whom you need to prepare a T4 slip, such as part-time and temporary employees, and employees absent with pay.

The bottom detachable portion of the PD7A form is the Remittance Voucher, which you complete and send, along with your payment, to the Receiver General.

When you aren't making a remittance for your regular reporting period, use the back of the PD7A form to write out a note that explains why; for example, maybe you don't have any employees during the period. This way, the CRA won't conclude that you are delinquent in your remittance. The back of the form also provides additional information on CRA's TeleReply service.

You can also access an electronic version of the PD7A, called the E-PD7A, which is available through certain financial institutions' online banking websites. Check the CRA's website (www.cra-arc.gc.ca) for details.

Knowing how often to file

Most businesses are regular monthly remitters and have to pay by the 15th of the month following the pay period. To become a quarterly (every three months) remitter, a business has to have both an average monthly withholding amount (AMWA) of less than $3,000 in either the first or the second preceding calendar year, and a perfect compliance history for all tax payments and filing of information returns over the last 12 months.

Businesses that have large withholding amounts to pay (over $50,000) have to make the payments at a bank. We believe this rule is in place to ensure that the bank account contains sufficient funds when the government accepts the payment.

You definitely don't want to be late in making your payments. You don't want to underpay, either. Mail out your payment well ahead of the due date, or pay at a bank a day ahead of the deadline. Keep in mind that the majority of the amount you pay is actually money that belongs to your employees. The CRA can assess a penalty when it receives the amounts you withheld past the due date.

The penalty is

- ✔ Three percent if the amount is one to three days late
- ✔ Five percent if the amount is four or five days late
- ✔ Seven percent if the amount is six or seven days late
- ✔ Ten percent if the amount is more than seven days late

If that's not enough to convince you to pay attention to these deadlines, the CRA can also charge you interest, on top of the penalty.

You don't want the CRA to charge you penalties and interest. Not only does your business have to deal with these extra costs, but it also can't claim these fines and penalties as business expenses on its tax return. This adds insult to injury, don't you think?

Workers' Compensation Program

You need to worry about more than just taxes when you figure out your obligations after you hire employees. All the provinces and territories require employers to carry *workers' compensation insurance,* which covers your employees in case they're injured on the job. Workers' compensation programs protect employees from the financial hardships associated with work-related injuries and occupational diseases. Employees don't pay for this protection; employers do. In certain types of industries where accidents happen relatively frequently, such as the construction industry, employers have to pay quite high premiums.

Besides covering the cost of some of the lost income for an injured worker, the different provincial programs protect businesses from being sued by their employees for similar benefits. The programs also cover health care costs resulting from work-related injuries and illnesses, and support the return to work by providing funding for reeducation, for example. They provide numerous training and education programs that help employers prevent injuries and illness. The added benefit of getting injured staff back on the job quickly means that a business can return to full productivity quickly. An employee's quick return to work may also lead to reduced insurance premiums in the future for your business.

The Association of Workers' Compensation Boards of Canada is a national resource that offers information about workers' compensation. On their website (`www.awcbc.org`), you can find a link for Employer Registration that then provides you with links for all provinces and territories. Follow these links to obtain the registration forms and download employer classification manuals, premium rate tables, and handbooks or policy manuals that cover how to properly follow the government guidelines for your business.

Maintaining Employee Records

When you consider all the federal and provincial filing requirements for employee benefits, you quickly realize that you must keep very good employee records. Otherwise, you have a hard time filling out all the necessary forms and providing detail on your employees and your payroll. If you use a manual bookkeeping system, you can best track employee information by setting up an employee journal and creating a separate journal page for each employee. (We show you how to set up journals in Chapter 5.)

The detailed individual records you keep on each employee should include the following basic information, most of which the business collects or determines as part of the hiring process:

- Name, address, phone number, and e-mail address
- Social Insurance Number
- Job title
- Department or division within the business
- Start date with the business
- Pay rate
- Pay period (weekly, biweekly, semi-monthly, or monthly)
- Whether paid hourly or salaried
- Claim code (taken from the TD1 form, which we discuss in Chapter 10)
- Benefits information
- Payroll deductions

If an employee asks to change the information on her TD1 or asks for benefits changes, you must update her record to reflect such changes.

Place the personal details that don't change each pay period at the top of the journal page. Here's a list of the common information contained in the bookkeeping records:

✔ Pay period end date

✔ Total hours worked

✔ For gross pay:

- Regular pay

- Overtime pay

- Total pay for the period, including any taxable benefits

- Cumulative year-to-date gross pay

✔ For deductions:

- Income tax

- CPP/QPP

- EI

- Union dues

- Optional deductions

- Total deductions

✔ For payment:

- Net amount

- Cheque number, if applicable

This preceding list obviously doesn't cover all the information that you need to keep in your records. You most likely want to keep track of several more sources of gross pay, as well as vacation pay, for example. Also, you probably want several additional deductions columns so that you can keep track of the many benefits that your business offers to employees. Later on, someone (such as the owner of the business) may ask you to provide this level of detail so that he can figure out the true costs of hiring employees. You may also need this information to come up with a budget for future benefit costs.

Keeping track of employee records with software

Clearly, employee journal sheets can get very lengthy very quickly. Preparing payroll and following all the necessary paperwork for the government can become overwhelming. For that reason, many small businesses use computerized accounting systems to monitor both payroll and employee records. Figure 11-1 shows you how to add an employee to the QuickBooks system. Figure 11-2 shows how you can set up the rate of pay and some deductions in the employee's QuickBooks record. To access these forms, click the Employee Centre link in QuickBooks.

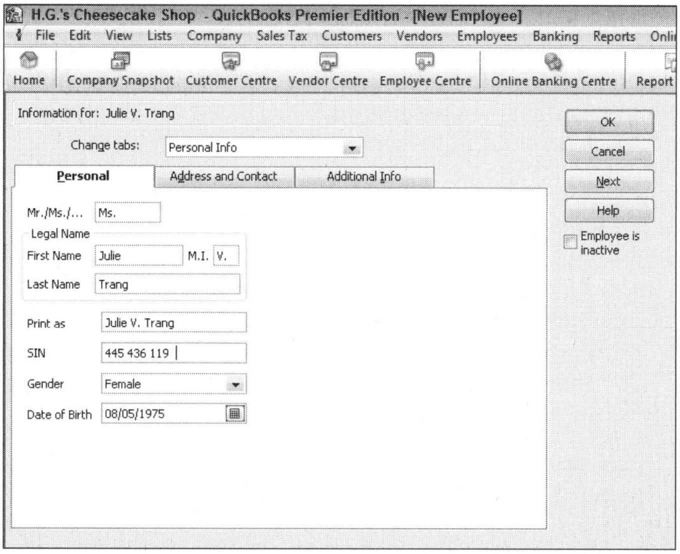

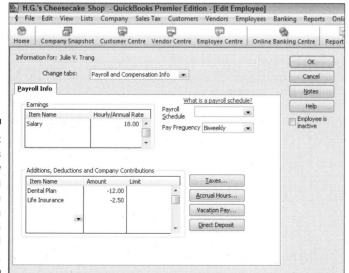

Figure 11-1: You can add new employee personal and contact information to QuickBooks.

Figure 11-2: QuickBooks can show you employee information about rate of pay and deductions.

Completing a Record of Employment (ROE) for departing employees

When an employee leaves the business's employment, you (as the book-keeper) must prepare the Record of Employment (ROE), which outlines the number of weeks of employment and the Employment Insurance (EI) that both the business and employee paid. The ROE is the single most important document in EI. Service Canada uses the information on the ROE to determine whether a person qualifies for EI benefits, the benefit rate, and the duration of her claim. The ROE also plays an important role in controlling the misuse of EI funds. You must issue a ROE, even if the employee has no intention of filing a claim for EI benefits.

You need to prepare a ROE within five days of an interruption in earnings that occurs when an employee leaves because of pregnancy, injury, illness, adoption leave, a layoff, a leave without pay, or dismissal. The employee needs this form to file a claim for EI benefits. If you're using QuickBooks to prepare your payroll, you can generate the necessary information to fill out an ROE automatically. Click the Employees command in the top menu bar in QuickBooks, and then click Payroll Forms to access the Process Record of Employment command.

When you create an ROE, also prepare a T4 slip because it will save you having to recall the information at the time the remaining T4s have to be prepared. (The CRA actually suggests that you do this, and we discuss in detail how you prepare T4 slips in Chapter 20.) From the CRA website (www.cra-arc.gc.ca), you can print PDF copies of T4 slips, which you complete by hand, or you can access a PDF T4 form that can be filled in online. Even if you use software to prepare your T4s, you can issue a handwritten T4 to the employee, particularly if you think you may have a hard time delivering a T4 to the employee in the following February. Make sure that the information accurately reflects your payroll records and keep a copy of the T4 that you provided to the employee. When preparing the T4 summary for the CRA the following February, make sure that you include this slip. If you're using software, have the software duplicate the T4 slip that you want to include in the summary, but don't mail the slip to your former employee if you have already given him one earlier.

Part IV

Preparing the Books for Year's (Or Month's) End

The 5th Wave   By Rich Tennant

"Isn't that our bookkeeper?"

In this part . . .

*E*ventually, every accounting period comes to an end, and whether it's the end of a month, a quarter, or a year, you need to check your work and get ready to prepare reports for the period.

This part introduces you to the part of the accounting cycle that involves summarizing and adjusting the accounts at the end of an accounting period. For example, you find out about the key adjustments that you need to make to record depreciation of your fixed assets. This part also shows you how to calculate and record your business's interest payments and income in the books and record bad debt expenses.

To round out the process, we show you how to prove out your books by checking your cash, testing your books' balances, and making any needed adjustments, accruals, or corrections.

Chapter 12

Depreciating Your Assets

. . . .

. . . .

*A*ll businesses use equipment, furnishings, and vehicles that last more than a year. Any asset that has a lifespan, or at least a useful life to the business, of more than a year is called a *fixed asset* or *property, plant, and equipment.* These assets may last longer than other assets, but even fixed assets eventually get old and need replacing.

And because the rules of accounting require your business to match its expenses with its revenue in any accounting period, you don't want to write off the full expense of a fixed asset in one year. After all, you'll certainly use the asset for more than one year.

Imagine how bad your income statement would look if you charged to an Expense account the cost of a $100,000 piece of equipment in just one year! That income statement would make it look like your business isn't doing well, and we all know that is not the case. Imagine the impact on a small business — $100,000 may eat up its entire profit, or maybe even put it in the position of reporting a loss.

Instead of expensing the full amount of a fixed asset in one year, you use an accounting method called *depreciation* to charge some of the cost of the asset to an expense on your income statement while your business uses up that asset.

Recording depreciation achieves two objectives. First, depreciation reduces the book value of the asset while it wears off. *Book value* or *carrying amount* — in the case of property, plant, and equipment — represents the cost of the asset less all the depreciation recorded against the asset to date, as reported on the balance sheet. Second, depreciation pieces out a portion of the cost of the asset to an expense that reduces your profit because of the use of that asset. You need to record a charge for depreciation expense on your income statement because this asset helped you earn revenue during the year. In this chapter, we introduce you to some of the various ways you can depreciate your fixed assets and explain how to calculate depreciation, how depreciation affects both the income statement and your income tax bill, and how to record depreciation in your books. Finally, we provide a short explanation of what to do if your fixed assets have become impaired.

Defining Depreciation

You may think of depreciation as something that happens to your car when it loses value as soon as you drive off the dealer's car lot. When you're talking about accounting, the definition of depreciation is a bit different.

Essentially, accountants use *depreciation* as a way to allocate or parcel out the costs of a fixed asset over the period in which the business can use the asset. You, the bookkeeper, record the full cost when your business buys the asset, but you gradually reduce the book value or carrying amount of the asset by subtracting a portion of that cost as a depreciation expense each year. Depreciation expenses don't involve the exchange of cash; they're solely done for accounting purposes, to achieve some fairness in the amount of expenses you record on your income statement. Most companies enter depreciation expenses into the books once a year, just before preparing their annual reports, but others calculate depreciation expenses monthly or quarterly. It all depends on how often you (or the accountant) prepare financial statements.

You may want to write off assets so that you can lower your tax bill. The Canada Revenue Agency (CRA) gets involved in depreciation for the same reason. As a business owner, you can't write off the cost of all major purchases in one year. Instead, the CRA has strict rules about how you can write off assets as tax-deductible expenses. We talk more about the CRA's rules in the section "Tackling Taxes and Depreciation," later in this chapter.

Knowing what you can and can't depreciate

Businesses don't depreciate all assets. You record low-cost items or items that aren't expected to last more than one year in Expense accounts, rather than Asset accounts. For example, office supplies are Expense items and not depreciated, but you record the office copier, which your business plans to use for more than one year, as a fixed asset and depreciate it each year.

Lifespan isn't the deciding factor for depreciation, however. Some specific assets exist that you never depreciate, though they last many years. One good example is land; you can always make use of land, and land never gets consumed or used up, so its carrying value doesn't depreciate. (You do need to reduce the carrying value of land in the rare situation when the land is impaired, however. We outline what needs to be done when that happens later on in this chapter.)

You also can't depreciate any property that you lease or rent, but if you make improvements to leased property, you can depreciate the cost of those improvements if they happen to last more than one year. In that case, you write off the monthly lease or rent payments as an Expense item and depreciate the lease improvements over their estimated useful life or the length of the lease, whichever is shorter. You are forced into this time limit, and that limit makes sense because you can't use the asset after the term of your lease is over and you aren't present to use the improvement.

You can't depreciate any items that you use outside your business, such as your personal car or home computer, but if you use these assets for both personal needs and business needs, you can depreciate a portion of them based on a percentage of time or some other measurement that proves how much you use the car or computer for your business activities.

You base the portion of a car that you can depreciate on the kilometres driven for business versus the kilometres driven for personal use. If you drive your car a total of 20,000 kilometres in a year and have records showing that you drove 10,000 of those kilometres for business purposes, you can charge 50 percent of the cost of operating the car as a business expense on your personal tax return. You apply that same calculated percentage to the total allowable amount of tax depreciation on the car. We discuss this kind of tax depreciation in the section "Capital cost allowance (CCA)," later in this chapter.

You can't claim your house expenses as business expenses if you already have an office at your place of business. You need to spend the majority of your business activities in your home office in order for the costs to become deductible for tax purposes. The CRA refers to the deductible portion of your home as your principal place of business.

Delving into cost basis

In order to calculate depreciation for an asset, you need to know the cost basis of that asset. The equation for cost basis is

Cost of the fixed asset + Retail sales tax (if any) + Shipping and delivery costs + Installation charges + Other costs = Cost basis

This list explains each of the items in the preceding equation:

- **Cost of the fixed asset:** What you paid for the equipment, furniture, structure, vehicle, or other asset.

- **Retail sales tax:** The provincial sales tax that you had to pay when you bought the fixed asset, if you happen to be located in a province where PST/RST was added to your invoice.

- **Shipping and delivery costs:** Any shipping or delivery charges you paid to purchase the fixed asset. You should also include any delivery insurance you paid.

- **Installation charges:** Any charges you paid in order to have the equipment, furniture, or other fixed asset installed on your business's premises.

- **Other costs:** Any other charges you need to pay to make the fixed asset usable for your business. For example, if you buy a new computer and need to set up certain hardware in order to use that computer for your business, you can add those setup costs as part of the cost basis of the fixed asset (the computer).

When calculating the cost basis of an asset, don't include in the cost of your purchase any GST/HST that you pay. Lucky for you, as a GST/HST registrant, you get to claim all the GST/HST back from the government. We discuss how to deal with these taxes in Chapter 5.

Reducing the Book Value or Carrying Amount of Fixed Assets

After you decide on the useful life of a fixed asset and calculate its cost basis (see the preceding sections), you have to decide how to go about reducing the asset's book value or carrying amount by using a technique or method that you plan to use from this point forward. The technique you select should make sense in relation to the type of fixed asset your business owns and the way that your business uses that asset.

Evaluating your depreciation options

When calculating the depreciation of your fixed assets each year, you have a choice of several commonly used methods: Straight Line, Double-Declining Balance, Declining Balance, and Units of Production. In the following sections, we explain these methods, as well as the pros and cons of using each one.

To show you how the methods handle assets differently, we calculate the first year's depreciation expense by using the purchase of a truck on January 1, 2013, with a cost basis of $25,000. We assume that the business can sell the truck in five years for $5,000, which is called the *residual value.* We show you how to use the residual value as part of the calculations for two of the depreciation methods. You use the fourth method that we cover, Units of Production (sometimes called Units of Activity), when you can measure some sort of total units of production activity that you get out of an asset for the time you intend to use it. This method is perfect for depreciating the truck because the more kilometres you drive the truck, the higher the depreciation expense. The odometer meter on the truck gives you a very easy way to keep track of how much you use the truck.

You may have heard the term *salvage value,* which refers to a depreciable asset that your business can't use any longer. The meaning of salvage value is similar to that of residual value, except that it refers to a small value, some-times also called *scrap value.* You ignore the salvage value when you calculate depreciation because it's a very small amount.

Straight Line method

When you depreciate assets by using the *Straight Line method,* you spread the cost of the asset evenly over the number of years your business plans to use the asset. Straight Line is a very common method for the depreciation of assets, and it's also the easiest one to use.

The formula for calculating Straight Line depreciation is

(Cost basis of fixed asset – Residual value) ÷ Estimated useful life in years = Annual depreciation expense

For the truck in our example, the cost basis is $25,000, the residual value is $5,000, and we assume an estimated useful life of five years. With these figures, we calculate the annual depreciation expense of this truck based on the Straight Line depreciation method:

($25,000 – $5,000) ÷ 5 = $4,000

Each year, the business's income statement should include $4,000 as a depreciation expense for this truck. You add this $4,000 depreciation expense to the accumulated depreciation account for the truck. The accumulated depreciation account appears below the truck's original cost on the balance sheet. You subtract the accumulated depreciation from the cost of the truck to show a net book value or net carrying amount. In turn, the net book value should equal the depreciation that you haven't yet recorded plus the residual value that you can get from selling the truck at the end of its useful life.

Double-Declining Balance method

If you think your asset loses a greater portion of its usefulness in the early years of its life, you can speed up its depreciation by using the *Double-Declining Balance method.* This method allows you to charge higher depreciation expenses in the earlier years of useful life and lower depreciation in later years. You use this method when you expect that your business will use the fixed asset less in later years. You may also expect that the asset won't be as productive for the business in later years.

You calculate the depreciation with the Double-Declining Balance method by using this formula:

2 × (1 ÷ Estimated useful life) × Book value at the beginning of the year = Depreciation expense

We calculate our example truck's depreciation expense by using the Double-Declining Balance method:

2 × (1 ÷ 5) × $25,000 = $10,000

So, the depreciation expense for the first year of using the truck is $10,000. If you do the same calculation for the remaining years of useful life, you get the following results:

✔ **Year 2:** $6,000

✔ **Year 3:** $3,600

✔ **Year 4:** $400

✔ **Year 5:** $0

When you calculate the yearly depreciation by using this method, you ignore the residual value.

You write off close to 80 percent of the value of the truck to expense in the first three years. Clearly, the Double-Declining Balance method of depreciation reduces the book value of an asset very quickly.

Declining Balance method

If you want to calculate a declining amount of depreciation from year to year but feel the rate of the Double-Declining Balance method is too high, the Declining Balance method offers an alternative. The *Declining Balance method* works in exactly the same way as the Double-Declining Balance method: You need to come up with a fixed percentage rate that you use consistently every year. You still expect the amount of the depreciation to decline from year to year, but not at as fast a pace as with the Double-Declining Balance method.

In the truck example we use in the preceding sections, the Double-Declining Balance method works out to a fixed percentage of 40 percent: $2 \times (1 \div 5)$.

When you use the Declining Balance method, you may set your annual rate at 20 percent $(1 \div 5)$ instead. Your choice depends on the percentage you think is fair for the asset you use in your business.

Units of Production or Units of Activity method

The *Units of Production (UOP) method* of depreciation works well when you want to record depreciation in an amount that is in proportion with how much you use the asset. The more you use the asset, the more depreciation expense you record. You calculate depreciation by using the Units of Production method by following these steps:

1. **Find the UOP rate.**

   Use this formula:

   (Cost – Residual value) ÷ Estimated number of units to be produced during estimated useful life = UOP rate

2. **Find the depreciation expense.**

Use this formula:

Units produced during the year × UOP rate = Depreciation expense for the year

You can use the UOP depreciation method only if you can estimate the total units of production or activity that an asset can produce or deliver. You can't use the UOP method for depreciating a building, for example.

Choosing and changing a depreciation method

With four different methods for depreciating your business's assets, you're probably wondering which method you should use. Your accountant is the best person to answer that question. She can look at the way your business operates and determine which method makes the most sense when you consider the different types of fixed assets.

Depreciation doesn't involve the use of cash. When talking about accounting, depreciation is purely a way to show how quickly you're using up an asset.

Keep in mind the possibility that you may decide to change the way you use the assets you are depreciating. The intended use of most assets in your business will be pretty straightforward; for example, you purchase a vehicle in order to use it for transportation for the duration of its useful life. On the other hand, changes to your business activities may require you to change the way you use some specialized or unique types of fixed assets. For example, a building that has previously been used as a warehouse to store inventory is converted into a rental property used as a restaurant. If and when a change in use happens, you need to look at the assets you already own and have already depreciated with a new set of eyes. Think of these assets as if you had just bought them at their recorded book value. If you decide to use a different logical method of depreciating your fixed asset, then start using that new method as soon as the change in the asset's intended use changes. Telling whoever is using your financial statements that you have implemented this change in your method of depreciation is a good idea; you communicate this in the notes to the financial statements.

Tackling Taxes and Depreciation

Depreciation calculations for tax purposes are a completely different animal than the calculations you use to record depreciation for accounting purposes (which we talk about in the section "Reducing the Book Value or Carrying Amount of Fixed Assets," earlier in this chapter). The Income Tax Act essentially says that the CRA doesn't recognize depreciation as a deductible expense. Instead, you have to claim *capital cost allowance (CCA),* the depreciation technique used by the CRA for depreciable assets. Your business doesn't have to take this deduction when you calculate taxable income, but most businesses prefer to write off the highest expense legally permissible and reduce their tax bills by the greatest amount.

So, why would your business not record a CCA deduction on its tax return? It doesn't happen every year, we hope, but if your business has a bad year and has a loss, you may not want to make that loss any larger for tax purposes by claiming CCA. A bigger loss can't reduce the taxes owing, because there are none owing already. You can save the CCA deduction for a later year — although you're not allowed to double up in a later year.

Capital cost allowance (CCA)

To understand how capital cost allowance (CCA) works, compare it to the Declining Balance method we explain in the section "Declining Balance method," earlier in this chapter. Two main differences exist between these two methods:

- ✔ You can't estimate or choose the percentage rates that you use when you determine the capital cost allowance; the Income Tax Act provides the percentages that you have to use. These percentage rates are based on classes of assets, also defined by the Act.

- ✔ In the year you buy an asset, you get to claim half of a year's CCA, no matter when you bought the asset in the year. This claim is commonly referred to as the *half-year rule.*

This part of the tax regulations is supposed to encourage businesses to buy new property in order to stimulate the economy. The Income Tax Act assigns quite generous rates for the different categories of fixed assets. Table 12-1 gives you a short list of the most common classes of depreciable fixed assets and their corresponding CCA rates.

Table 12-1	Capital Cost Allowance Classes and Rates	
Class No.	*Description*	*Rate*
1	Buildings purchased after 1987	4%
3	Buildings purchased before 1988	5%
8	Machinery, equipment, and furniture	20%
10	Vehicles and computer hardware	30%
12	Computer software and small tools	100%

You always have differences between what you record in your books as depreciation expenses and what you record as CCA for tax purposes. The book value of assets on your balance sheet also differs from the corresponding amount the CRA recognizes as undepreciated capital cost (UCC). Accounting and tax preparation have different rules, and you can't find a way around those differences.

Figuring out the useful life of a fixed asset

You may be wondering how you can figure out the useful life of a fixed asset. You know that you need to get a good feel for how long your business can use an asset when you use the Straight Line method of depreciation. You also use that number of years in the formula to calculate the rate of depreciation if you use the Double-Declining Balance method.

Ask the opinion of the person in your business who actually uses the asset to find out how long he thinks the asset will remain useful to your business. When you decide on the useful life of an asset, you also need to try to predict what the asset's residual value is going to be. The longer you use an asset, the less you can expect to get for the asset after you finish using it.

Also, when you try to determine how long an asset will last, consider how well you intend to maintain it. Often, businesses don't have the time to properly maintain their assets, and so they end up paying for this choice in the long run by having to replace assets more often.

Your past experience and best judgment are often the best tools you have when you need to come up with these estimates.

Setting Up Depreciation Schedules

In order to keep good accounting records, you need to track how much you depreciate each of your assets in some form of a schedule. After all, your balance sheet reports only a total cost for all your assets in a category and a total accumulated depreciation amount for that category (for example, Vehicles). Most businesses maintain depreciation schedules in some type of spreadsheet program that exists outside their computerized accounting systems. Usually, one person manages assets and their depreciation. However, in a large business these tasks can turn into full-time jobs for several people. If that situation arises, often the computerized accounting system has some fixed asset component or module to deal with the financial details that you need to track for all fixed assets.

You can best keep track of depreciation by preparing a separate schedule for each asset account that you depreciate. For example, set up depreciation schedules for Buildings, Furniture and Fixtures, Office Equipment, and so on. Your depreciation schedule should include all the information that you need to determine annual depreciation, such as the original purchase date, original cost, and useful life. You can add columns to track the actual depreciation expenses and calculate the current book value of each asset. Table 12-2 shows a sample depreciation schedule for vehicles.

Table 12-2	Depreciation Schedule: Vehicles			
Date Put in Service	*Description*	*Cost*	*Useful Life*	*Annual Depreciation*
1/5/2011	Black car	$30,000	5 years	$5,000
1/1/2012	Blue truck	$25,000	5 years	$4,000

Depreciation can be more than just a mathematical exercise. As the book-keeper, planning for any major cash outflows is a very important part of your job. Keeping track of depreciation is a good way to monitor the age of your assets and know when you should plan for their replacement. While your business's assets age, they incur greater repair costs, so keeping depreciation schedules can help you plan repair and maintenance budgets, as well.

Considering Impairments of Fixed Assets

In Chapter 8, we discuss adjusting the value of your inventory to the lower of its cost and its net realizable value and explain the need to record a loss on the books whenever inventory for resale can't be sold for at least the amount that you paid for it. Accounting impairment rules for fixed assets are very similar. When you buy inventory, you intend to sell your goods at a profit, and so that those assets don't stay on your books for very long. In the case of fixed assets, you have them on your books for a much longer period of time, and so they have a better chance of becoming impaired during their useful lives. You have to monitor whether or not this has happened. For example, if a business owns a property in an area where there has been oil spill from a pipeline, the land has likely been impaired by the spill. You are on the front lines of the business's operations, and so you are likely the best person to notice the factors that may create an impairment of any of the fixed assets.

You can't postpone the pain of recording a loss of a fixed asset any more than you can prevent losing some of your inventory or some accounts receivable, for that matter. (We discuss in Chapter 9 the reduction of the book value of accounts receivable due to bad debts.)

When you purchase a fixed asset, you determine you'll get your money's worth when you negotiate a purchase price. Don't stop your test of value there. Down the road, whenever you have a suspicion that your fixed asset has lost its usefulness or that you won't be able to recover its book value in the future, you have to pause and try to measure and record that asset's impairment.

Intangible assets are particularly susceptible to impairment. Due to their nature, intangible assets such as patents have value to your business in relation to some sort of business activity. If you change the business activity in question, you'll likely lose a great deal of the usefulness of the patent.

Your business has to follow some complex technical rules concerning measuring the amount of an impairment that must be recorded. You need to get the business's accountant involved in that aspect of the task. When the accountant arrives at a figure, the entry to record the impairment causes a reduction of the book value of the fixed asset, with a credit entry to the asset and a debit entry to increase a Loss on Impairment account listed on the income statement.

Recording Depreciation Expenses

Recording a depreciation expense calls for a rather simple entry into your accounting system.

After you calculate your depreciation expense — no matter which method you use to calculate that expense — you record it as follows. In this example, the depreciation expense is $4,000:

Account	*Debit*	*Credit*
Depreciation Expense	$4,000	
—Accumulated Depreciation: Vehicles		$4,000

The debit increases the Depreciation Expense account, and the credit increases the Accumulated Depreciation: Vehicles account. On the income statement, you subtract the Depreciation Expense from Sales, and on the balance sheet, you subtract the Accumulated Depreciation: Vehicles from the Cost of Vehicles to arrive at the net book value.

In Chapter 17, we show you how to enter depreciation and other adjusting journal entries by using the General journal.

Chapter 13

Paying and Collecting Interest

. . . .

In This Chapter

▶ Understanding the types of interest calculations

▶ Making the most of interest income

▶ Calculating loan interest

. . . .

Few businesses can make major purchases without having to take out loans. Whether your business needs loans for vehicles, buildings, or other business needs, you must pay *interest,* a percentage of the amount loaned, to whoever loans you the money.

Some businesses loan their own money and receive interest payments as an additional source of revenue. In fact, you can consider a savings account a type of loan because by placing your money in this type of account, you're giving the bank the opportunity to loan that money to others. So, the bank pays you interest for the use of your money, which is a type of income for your business.

This chapter reviews different types of loans and how to calculate and record interest expenses for each type. In addition, we discuss how you calculate and record interest income in your business's books.

The amount of interest you pay or collect is usually communicated as a percentage rate applied to the principal balance over a specific period of time. You will notice that your bank generally quotes you an annual rate of interest. Banks follow this convention so that you can easily compare different loan alternatives with repayment terms that are not of equal length, or different types of investment alternatives. When you're thinking of making an investment in shares, you may be interested in the dividend yield, and for bonds, the interest yield. You can readily obtain these quoted percentages from brokers or investment sites on the web. These yields are always given in annual terms, even though the interest or dividends aren't paid on an annual basis.

Deciphering Types of Interest

Any time you make use of someone else's money, such as a bank's, you have to pay interest for that use — whether you're buying a house, a car, or some other item you want. The same is true when someone else uses your money. For example, when you buy a bond or deposit money in a money market account, you're paid interest for allowing the use of your money while it's on deposit.

The bank that has your money likely combines your money with that of other depositors and loans that money out to other people so that the bank can make more interest than it's paying you. That's why when you can get low interest rates on loans, you then earn even lower interest rates on savings.

Banks actually use two types of interest calculations:

- **Simple interest:** Calculated only on the principal amount of the loan
- **Compound interest:** Calculated on the principal and on interest earned

Simple interest

Simple interest is simple to calculate. Here's the formula for calculating simple interest:

$$\text{Principal} \times \text{Interest rate} \times \text{Number of years} = \text{Interest}$$

To show you how interest is calculated, we assume that someone invested $10,000 in a term deposit at the bank, earning 3 percent (0.03) interest for three years. (You know that the 3 percent is an annual rate of interest, based on the convention we explain earlier in this chapter.) So, the interest earned over three years is

$$\$10,000 \times 0.03 \times 3 = \$900$$

Simple interest is calculated on the principal amount only. You have to have clear understanding of what is the principal amount of your loan at all times. You, as the borrower, need to know the cost of borrowing and consequently the amount of the interest expense that you will have to pay over the term of the loan. Similarly, the lender, usually a bank, needs to be satisfied with the amount of interest income that will be earned by letting you use their cash.

Compound interest

You compute compound interest on both the principal and any interest earned up to that point in time. You must calculate the interest each year and add it to the balance before you can calculate the next year's interest payment, which will be based on both the principal and interest earned.

Here's how you calculate compound interest:

$$\text{Principal} \times \text{Interest rate} = \text{Interest for Year One}$$

$$(\text{Principal} + \text{Interest earned}) \times \text{Interest rate} = \text{Interest for Year Two}$$

$$(\text{Principal} + \text{Interest earned}) \times \text{Interest rate} = \text{Interest for Year Three}$$

You repeat this calculation for all years of the deposit or loan. However, with a loan, if you pay the total interest due each month or year (depending on when your payments are due), you don't have any interest to compound.

To show you how compound interest affects earnings, we calculated the three-year term deposit of $10,000 at 3 percent (0.03):

- ✔ **Year One interest:** $10,000 × 0.03 = $300.00
- ✔ **Year Two interest:** ($10,000 + $300) × 0.03 = $309.00
- ✔ **Year Three interest:** ($10,000 + $300 + $309) × 0.03 = $318.27
- ✔ **Total interest earned:** $300.00 + $309.00 + $318.27 = $927.27

You earn an extra $27.27 during the first three years of that term deposit if the interest is compounded. When working with much larger sums or higher interest rates for longer periods of time, compound interest can make a big difference in how much you earn or how much you pay on a loan.

Ideally, you want to find a savings account, certificate of deposit, or other savings investment that earns compound interest. But, if you want to borrow money, look for a simple-interest loan.

Also, not all accounts that earn compound interest are created equal. Watch carefully to see how frequently the interest is compounded. In the preceding example, interest is compounded annually. But, if you can find an account for which interest is compounded monthly, you can earn even higher interest. Monthly compounding means that interest earned is calculated and added to the principal each month before calculating the next month's interest, which results in a lot more interest than you get from a bank that compounds interest just once a year.

Handling Interest Income

The income that your business earns from its savings accounts, certificates of deposit, or other investments is called *interest income*. As the bookkeeper, you're rarely required to calculate interest income by using the simple-interest or compound-interest formulas described in the preceding sections. In most cases, the bank sends you a monthly, quarterly, or annual statement that has a separate line item reporting interest earned.

When you get your monthly bank statement, you then reconcile the books. *Reconciliation* is a process in which you prove out whether the amount the bank says you have in your account is equal to what you think you have in your account. We talk more about reconciling bank accounts in Chapter 14. The reason we mention it now is that the first step in the reconciliation process involves recording any interest earned or bank fees in the books so that your balance matches what the bank shows. Figure 13-1 shows you how to record $60 in interest income by using QuickBooks.

Figure 13-1: In QuickBooks, you enter interest income at the beginning of the account reconciliation process.

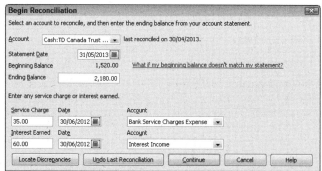

If you're keeping the books manually, a journal entry to record interest will look similar to this:

Account	Debit	Credit
Cash	$60	
—Interest Income		$60

To record interest income from bank.

When preparing financial statements, you show interest income on the income statement (see Chapter 19 for more information about the income statement) in a section called Other Income. Other income includes any income your business earned that wasn't directly related to your primary business activity, which is selling your goods or services.

Delving into Loans and Interest Expense

Businesses borrow money for both *short-term periods* (periods of less than 12 months) and *long-term periods* (periods of more than one year). Short-term debt usually involves some form of credit card debt or line-of-credit debt. Long-term debt can include, for example, a 3-year car loan, a 20-year mortgage, or any other type of debt where your business repays the principal amount over more than one year.

Short-term debt

Any money due in the next 12-month period is shown on the balance sheet as short-term or current debt. Any interest paid on that money is shown as an interest expense on the income statement.

In most cases, you don't have to calculate your interest due. The bank sends you a statement that gives you a breakdown of the principal and interest that your business owes and the dates when you need to make payments. Often, the agreement from the bank allows it to withdraw directly from your chequing account the charge for interest every month. Looking at the bank debit memo or the bank statement provides you with the amount of the interest expense that you need to record.

How credit card interest is calculated

When you get a credit card statement for your personal credit card, line items in a summary page always show you the amount of new charges, the amount you need to pay in full to avoid all interest charges, and the amount of interest charged during the current month on any balance that remains unpaid since the previous month's statement. If you decide you don't want to pay your credit card balance in full, interest on most credit cards is calculated by using a daily periodic rate of interest, which is compounded each day based on any unpaid balance. Yes, credit cards use a type of compound interest. When you don't pay your credit card bill in full, the credit card company calculates interest on the unpaid principal balance, plus any unpaid interest. When you take a cash advance by using your credit card, the interest charges on that amount start immediately.

On many credit cards, if you haven't paid your balance due in full by the due date, the credit card company will start charging you interest on new purchases starting immediately after the due date. When opening a credit card account for your business, make sure you understand how the credit card company calculates interest and when it starts charging interest on new purchases. Some issuers give a grace period of 20 to 30 days before charging interest, but others don't give any type of grace period at all.

If you take a cash advance using your credit card, some credit card companies charge a transaction fee based on the total amount of cash advanced. This fee may also apply when you transfer balances from one credit card to another. Although the credit card company entices you with a low introductory interest rate to get you to transfer your balance, make sure to read the fine print. You may have to pay a transaction fee on the full amount transferred, which in effect makes the credit card's introductory percentage rate much higher.

Using credit lines

As a small-business owner, you get better interest rates by using a line of credit with a bank rather than using a credit card. Interest rates are usually lower on lines of credit. Typically, a business owner uses a credit card for purchases, but if she can't pay the bill in full on the due date, she draws money from her line of credit to pay off the credit card balance, rather than carry over the balance and pay a higher interest rate. Clearing any credit card balances owing each month is a good idea, because you may want the flexibility of having enough credit to be able to make large purchases in upcoming months. You may otherwise be barred from making large purchases if you have reached the credit limit set by your credit card company.

Some banks have a system whereby they cover your credit card balance daily by applying charges to your credit line. This arrangement gives you several advantages:

- You have the convenience of the credit card when making purchases on the go.
- You don't have to keep track of your credit card limit or have to make payments by a certain deadline.
- The rate of interest charged on a credit line is usually negotiated at a rate of interest that's far lower than the rate charged on credit cards.

When your business first receives the money from the credit line, you record the cash receipt and the liability. Just to show you how this transaction works, we record the receipt of a credit line of $1,200. Here's what the journal entry would look like:

Account	**Debit**	**Credit**
Cash	$1,200	
—Bank Line of Credit		$1,200

  To record receipt of cash from bank line of credit.

In this entry, you increase the Cash asset account and the Bank Line of Credit liability account balances. If you're using a computerized accounting program, you record the transaction by using the Make Deposits screen, as shown in Figure 13-2.

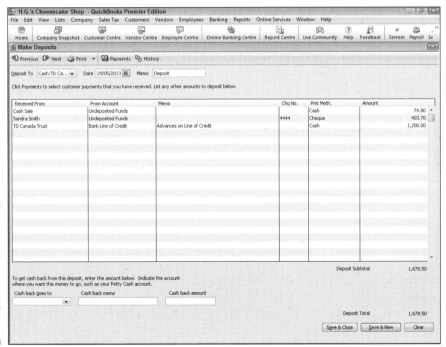

Figure 13-2: Recording the receipt of cash from your business's bank line of credit.

When you make your first payment, you must record the reduction of cash, the amount paid on the principal of the loan, and the amount paid in interest. Here's what that journal entry looks like:

Account	*Debit*	*Credit*
Bank Line of Credit	$100	
Interest Expense	$80	
—Cash		$180

      To make monthly payment on bank line of credit.

This journal entry reduces the amount due in the Bank Line of Credit account, increases the amount paid in the Interest Expense account, and reduces the amount in the Cash account.

If you're using a computerized system, you simply complete a cheque form and indicate which accounts are affected by the payment, and the system updates the accounts automatically. Figure 13-3 shows you how to record a loan payment in QuickBooks.

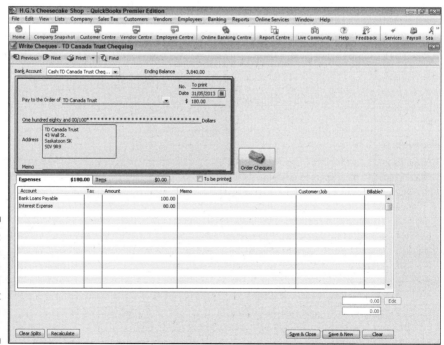

Figure 13-3:
Recording a loan principal and interest payment in QuickBooks.

As you can see in Figure 13-3, at the same time that you prepare the cheque for printing, you can add the accounts that are affected by that payment by splitting the detail expense information. We indicate that we should record $100 of that payment in the Bank Line of Credit account and $80 as Interest Expense. At the top of the cheque, we indicate which bank account we want to use to make the payment. QuickBooks can then update all affected accounts. You don't need to do any additional postings to update your books.

Long-term debt

Most businesses take on some form of debt that they plan to pay over a period of time that's longer than 12 months. You will find that long-term debt makes day-to-day cash flow management easier for you because you can plan years in advance the amount of the principal payments that will come due and organize your financing accordingly. This debt may include car loans, mortgages, or promissory notes. A *promissory note* is a written agreement in which you promise to repay someone or a business a set amount of money as principal at some point in the future plus interest at a stated interest rate. The interest payment can be monthly, yearly, or some other term specified in the note. Most instalment loans are types of promissory notes.

Recording a long-term debt

When a business first takes on a long-term debt, the bookkeeper records that debt in the books in much the same way as a short-term debt:

Account	Debit	Credit
Cash	$XXX	
—Notes Payable		$XXX

    To record receipt of cash advance from bank promissory note.

You also record payments in a manner similar to short-term debt:

Account	Debit	Credit
Notes Payable	$XXX	
Interest Expense	$XXX	
—Cash		$XXX

    To record payment of principal and interest on bank promissory note.

You record the initial long-term debt and make payments the same way in QuickBooks that you do for short-term debt (which we explain in the section "Using credit lines," earlier in this chapter).

Although you don't enter the initial information very differently, a big difference exists between how you show short- and long-term debt on the balance sheet. All short-term debt appears in the Current Liability section of the balance sheet. (This is one of the reasons that you use Other Current Liability as a type of account in your Chart of Accounts. We discuss how to set up your Chart of Accounts in Chapter 3.)

You split up long-term debt and show it in different line items. You put the portion of the debt principal that's due in the next 12 months in the Current Liabilities section, which is usually a line item named something like Current Portion of Long-Term Debt. You place the remaining balance of the long-term debt due beyond the next 12 months in the Long-Term Liability section of the balance sheet as Notes Payable.

How you split your debt between current and long-term debt is very important when measuring your business's liquidity. Liquidity is a measure of your business's ability to pay its debts that are due in the next 12 months. Liquidity is generally expressed as a ratio. We discuss liquidity ratios in Chapter 18.

You can find some of the information concerning due dates, any security offered as collateral on the loans, and the interest rates on the loans in the information that you or your accountant includes in the notes portion of your business's financial statements. This information tells you when your business needs to make large cash payments in the future.

Major purchases and long-term debt

Sometimes, a long-term liability is set up at the same time that you make a major purchase. You may pay some portion of the amount due on the purchase in cash as a down payment and the remainder as a promissory note. To show you how to record such a transaction, we assume that a business has purchased a truck for $25,000, made a down payment of $5,000, and signed a note at an interest rate of 6 percent for the remaining $20,000. Here's how you record this purchase in the books:

Account	Debit	Credit
Vehicles	$25,000	
—Cash		$5,000
—Notes Payable — Vehicles		$20,000

To record the purchase of the blue truck.

You then record payments of principal and interest on the note in the same way as any other loan payment:

Account	*Debit*	*Credit*
Notes Payable — Vehicles	$XXX	
Interest Expense	$XXX	
—Cash		$XXX

To record payment on note issued to purchase the blue truck.

When you record the payment on a long-term debt for which you have a set instalment payment, you may not get a breakdown of interest and principal included in every payment. For example, when you take out a car loan, you sign an agreement that states your obligation to pay a fixed payment due each month. You can make arrangements with your bank to start pre-authorized payments that will be triggered automatically every month. When you get your monthly bank statements, you see the total payment coming out of your business's bank account. Each payment includes principal and interest, but you don't get any breakdown detailing how much of the payment goes toward interest and how much goes toward principal.

Separating principal and interest

Why does not having the breakdown between principal and interest cause problems for recording payments? Each payment includes a different amount for principal and for interest. At the beginning of the loan, the principal is at its highest balance, so the amount of interest due is much higher than later in the loan term, when the balance is lower, because you've had a chance to make principal payments. Many times, in the first year of payments on notes or mortgages payable for high-priced items, such as a mortgage on a building, you're paying more interest than principal.

In order to record long-term debt for which you don't receive a breakdown each month, you need to ask the bank that gave you the loan for an amortization schedule. An *amortization schedule* lists the total payment, the amount of each payment that goes toward interest, the amount that goes toward principal, and the remaining balance that your business still owes on the note.

Some banks provide an amortization schedule automatically when you sign all the paperwork for the note. If your bank can't give you one, you can easily get one online by using an amortization calculator. You can also use any worksheet software to build one yourself.

By using worksheet software, we list the principal/interest breakdown for the first six months of payment on the truck in a six-month amortization chart.

You can see from Table 13-1 that the amount paid to principal on a long-term note gradually increases, and the amount of interest paid gradually decreases while your business pays off the note's principal balance.

Table 13-1	Six-Month Amortization Chart for Truck Payments		
Total Payment	**Principal**	**Interest**	**Remaining Note Balance**
			$20,000.00
$386.66	$286.66	$100.00	$19,713.34
$386.66	$288.09	$98.57	$19,425.25
$386.66	$289.53	$97.13	$19,135.72
$386.66	$290.98	$95.68	$18,844.74
$386.66	$292.44	$94.22	$18,552.30
$386.66	$293.90	$92.76	$18,258.40

Referring to the first payment line of our six-month amortization chart in Table 13-1, you have the information you need to record the first payment on the truck note:

Account	**Debit**	**Credit**
Notes Payable — Vehicles	$286.66	
Interest Expense	$100.00	
—Cash		$386.66

To record monthly principal and interest payment on note for blue truck.

In the amortization chart in Table 13-1, the amount paid toward interest is slightly less each month, and the balance on the note that's still due gradually reduces. Also, the amount paid toward the principal of that note gradually increases while less of the payment is used to pay interest.

By the time you start making payments for the final year of the loan, interest costs drop dramatically because the principal balance on the note is so much lower. For the first payment of Year Five (the last year of the note), the business pays $22.46 in interest and $364.20 for principal. The business has a remaining balance of $4,128.14 after that payment. After the last loan payment, the principal balance is nil.

While you lower your principal balance, much less of your payment goes toward interest and much more goes toward reducing principal. For that reason, many financial specialists advise you to pay down principal as fast as possible if you want to reduce the term of a loan.

Chapter 14

Proving Out the Cash

● ●

In This Chapter

▶ Knowing the importance of proving out the books

▶ Counting your business's cash

▶ Finalizing the cash journals

▶ Balancing out your bank accounts

▶ Posting cash-related adjustments

● ●

*A*ll business owners — whether the business is a small, family-owned corner store or a major international conglomerate — like to periodically test how well their businesses are doing. Business owners also want to be sure that the numbers in their accounting systems actually match what's physically in their stores and offices. After they check out what's in the books, these business owners can prepare financial statements and reports to determine the business's financial success or failure during the last month, quarter, or year. This process of verifying the accuracy of your cash is called *proving out.* When you talk to other bookkeepers, they may refer to this part of the process as doing the month-end or doing the year-end on the books.

The first step in proving out the books involves counting the business's cash and verifying that the cash numbers in your books match the actual cash on hand and in bank accounts at a particular point in time. This chapter explains how you can test to be sure your business has accurate cash counts, finalize the Cash journals for the accounting period, prove out the bank accounts, and post any necessary adjustments or corrections to the General Ledger.

Why Prove Out the Books?

You're probably thinking that proving out the books sounds like a huge task that takes a lot of time. You're right — it's a big job, but it's also a very necessary one to do on a regular basis so that you can be sure what you have recorded in your accounting system realistically measures and tracks what's actually going on in your business.

With any accounting system, mistakes can be made, and unfortunately, any business can fall victim to incidents of theft or embezzlement. One of the ways to be sure that none of these problems exist in your business is to periodically prove out the books. The process of proving out the books is a big part of the accounting cycle, which we discuss in Chapter 2. The first three steps of the accounting cycle — recording transactions, making journal entries, and posting summaries of those entries to the General Ledger — involve tracking the flow of cash and other transactions throughout the accounting period. All three steps are part of the process of recording a business's financial activities. You conduct the rest of the steps in the accounting cycle at the end of the period to help prove out the accuracy of your books. These steps include running a trial balance (see Chapter 16), possibly creating a worksheet (see Chapter 16), adjusting journal entries (see Chapter 17), preparing financial statements (see Chapters 18 and 19), and at the end of the year, closing the books (see Chapter 22). Most businesses prove out their books every month.

Of course, you don't want to shut down your business for a week while you prove out the books, so select a day during each accounting period on which you plan to take a financial snapshot of the state of your accounts. For example, if you're preparing monthly financial reports at the end of the month, you test the amount of cash your business has on hand as of that certain time and day, such as 6 p.m. on June 30 after your store closes for the day. You base the rest of the testing process —including running a trial balance, preparing the adjusting journal entries, and drafting financial statements — on what happened before that point in time. When you open the store and sell more products the next day and buy new things to run your business, those transactions and any others that follow the point in time of your test become part of the next accounting cycle.

Making Sure Ending Cash Is Right

Testing your books starts with counting your cash. Why start with cash? Because the accounting process starts with transactions, and transactions occur most often when cash exchanges hands, either to buy things you need to run the business or to sell your goods or services. Cash is the busiest account in your books. Before you can even begin to test whether the books are right, you need to know whether your books have captured what's happened to your business's cash and whether the amount of cash shown in your books actually matches the amount of cash you have on hand.

We're sure you've heard the well-worn expression "Show me the money!" Well, in business, that idea is the core of your success. Everything relies on your cash profits, which you can take out of your business or use to expand your business.

In Chapter 9, we discuss how a business proves out the cash taken in by each of its cashiers. That daily process gives a business good control of the point at which cash comes into the business from customers who buy the business's goods or services. It also measures any cash refunds given to customers who return items. But the points of sale and return aren't the only times cash comes into or goes out of the business.

If your business sells products on account (refer to Chapter 9), the bookkeeping staff responsible for tracking customer accounts actually collect some of the cash from customers at a later point in time. And when your business needs something, whether products that you plan to sell or supplies that various departments need, you must pay cash to vendors, suppliers, and contractors. Sometimes, you pay cash on the spot, but many times, you record the bill in the Accounts Payable account and pay it at a later date. All these transactions involve the use of cash, so the amount of cash on hand in the business at any one time includes not only what you have in the cash registers, the business's safe, and the petty cash box, but also what the business has on deposit in its bank accounts. You need to know the balances of those accounts and test those balances to be sure they're accurate and match what's in your business's books. We talk more about how to check your bank accounts against your books in the section "Reconciling Bank Accounts," later in this chapter.

So, your snapshot in time of your business's cash includes not only the cash on hand but also any cash your business may have in the bank. You show the total cash figure as an asset named Cash on the first line of your business's financial statement, the *balance sheet.* The balance sheet shows all that the business owns (its assets) and owes (its liabilities), as well as the equity that the owners have in the business. (We talk more about the balance sheet and how you prepare one in Chapter 18.)

The actual cash you have on hand is just one tiny piece of the cash moving through your business during the accounting cycle. You can find the true detail of what cash has flowed into and out of the business in your Cash journals. Summarizing those journals, which we discuss in the following section, is the next step in the process of figuring out how well your business is doing

Summarizing the Cash Journals

As we explain in Chapter 5, if you keep the books manually, you can find a record of every transaction that involves cash in one of two Cash journals: the Cash Receipts journal (cash that comes into the business) and the Cash Disbursements journal (cash that goes out of the business).

If you use a computerized accounting system, you don't have these Cash journals, but you have many different ways to find out the same detailed information that they contain. Figure 14-1 shows the types of sales reports that QuickBooks can automatically generate for you. You can also run reports that show you all the business's sales by customer, by item, or by sales representative, as well as list any open sales orders. Figure 14-2 shows the various purchase reports that QuickBooks can automatically run for you. You can run these reports by vendor or by items bought, as well as list any open purchase orders.

In addition to the sales and purchase reports shown in Figures 14-1 and 14-2, you can generate other transaction detail reports, including customers and receivables; jobs, time, and mileage; vendors and payables; inventory; employees and payroll; and banking. One big advantage of a computerized accounting system when you're trying to prove out your books is the number of different ways that you can develop reports to check for accuracy in your books if you suspect an error.

Figure 14-1:
By using QuickBooks, you can easily generate reports that show your business's sales organized by customer, items sold, or sales representative.

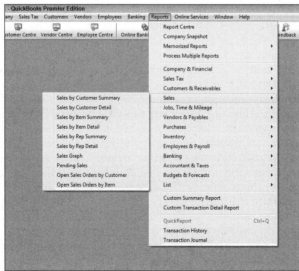

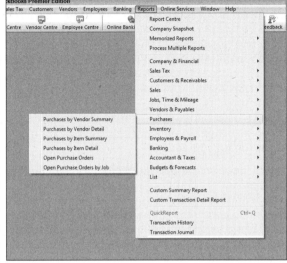

Figure 14-2:
By using QuickBooks, you can produce reports that show your business's purchases by vendor or by items bought.

Finalizing cash receipts

If all your books are up to date, when you summarize the Cash Receipts journal on whatever day and time you choose to prove out your books, you should come up with a total of all cash received by the business at that time. Unfortunately, in the real world of bookkeeping, things don't come out so nice and neat. In fact, you probably wouldn't even start entering the transactions from that particular day into the books until the next day, at the earliest. At that time, you enter the cash reports from all cashiers and others who handle incoming cash (such as the Accounts Receivable staff, who collect money from customers buying on account) into the Cash Receipts journal.

After entering all the transactions from the day in question, the books for the period you're looking at may still be incomplete. Sometimes, you must make adjustments or corrections to the ending cash numbers. For example, you may not yet have recorded monthly credit card fees and interest received from the bank in your Cash journals. As the bookkeeper, you must be sure that you record all bank fees related to cash receipts, as well as any interest earned, in the Cash Receipts journal before you summarize the journals for the period you're analyzing.

Remembering credit card fees

When your business allows customers to use credit cards, you must pay fees to the bank that processes these transactions, which is probably the same bank that handles all your business accounts. These fees actually lower the amount you take in as cash receipts, so you must adjust the amount that you record as cash receipts to reflect those costs of doing business. Monthly credit card fees vary greatly, depending on the bank you're using, but here are some of the most common fees that a bank may charge your business:

- **Address verification service (AVS) fee:** To avoid accepting fraudulent credit card sales. Businesses that use this service take orders by phone or via the Internet, and therefore don't have the credit card in hand to verify a customer's signature. Banks charge this fee for every transaction that they or their agent verify.

- **Discount rate:** All companies that use credit cards must pay this fee; it's based on a percentage of the sale or return transaction. The rate that a bank may charge your business varies greatly, depending on the type of business you conduct and the volume of your sales each month. Companies that use a terminal to swipe cards and electronically send transaction information usually pay lower fees than companies that use paper credit card transactions because the electronic route creates less work for the bank and eliminates the possibility of key-entry errors by employees.

- **Secure payment gateway fee:** Allows the merchant to process transactions securely. Businesses that transact business over the Internet have to pay this fee. If your business sells products online, you can expect to pay this fee based on a set monthly amount.

- **Customer support fee:** Charged to businesses that want bank support for credit card transactions 24 hours a day, 365 days a year. Businesses such as mail-order catalogues that allow customers to place orders 24 hours a day look for this support. Sometimes, businesses even want this support in more than one language if they sell products internationally.

- **Monthly minimum fee:** The least a business is required to pay for the ability to offer its customers the convenience of using credit cards to buy products. This fee usually varies between $10 and $40 per month.

Even if your business doesn't generate any credit card sales during a month, you still have to pay this minimum fee. As long as your business generates enough sales to cover the fee, you shouldn't have a problem. For example, if the fee is $10 and your business pays 2 percent per sale in discount fees, you need to sell at least $500 worth of products each month to cover that $10 fee ($500 × 0.02 = $10). When deciding whether to accept credit cards as a payment option, be sure you're confident that you can generate enough business through credit card sales to cover that fee. If not, you may find that accepting credit cards costs you more than the sales you generate by offering that convenience.

✔ **Transaction fee:** A standard fee charged to your business for each credit card and debit card transaction that you submit for authorization. You pay this fee even if the cardholder is denied and you lose the sale.

✔ **Equipment and software fees:** Charged to your business based on the equipment and computer software that you use in order to process credit card and debit card transactions. You have the option of buying or leasing credit card equipment and related software.

✔ **Chargeback and retrieval fees:** Charged if a customer disputes a transaction.

When deciding whether to accept credit cards as a form of payment, you must consider what your competition is doing. If all your competitors offer the convenience of using credit cards and you don't, you may lose sales if customers take their business to competitors who accept credit cards.

Reconciling your credit card statements

Each month, the bank that handles your credit card sales sends you a statement listing

✔ All your business's transactions for the month

✔ The total amount that your business sold through credit card sales

✔ The total fees charged to your account

If you find a difference between what the bank reports was sold on credit cards and what the business's books show regarding credit card sales, you need to play detective and find the reason for the difference. In most cases, the error involves the bank charging back one or more sales because a customer disputes the charge. In this case, you adjust the Cash Receipts journal to reflect that loss of sale, which should make the bank statement and business books match up.

For example, suppose customers disputed $200 in credit card sales. The entry to adjust for this transaction in the books looks like this:

Account	Debit	Credit
Sales	$200	
—Cash		$200

To reverse disputed credit sales recorded in June.

This entry reduces the total Sales for the month, as well as the amount recorded in the Cash account. If the dispute is resolved and your business can later retrieve the money, you re-enter the sale when your business receives the cash.

You also record any fees related to credit card sales in the Cash Disbursements journal. For example, if credit card fees for the month of June total $200, the entry in the books looks like this:

Account	Debit	Credit
Credit Card Fees Expense	$200	
—Cash		$200

To record the credit card fees for the month of June.

Summarizing the Cash Receipts journal

When you're sure that you've properly entered all cash receipts, as well as any corrections or adjustments to those receipts, in the books (refer to the preceding sections), you summarize the Cash Receipts journal as we explain in detail in Chapter 5. After summarizing the Cash Receipts journal for the accounting period that you're analyzing, you know the total cash that the business took in from sales, as well as from other channels.

In the Cash Receipts journal, cash receipts usually appear in two columns:

- **Sales:** Cash received when the customer purchases the goods by using cash, a cheque, or a bank credit or debit card.

- **Accounts Receivable:** Cash received from collecting outstanding accounts receivable from sales in which the business doesn't receive any cash when the customer purchases the item. Instead, the customer buys on account and is now paying cash for the purchase at a later date. (We talk more about Accounts Receivable and collecting money from customers in Chapter 9.)

After you add all receipts to the Cash Receipts journal, you can post entries for cash collections to the Accounts Receivable General Ledger account and the individual customer accounts. Typically, you send invoices to customers along with the shipment of inventory or right after you send a shipment. At the end of the month, you then send reminder statements to customers who still owe you.

In addition to the Sales and Accounts Receivable columns, your Cash Receipts journal should have at least two other columns:

✔ **General:** Lists all other cash received, such as owner investments in the business or proceeds from a loan advanced by the bank.

✔ **Cash:** Contains the total of all cash received by the business during an accounting period.

We show you in Chapter 5 two weeks' worth of transactions recorded in H.G.'s Cheesecake Shop's Cash Receipts journal. There, we describe and illustrate how you post the information from the journal to the accounts in your books.

Finalizing cash outlays

After you summarize the Cash Receipts journal (as we discuss in the preceding section), you next need to summarize the Cash Disbursements journal. Add any adjustments related to outgoing cash receipts, such as bank credit card fees, to the Cash Disbursements journal.

Before you finalize the journal, be certain that you've added any bills that the business paid at the end of the month to the Cash Disbursements journal. (Refer to Chapter 5 for an example of how to post information from the Cash Disbursements journal to the accounts in your books.)

You accrue bills that relate to financial activity for the month that you're reporting but that your business hasn't yet paid. To *accrue* means to record in the books so that you can match expenses to the revenue for the month. You need to record these accruals to fully implement accrual accounting. We discuss the need to record and report transactions by using the accrual method in Chapter 2. We also discuss why you need to record accruals of expenses in Chapter 17.

You accrue bills that your business hasn't yet paid in the Accounts Payable account. If you look through the bills that you've put in your accordion file to await entry or payment, you may find the information you need to properly record all the necessary accruals. For example, suppose that your business prints and mails flyers to advertise a sale during the last week of the month. Your business hasn't yet paid a bill for the flyers totalling $500. Here's how you enter the bill in the books:

Account	*Debit*	*Credit*
Advertising Expense	$500	
—Accounts Payable		$500

To accrue the bill from Jack's Printing for June sales flyers.

This entry increases advertising expenses for the month and increases the amount due in Accounts Payable. When you pay the bill, you debit the Accounts Payable account (to reduce the liability) and credit the Cash account (to reduce the amount in the account). You make the payment entry in the Cash Disbursements journal when your business pays out the cash.

When proving out the cash, you should also review any accounts in which you've accrued expenses for later payment, such as expenses related to payroll benefits, so that you can be sure you have all accrual accounts up to date. These accounts are actually liability accounts for benefits that your business needs to pay in the future. We discuss how to record these liabilities related to payroll in Chapter 11.

Reconciling Bank Accounts

Part of proving out cash involves checking that what you have in your bank accounts actually matches what the bank thinks you have in those accounts. This process is called *reconciling* the bank accounts.

Before you tackle reconciling your accounts with the bank's records, be sure that you've made all necessary adjustments to your books. We suggest in the section "Making Sure Ending Cash Is Right," earlier in this chapter, that you search for transactions that the bank has recorded but that you don't have recorded in your books. You can do this by viewing your bank account online or waiting to look at your bank account statement. By doing this search, you'll likely find the majority of the missing transactions from your Cash account. When you make adjustments to your Cash accounts, you identify and correct any cash transactions that you may not have properly entered into the books. You also make adjustments to reflect interest income or payments, bank fees, and credit card charges.

If you've done everything right, your accounting records should match the bank's records when it comes to how much cash you have in your accounts, after taking into account any timing differences between when you and the bank record transactions. The day you summarize your books probably isn't the same date that the bank prints your bank statement, so do your best at balancing the books internally without actually reconciling your chequing account. Correcting any problems during the process of proving out can minimize problems that you may face reconciling the cash accounts when you actually pick up that bank statement.

You've probably reconciled your personal chequing account on a regular basis because you understand the benefit of staying on top of your personal record keeping. Reconciling business accounts is a similar process. Table 14-1 shows one common format for reconciling your bank account.

Table 14-1	Bank Reconciliation	
	Balance per bank statement	*$XXX*
Add	Deposits in transit (those not shown on the bank statement)	$XXX
Deduct	Outstanding cheques (cheques that haven't arrived for payment at the bank)	($XXX)
Add or deduct	Bank errors in deposits or payments, if any	$XXX
	Reconciled updated bank balance	$XXX
	Balance in Cash per the updated General Ledger (which should be the same)	$XXX
	Difference (which should be zero)	$XXX

If you find bank errors, communicate them to the bank as soon as possible. The bank can probably record the necessary corrections only if you notify them. If you fail to notify the bank, your accounts will remain out of balance until the bank finds out about its error some other way and then makes the necessary correction. Until corrected, the error will remain a reconciling item on all your subsequent bank reconciliations and continue to cause a difference between the amount of cash in your bank account and the amount of cash in your General Ledger. Until corrected, the reconciling item for the error will come back to haunt you the next time you try to reconcile the bank account.

Tracking down errors

Ideally, your balance and the bank's balance (adjusted for transactions not yet shown on the statement due to timing differences) should match. If they don't, you need to find out why:

- ✔ **If the bank balance is higher than your General Ledger book balance:** Check that all the deposits listed by the bank appear in the Cash account in your books. If you find that the bank lists a deposit that you don't have, you need to do some detective work to figure out what that deposit was for and add the detail to your accounting records. Also, check for amount differences between what the bank recorded and what you recorded in the books. You (or the bank) may have made a mathematical error when entering a transaction. A more unusual explanation may be that the bank placed a deposit in your bank account that doesn't belong to your business. Also, check that all cheques you've sent out for payment have cleared your bank statement. Your bank balance may be missing several cheques you sent out recently as payments if your vendors haven't had the chance to receive and deposit them in their bank accounts. You need to list those cheques in Outstanding Cheques.

✔ **If the bank balance is lower than your balance:** Check that your Cash account lists all cheques listed by the bank. Also, check that the amounts of all cheques correspond between your Cash account and the bank's statement to ensure that neither the bank nor you have made any entry errors. In spite of the internal controls you set up, you may have missed one or two cheques that your business wrote but you didn't properly record. Also, you may have listed a deposit in your Cash account that the bank hasn't yet put on its statement; for example, maybe you placed the money in the overnight deposit box over the weekend and the bank hasn't had a chance to post the deposit to your bank account. If you notice a missing deposit on the bank statement, be sure you have your proof of deposit. Log into your bank's online banking site and look at the transactions immediately after the last date that appears on the bank statement. If the deposit doesn't appear, wait a couple of business days. If the deposit doesn't appear within a reasonable period of time, get in touch with the bank to follow up.

✔ **If all deposits and cheques are correct but you still see a difference:** Your only option is to check your math and make sure that you entered all cheques and deposits correctly.

Sometimes, you may think that rooting out every little difference is really not worth the time it takes. Think again! The types of errors that cause your bank statement and your books to not match up may be quite large but just happen to offset each other in size. For example, you have an unrecorded receipt and an unrecorded payment that are in very similar amounts. Could the unrecorded payment be unauthorized? This type of activity gives you a red flag, suggesting possible fraud or embezzlement, which you must diligently detect. (We talk about fraud and embezzlement in Chapter 7.) Tracking down a discrepancy can also help you detect a loophole in your bookkeeping system that causes you to omit transactions. You want to fix that loophole right away to strengthen your internal control system and to prevent errors. You never know exactly what accounts are affected by an error or how that difference may affect your profit or loss.

Your bank has probably given you (as the bookkeeper) or the owner access to view the business bank account's transactions online. Use this capability to view transactions that immediately follow the month end. You may be able to confirm the amounts of outstanding balances for deposits or find out when the bank clears cheques that remained outstanding as of the date of the bank reconciliation.

You can use the tricks that you've figured out for reconciling your own personal bank account when you reconcile your business's bank account. If the amount of the difference between the bank balance and the General Ledger balance is exactly divisible by two, take half of the difference and search for that amount in your cash receipts or cash disbursements journal. Here's why: If you enter an increase to an account as a decrease (you accidentally flip the entry), that mistake doubles the effect on the accounts to which you record the transaction.

Here's another trick to detect errors, which you can use if you accidentally transpose numbers or record an amount with missing or extra zeros (called *slides*). When you make this kind of error, you can exactly divide the amount of the difference between the bank balance and the General Ledger account balance by 9. For example, if you enter 798 as 789, the difference is 9. Or if you enter 790 as 79, the difference of 711 is exactly divisible by 9 (giving you 79).

Using a computerized system

If you use a computerized accounting system, you can reconcile your cash accounts and your bank statement much more easily than if you keep your books manually. In QuickBooks, for example, when you start the reconciliation process, a screen pops up in which you can add the ending bank statement balance and any bank fees or interest earned. Figure 14-3 shows you that screen. In this example, we've added $4,900.25 as the ending balance and $20 in bank fees. (The bank fees are automatically added to the Bank Fees Expense account.) Figure 14-3 also shows that $60 was earned in interest. The amount will be added automatically to the Interest Revenue account.

Figure 14-3:
When you start the reconciliation process in QuickBooks, you enter the bank's ending balance and any bank service charges or interest earned on a particular account.

Begin Reconciliation

Select an account to reconcile, and then enter the ending balance from your account statement.

Account	Cash	last reconciled on 31/05/2012.
Statement Date	30/06/2013	
Beginning Balance	4,101.25	What if my beginning balance doesn't match my statement?
Ending Balance	4,900.25	

Enter any service charge or interest earned.

Service Charge	Date	Account
20.00	30/06/2013	Bank Service Charges Expense

Interest Earned	Date	Account
60.00	30/06/2013	Interest Income

Locate Discrepancies | Undo Last Reconciliation | Continue | Cancel | Help

After you click Continue, a screen appears that lists all the cheques your business has written since the last reconciliation, as well as all deposits and transfers. Put a check mark next to the cheques, deposits, and transfers that have cleared on the bank statement if the amounts recorded by the bank correspond exactly with the amounts shown in QuickBooks, as we've done in Figure 14-4.

When you retrace the amounts entered by the bank, keep an eye out for differences in the amounts that appear on the bank statement. Follow up and correct any discrepancies immediately, before you finalize the reconciliation. In Figure 14-4, three cheques dated late in the month that appear in the Cheques and Payments column don't have check marks. These cheques appear as reconciling items on the bank reconciliation because they didn't clear the bank account by the time the bank created your statement. The sum of these three outstanding cheques appears under Uncleared Transactions as a deduction in the Reconciliation Summary shown in Figure 14-5.

In Figure 14-4, two deposits made late in the month that appear in the Deposits and Other Credits column don't have check marks. These deposits appear as reconciling items on the bank reconciliation because they weren't added to your bank account by the time the bank created your statement. The sum of these two outstanding deposits appears under Uncleared Transactions as an addition in the Reconciliation Summary found in Figure 14-5.

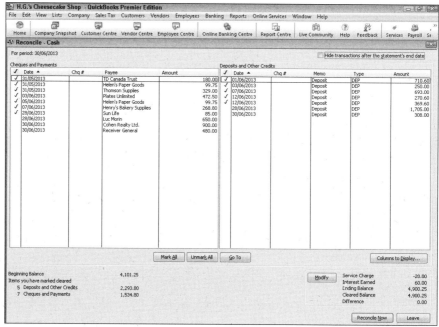

Figure 14-4: To reconcile the chequing account using QuickBooks, put a check mark next to all the cheques, deposits, and transfers that have cleared the account.

When the difference is zero, you can move forward by clicking Reconcile Now.

QuickBooks automatically reconciles the account and provides reports that indicate any differences. It also provides a *reconciliation summary,* shown in Figure 14-5, that includes the beginning balance, the balance after QuickBooks records all cleared transactions, and a list of all transactions that haven't yet been cleared.

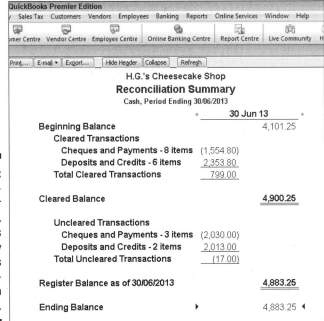

Figure 14-5: After reconciling your accounts, QuickBooks automatically provides a reconciliation summary.

Posting Adjustments and Corrections

After you summarize the Cash Receipts and Cash Disbursements journals (which we talk about in the section "Summarizing the Cash Journals," earlier in this chapter), as well as reconcile your business's bank account with your accounting system (as discussed in the section "Reconciling Bank Accounts," earlier in this chapter), you post any adjustments or corrections that you uncover to any other journals that may be affected by the change, such as Accounts Receivable or Accounts Payable. If you make changes that don't affect any journal accounts, you record the adjustments using the General Journal and post the entries directly to the General Ledger. We show you how to record General Journal entries in Chapter 17.

For example, if you find that you haven't entered several customer payments in the Cash Receipts journal, you also need to post those payments to the Accounts Receivable ledger and the customers' accounts. You need to do the same if you find payments on outstanding bills that you haven't entered into the books. In that case, you post the payments to the Accounts Payable ledger, as well as to the individual vendors' accounts.

Chapter 15

Finalizing the Journals

In This Chapter

▶ Making sure your journals are correct

▶ Posting adjustments to the General Ledger

▶ Examining your journals in a computerized system

As the old saying goes, "The devil is in the details." When it comes to your bookkeeping, especially if you keep your books manually, those details are in the journals that you keep. And those small details can get you every time.

If you use a computerized accounting system to do your books, you don't need to summarize and post your journals, but you can still run a series of reports to verify that all the information in the computer accounting system matches what you have on paper. We talk about how to do that briefly in this chapter.

This chapter focuses primarily on how to prove out (sometimes referred to as *balance*) your journals and post them at the end of an accounting period. (Chapter 14 looks at this process for Cash journals, in particular, if you're interested.) You can also find out how to post all corrections and adjustments to the General Ledger after you make them in the appropriate journal. (To find out how to set up your journals, flip to Chapter 5.)

Prepping to Post: Checking for Accuracy and Tallying Things Up

While you prepare to post to the books, you first need to total the amounts you've recorded in your journals, which is called *summarizing the journals*. During this process, look for blatant errors and be sure that the entries accurately reflect the transactions during the accounting period.

Even the smallest error in a journal can cause a lot of frustration when you try to run a trial balance, so do a thorough search for errors before you post each journal for the month. You can much more easily find an error at this point in the process than if you have to track it back through all your various accounts.

Paying attention to initial transaction details

Do a quick check to be sure the transaction details in your journals are accurate. Chapter 14 tells you how to do this type of check on the Cash journals. Because you follow the rules of accrual accounting, not all transactions involve cash. In accrual accounting, non-cash transactions can include customer purchases made on account (which you track in the Accounts Receivable account) and bills that you plan to pay in the future (which you track in the Accounts Payable account). You may also have created other journals to track transactions in your most active accounts, and you probably also keep details about sales in the Sales journal and payroll in the Payroll journal.

In the Payroll journal, make sure that you've added all payrolls for the month, including all the proper details about salaries, wages, withholding taxes, and benefits. Also, verify that you've recorded all employer and employee withholding taxes that your business needs to remit. These taxes include the employer's portion of Canada Pension Plan/Québec Pension Plan (CPP/QPP) and Employment Insurance (EI). (We talk more about the employer portion of benefit costs in Chapter 11.)

Summarizing journal entries

The first step in checking for accuracy in your journals is summarizing them, which we explain in Chapter 5. Summarizing your journals primarily involves totalling all the columns in the journal. This summary process gives you totals for the accounts that each journal tracks. For example, summarizing the Accounts Receivable journal gives you a grand total of all transactions for that period that involved customer credit accounts. Figure 15-1 shows a summary of an Accounts Receivable journal.

The Accounts Receivable control account in the General Ledger includes transactions from the Sales journal (where you first record customer purchases on account) and the Cash Receipts journal (where you first record customers' payments toward their outstanding amounts), as well as any credit memos for customer returns and allowances. The example in Figure 15-1 is only a few lines long, but in most businesses the Accounts Receivable journal is very active. Bookkeepers for food wholesalers, for example, post transactions every day that their warehouse is open during the month. When you summarize the Accounts Receivable account in the General Ledger, you arrive at a *closing balance.* This total corresponds to the sum of all the accounts outstanding from your customers as of that date. The entries posted in summary to the Accounts Receivable control account show the total of all financial activity recorded concerning the accounts receivable for the month. Figure 15-1 shows a closing balance of $2,296, which is the amount outstanding from customers.

Each transaction in the General Ledger should have a reference number next to it, which tells you where the detail for that transaction first appears in the journals. You may need to review this information later when you're proving out the books. When you check for errors in the General Ledger, you may need to review the original source information used to enter some transactions in order to double-check that an entry's accurate.

In addition to the Accounts Receivable control account in the General Ledger, you also have individual ledger pages for each customer; these pages detail each customer's purchases on account and any payments made toward those purchases. At the end of an accounting period, you prepare an *aging summary* that details all outstanding customer accounts. This report shows you what money customers owe your business and how long they've owed it. (We talk more about managing customer accounts in Chapter 9.)

Figure 15-1:
The
Accounts
Receivable
General
Ledger
account
activity and
running
balance.

H.G.'s Cheesecake Shop						
Accounts Receivable						
Date		Description	Ref.	Debt	Credit	Balance
June	1	Beginning Balance				2,000.00
	5	Credit memo No. 123	GJ 16		60.00	1,940.00
	30	Sales	S 20	886.00		2,826.00
	30	Cash Receipts	CR 17		530.00	2,296.00

For the purpose of proving out and reconciling the accounts receivable, the aging report or summary gives you a quick summary that ensures the customer accounts information matches what's in the Accounts Receivable control account in the General Ledger. Table 15-1 shows what an aging summary looks like at the same point in time, which in this case is the end of the month.

Table 15-1	Aging Summary: Accounts Receivable as of June 30, 2013			
Customer	*Current*	*31–60 Days*	*60–90 Days*	*> 90 Days*
S. Smith	$300			
J. Jones	$100	$300	$200	
S. Wong	$500	$240		
V. Wang	$400	$256		
Totals	$1,300	$796	$200	

In this sample Accounts Receivable Aging Summary, the total amount outstanding from customers matches the balance total in the Accounts Receivable journal of $2,296. Therefore, the bookkeeper has accurately entered all customer accounts in the books, and she shouldn't encounter any errors related to customer accounts when she runs a trial balance, which we explain in Chapter 16.

If you find a difference between the information in your control account in the General Ledger and your aging summary, review your customer account transactions to find the problem. You may have committed a mathematical error when you recorded, added, or transcribed amounts from the ledger and the aging summary. In addition, an error may be the result of

✔ Recording a sales transaction in the Sales journal without recording the details of that transaction in the customer's account.

✔ Recording a sales transaction directly into the customer's account without recording it in the Sales journal. If you omit this amount from your Sales journal, it also doesn't appear in the totals that you post to the Accounts Receivable control account in the General Ledger.

✔ Recording in the customer's account when your business collects what a customer owes without recording the cash receipt in the Cash Receipts journal. Therefore, you don't post that amount in the Accounts Receivable control account in the General Ledger.

✔ Recording when your business collects what a customer owes in the Accounts Receivable control account in the General Ledger without recording the cash receipt in the customer's account.

You need to perform a reconciliation (prove the equality) of the sum of the amounts in the individual customer records to the Accounts Receivable control account in the General Ledger. The preparation of this monthly reconciliation adds a key internal control procedure. Imagine trying to collect from customers when you don't even know who they are or how much each one owes your business.

The process of summarizing and reconciling the Accounts Payable control account in the General Ledger is similar to that of the Accounts Receivable account. For Accounts Payable, you can prepare an aging summary for your outstanding bills, as well. That summary should look something like Table 15-2.

Table 15-2	Aging Summary: Accounts Payable as of June 30, 2013			
Vendor	*Current*	*31–60 Days*	*60–90 Days*	*> 90 Days*
A. Bank	$150			
Cohen Realty	$800			
Helen's Paper Goods		$250		
Henry's Bakery Supplies		$500		
Plates Unlimited	$400	$200		
Totals	$1,350	$950		-

The total of outstanding bills on the Accounts Payable Aging Summary should match the total shown on the Accounts Payable control account in the General Ledger as of the end of the accounting period. If yours match, you're ready to prepare a trial balance. If they don't, you must figure out the reason for the difference before you close out the Accounts Payable journal. The problem may be mathematical errors or the result of

✔ Recording a bill due in the Accounts Payable control account in the General Ledger without recording it in the vendor's account.

✔ Recording a bill due in the vendor's account without recording it in the Accounts Payable control account in the General Ledger.

✔ Making a payment to the vendor and recording it in the vendor's account without recording it in the Accounts Payable control account in the General Ledger.

✔ Making a payment to the vendor and recording it in the Accounts Payable control account in the General Ledger but neglecting to record it in the vendor's account.

Correct any problems and continue to look for any errors until you reconcile your control account in the General Ledger to your detailed accounts. If you suspect you may be working with incorrect data, you don't want to do a trial balance because you create a balance filled with errors, so you can't generate accurate financial reports. Also, if you know errors exist, the books likely won't balance anyway, so you just waste your time if you do a trial balance.

Analyzing summary results

You may be wondering how you can find problems in your records by just reviewing a page in a journal. Well, that skill comes with experience and practice. While you summarize your journals each month, you become familiar with the expected level of transactions and the types of transactions that occur month after month. If you don't see a transaction that you expect to find, take the time to research the transaction to find out why it's missing. The transaction may not have taken place, or someone may have forgotten to record it.

For example, suppose that when you're summarizing the Payroll journal, you notice that the payroll for the 15th of the month seems lower than normal. When you check your details for that payroll, you find that you recorded the amount paid to hourly employees but didn't record the amount paid to salaried employees. For that particular payroll, the payroll company experienced a computer problem after running some checks and, as a result, sent the final report on two separate pages. When you recorded the payroll numbers, you didn't realize you had a separate page for salaried employees, so the final numbers that you entered into the books didn't reflect the full amount paid to employees.

While you post and reconcile the books each month, you get an idea of the numbers that you can expect for each type of journal. After a while, you can pick out problems just by scanning a page — no detailed research required!

Planning for cash flow

The process you go through each month while you prepare to post and reconcile your books helps you plan for future cash flow. Reviewing the

Accounts Receivable and Accounts Payable Aging Summaries tells you what additional cash you can expect from customers during the next few months and how much cash you'll need in order to pay bills for the next few months.

If you notice that your Accounts Payable Aging Summary indicates that your business has more and more bills slipping into past-due status, you may need to find another source for cash, such as a credit line from the bank. For example, the Accounts Payable Aging Summary given in Table 15-2 reveals that the business hasn't paid three key vendors — Helen's Paper Goods, Henry's Bakery Supplies, and Plates Unlimited — on time. Late payments can hurt your business's working relationship with vendors; those vendors may refuse to deliver goods unless your business pays cash up front. And if you can't get the inventory you need, you may have trouble filling customer orders on time. You must act quickly to find a way to improve cash flow before your vendors cut you off. (For more on Accounts Payable management, check out Chapter 8.)

You may also find that your Accounts Receivable Aging Summary reveals that certain previously good customers are gradually becoming slow-paying or non-paying customers. For example, Table 15-1 shows that J. Jones's account is past due, and at least some portion of his account is overdue by more than 60 days. The bookkeeper dealing with these accounts may need to consider putting a hold on that account until the business receives payment in full. (For more on Accounts Receivable management, check out Chapter 9.)

Posting to the General Ledger

An important part of summarizing and reconciling your books is posting to the General Ledger any corrections or adjustments that you make while you proceed through this process. For example, suppose you find that someone recorded a customer purchase directly in the customer's account record but not in the Accounts Receivable control account in the General Ledger. You have to research how someone originally recorded that transaction. If the only record was a note in the customer's account, both the Sales account and the Accounts Receivable account are affected by the mistake, and the correcting entry looks like this:

Account	*Debit*	*Credit*
Accounts Receivable	$100	
—Sales		$100

To record sale to J. Jones on 6/15/2013 — corrected 6/30/2013.

If you find this type of error, where a customer's purchase is posted in the customer's account record but not in the Accounts Receivable control account, the Sales transaction record for that date of sale isn't accurate — which means that someone bypassed your standard bookkeeping process when recording the sale. You may want to research that part of the issue, as well, because this incident may have more than just a recording problem behind it. Someone in your business may be allowing customers to take products, purposefully not recording the sale appropriately in your books, and pocketing the money instead. Or a salesperson may have recorded a sale for a customer that never took place. In that case, when you bill the customer, he'll likely question the bill, so you'll find out about the problem at that point.

The process of proving out and reconciling your journals, or any other part of your bookkeeping records, gives you a good opportunity to review your internal controls, as well. While you find errors during the process, keep an eye out for ones (probably similar errors that appear frequently) that may indicate bigger problems than just bookkeeping mistakes. Repeat errors may call for you to provide additional staff training to be sure everyone's following your bookkeeping rules to a T. Or such errors may be evidence that someone in the business is deliberately recording false information. Whatever the explanation, you need to take corrective action. (We cover internal controls in depth in Chapter 7.)

Checking Out Computerized Journal Records

Although you don't have to summarize, reconcile, and post to the General Ledger if you keep your books by using a computerized accounting system, run a spot-check (at the very least) of what you have in your paper records versus what you have on your computer — because if a flaw exists in the programming of the accounting software run by your computer, errors will keep occurring until the software is fixed. Simply run a series of reports by using your computerized accounting system and then check to be sure that those computer records match what you have in your files.

You can go to the Reports command that appears in the top menu bar of QuickBooks, where you will find Vendors & Payables drop-down menu. As shown in Figure 15-2, when you click on Vendors & Payables, several possible report formats appear, even in graph form, to illustrate your outstanding bills.

Figure 15-2:
QuickBooks allows you to run a number of reports concerning vendors and payables. Essentially, these reports tell you how much money your business owes to others.

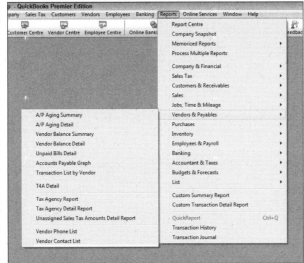

Figure 15-3 shows you the kind of detail that you get when you select the A/P Aging Summary report from the list of available reports shown in Figure 15-2. The A/P Aging Summary is divided into

- ✔ Current bills
- ✔ Bills overdue by 1 to 30 days
- ✔ Bills overdue by 31 to 60 days
- ✔ Bills overdue by 61 to 90 days
- ✔ Bills overdue by more than 90 days

Obviously, you want to avoid having any entries in the last two A/P Aging Summary columns — overdue by more than 60 days. You can expect a supplier or vendor whose bills appear in these columns to soon cut you off from additional credit until you pay your account's outstanding balance.

In addition to locating your bill-paying problem areas, you can also use the information in the A/P Aging Detail report to verify that the paper bills you have waiting to be paid in vendor files match what you have on your computer. You don't need to check each and every bill, but do a spot-check of several bills to make sure they match your computer records. You want to verify the accuracy of your records, as well as make sure that no one's entering and paying duplicate or nonexistent bills.

Figure 15-3:
When you run an Accounts Payable Aging Detail report in QuickBooks, you get a listing of all outstanding bills, the dates of the invoices, and the dates they're due.

H.G.'s Cheesecake Shop - QuickBooks Premier Edition

File Edit View Lists Company Sales Tax Customers Vendors Employees Banking Reports Online Services Window Help

Home | Company Snapshot | Customer Centre | Vendor Centre | Employee Centre | Online Banking Centre | Report Centre | Live Community | Help | Feedback | Services | Payroll | Se

A/P Aging Detail

Modify Report... | Memorize... | Print... | E-mail ▾ | Export... | Hide Header | Refresh

Dates Custom ▾ | 31/05/2013 | Interval (days) 30 | Through (days past due) 90 | Sort By Default ▾

H.G.'s Cheesecake Shop
A/P Aging Detail
As of 31 May 2013

Type	Date	Name	Due Date	Open Balance
Current				
Bill	31/05/2013	Cohen Realty Ltd.	01/06/2013	900.00 ◀
Bill	08/05/2013	Henry's Bakery Su...	07/06/2013	268.80
Total Current				1,168.80
1 - 30				
Bill	23/04/2013	Helen's Paper Go...	03/05/2013	99.75
Bill	25/04/2013	Thomson Supplies	05/05/2013	329.00
Bill	10/05/2013	Plates Unlimited	20/05/2013	472.50
Bill	17/05/2013	Thomson Supplies	27/05/2013	126.00
Total 1 - 30				1,027.25
31 - 60				
Total 31 - 60				
61 - 90				
Total 61 - 90				
> 90				
Total > 90				
TOTAL				2,196.05

When it comes to cash flow out of the business, keep tight controls on who can actually sign cheques and how you record the information that explains those cheques. In Chapter 7, we talk about the importance of separating duties to protect each aspect of your bookkeeping system from corruption.

You can also run reports in QuickBooks that show the information recorded in your Accounts Receivable account. Figure 15-4 shows you a list of possible reports to run from the Customers & Receivables page. In addition to the A/R Aging Summary, A/R Aging Detail, and Accounts Receivable Graph reports, you can also run a report for Open Invoices, which lists outstanding customer invoices or statements, and Collections, which lists not only overdue customers but also how much they owe and their contact information.

Again, run spot-checks on a few customer accounts to be sure your paper records of their accounts match the information in your computerized system. Someone may have entered a customer's purchase into the computer in error, and you may end up sending the bill to the wrong person.

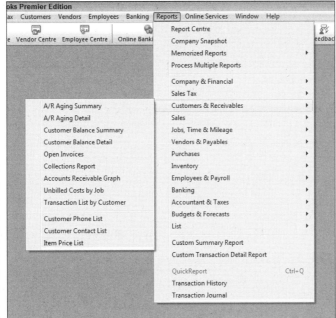

Figure 15-4:
In
QuickBooks,
you can run
a series of
reports that
summarizes
customer
accounts.

Some businesses double-check their Accounts Receivable bookkeeping for accuracy by sending surveys to customers periodically (usually twice a year) to see whether those customers' accounts are correct. If you choose to send these kinds of surveys, include with the customer's bill a postage-paid card asking whether the account is correct and giving the customer room to indicate any account problems before she mails the card back to your business. In most cases, a customer whom your business incorrectly bills will contact you soon after getting that bill — especially if your business bills him for more than he anticipated.

In addition to keeping actual accounts, such as Accounts Payable or Accounts Receivable, your computerized accounting system keeps a journal of all your business's transactions. This journal contains details about all your transactions over a specified time period and the accounts that each transaction affected. Figure 15-5 is a sample computerized journal page.

Figure 15-5:
A computerized accounting system keeps a journal of all transactions, which you can review during the summarizing and reconciling process.

				H.G.'s Cheesecake Shop — QuickBooks Premier Edition				

H.G.'s Cheesecake Shop
Journal
June 2013

Trans #	Type	Date	Num	Name	Account	Debit	Credit
64	Invoice	10/06/2013	60	Patricia Perry	Accounts Receiva...	308.00	
				Patricia Perry	Sales		280.00
				Patricia Perry	Inventory Asset		200.00
				Patricia Perry	Cost of Goods Sold	200.00	
				Receiver General	GST/HST Payable		14.00
				Saskatchewan Fin...	PST Payable (Sas...		14.00
						508.00	508.00
65	Invoice	10/06/2013	61	Karen Taylor	Accounts Receiva...	693.00	
				Karen Taylor	Sales		630.00
				Karen Taylor	Inventory Asset		465.00
				Karen Taylor	Cost of Goods Sold	465.00	
				Receiver General	GST/HST Payable		31.50
				Saskatchewan Fin...	PST Payable (Sas...		31.50
						1,158.00	1,158.00
66	Payment	30/06/2013		Charlie's Garage	Undeposited Funds	308.00	
				Charlie's Garage	Accounts Receiva...		308.00
						308.00	308.00
67	Deposit	30/06/2013			Cash	308.00	
				Charlie's Garage	Undeposited Funds		308.00
						308.00	308.00
68	Payment	28/06/2013		Jack Jones	Undeposited Funds	1,705.00	

If you need to be reminded of how you recorded a transaction into your computerized accounting system, run the Journal report by date, isolating all transactions that took place at a particular time or within a range of time. Running a report by date can help you locate the source of an error in your books; if you find a questionable transaction, you can open the detail of that transaction to see how it was entered and where you can find the original source material.

Chapter 16

Checking Your Accuracy — by Trial and Hopefully No Error

In This Chapter

▶ Putting your balances on trial

▶ Finding and correcting errors

▶ Preparing a worksheet

▶ Generating reports from your computerized system

After you summarize and post all your journals and do your darnedest to catch any and all errors (flip back to Chapter 15 for instructions on how to go error hunting), the time comes to test your work. If you've entered all double-entry transactions in the books correctly, the books balance out, and your trial's a success!

Unfortunately, few bookkeepers get their books to balance on the first try. And in some cases, the books balance but errors still exist. This chapter explains how you do a trial balance of your books and gives tips on finding any errors that may be lurking. You can also find out how to take your first step to developing financial statements and reports, which we explain in Part V, by creating a worksheet.

Working with a Trial Balance

When you first start entering transactions in a dual-entry accounting system, you may think, "This is a lot of work, and I don't know how I'm ever going to use all this information." You enter all your transactions by using debits and credits without knowing whether they actually produce financial information that you can use to gauge how well your business is doing. Only after you post your journals and prepare your first set of financial reports do you truly see the value of double-entry accounting. Trust us.

The first step toward creating usable reports that help you interpret your financial results is doing a trial balance. Basically, a *trial balance* is a worksheet prepared manually or spit out by your computer accounting system that lists all the accounts in your General Ledger at the end of an accounting period (whether that's at the end of a month, the end of a quarter, or the end of a year). The trial balance lists the accounts in the order of your Chart of Accounts. If you're searching for the balance of a particular account, you can easily find the account you need if you know that account's location in the Chart of Accounts.

Building your trial balance

If you enter transactions manually, you create a trial balance by listing all the accounts with a debit balance in one column and all of the accounts with a credit balance in a separate column. (We talk more about debits and credits in Chapter 2.) After you prepare the list, you total both the debit and credit columns. If the totals at the bottom of the two columns are the same, the trial is a success and your books are in balance.

You can do a shortcut of this procedure by running a tape of the balances on an adding machine. Enter the debits balances as additions and the credit balances as deductions. At the end, the tape should have a running balance of zero. (We've seen plenty of people give a cheer when that happens.) Bookkeepers sometimes use this shortcut procedure during the accounting cycle if they suspect that the General Ledger is somehow out of balance. Running this tape early in the month can eliminate the need to sift through a whole month's worth of transactions to figure out why the books are out of balance. Our motto is, "Why wait for spring? Do it now!"

The primary purpose of the trial balance is to prove that, at least mathematically, your debits and credits are equal. If any errors exist in your calculations — or in how you summarized the journals or posted the summaries to the General Ledger — you uncover them in the trial balance when the columns don't come out equal. Also, if you entered any transactions out of balance, you see the mistake when you add the columns of the trial balance.

Follow these four basic steps to develop a trial balance:

1. **Prepare a worksheet that has three columns: one for account titles, one for debits, and one for credits.**

2. **Fill in all the account titles and record their balances in the appropriate debit or credit columns.**

3. **Total the debit column and the credit column.**

4. **Compare the column totals.**

Figure 16-1 shows a sample trial balance for a business as of June 30, 2013. The debit column and the credit column both equal $65,730, making this a successful trial balance.

A successful trial balance doesn't guarantee that your books are totally free of errors; it just means that you've entered all your transactions in balance. You still may have errors in the books related to how you entered your transactions, including

✔ You forgot to put a transaction in a journal or in the General Ledger.

✔ You forgot to post a journal entry to the General Ledger.

✔ You posted a journal entry twice in either the General Ledger or in the journal itself.

✔ You posted the wrong amount for both the debit and the credit.

✔ You posted a transaction to the wrong account.

If, by chance, entry errors (such as the ones in the preceding list) slip through the cracks, someone will probably notice the discrepancy when you prepare the financial reports.

Even with these potentially lurking errors, the trial balance provides the essential first step in developing your financial reports.

H.G.'s Cheesecake Shop Trial Balance June 30, 2013		
Account	Debit	Credit
Cash - Petty Cash	500	
Cash - Bank Chequing	2,500	
Accounts Receivable	1,000	
Inventory	1,200	
Equipment	5,050	
Vehicle	30,000	
Furniture	5,600	
Accumulated Depreciation		5,000
Accounts Payable		2,200
Bank Line of Credit		600
Bank Loans Payable		20,650
H.G. Capital		15,500
H.G. Drawings	0	
Sales		21,600
Sales Returns & Allowances	150	
Purchases	12,300	
Purchase Returns & Allowances		180
Automobile Expense	370	
Computer & Internet Expenses	220	
Depreciaton Expense	600	
Insurance Expense	400	
Interest Expense	70	
Office Supplies Expense	140	
Payroll Benefits Expense	270	
Rent Expense	1,000	
Salaries and Wages Expense	3,600	
Telephone Expense	310	
Utilities Expense	450	
Totals	65,730	65,730

Figure 16-1:
A sample trial balance.

Dealing with trial balance errors

If your trial balance isn't correct, you need to work backwards in your summarizing or posting process to find the source of the mathematical error. When you find errors after you complete a trial balance that fails, you need to identify and fix the problem. When they prepare trial balances, bookkeepers and accountants work with pencils, not pens — with pencils, you can erase mistakes and make corrections much more easily. Just follow these steps to find your mistake:

1. **Check your math.**

   Keep your fingers crossed and add up your columns again to be sure you didn't just make an addition error. That's the simplest kind of error to find. Correct the addition mistake and retotal your columns. If you're using an adding machine with a tape, you can retrace the amounts without having to reenter the figures in the adding machine.

2. **Check the columns.**

   Retrace the amounts from the General Ledger to the trial balance. You may have placed a balance in the wrong column. You may be able to zero in on this type of error by dividing the amount of the difference between your debit and credit column balances by two. Assuming you get a whole number, look for this number anywhere in your trial balance and make sure you listed this particular amount in the correct column. If you list an amount in the debit column instead of the credit column, or vice versa, the effect of your error on the column totals will be exactly double the size of the amount of your entry.

3. **Compare your balances.**

   Double-check the balances on the trial balance worksheet by comparing them to the totals from your journals and your General Ledger. Be sure you didn't make an error when transcribing the account balances to the trial balance. You can correct this type of problem pretty quickly and easily. Simply correct the incorrect balances and add up the trial balance columns again. Another way to come up with a revised total is to calculate the effect of your correction on the balances — apply the amount of the change to the amount you first arrived at for the totals.

4. **Check your journal summaries.**

   Double-check the math in all your journal summaries, making sure that all totals are correct and that any totals you posted to the General Ledger are correct. Running this kind of a check, of course, takes some time, but it's still easier than rechecking all your transactions. If you do find errors in your journal summaries, correct the errors, reenter the totals correctly, change the numbers on the trial balance worksheet to match your corrected totals, and retest your trial balance.

5. **Check your journal and General Ledger entries.**

Unfortunately, if Steps 1, 2, 3, and 4 fail to fix your problem, the only option left is to go back and check your actual transaction entries. The process can be time-consuming, but you can't communicate any of the financial use information in your books until your debits equal your credits.

If you have to check all your entries, scan through those entries, looking specifically for ones that appear questionable. For example, if you see an entry for office supplies that's much larger or much smaller than you normally expect, check the original source material for that entry to be sure it's correct. If you carefully reconciled the Cash, Accounts Payable, and Accounts Receivable accounts (as we explain in Chapters 14 and 15), you can concentrate your efforts on accounts that have separate journals. After you find and correct the error or errors, run another trial balance. If things still don't match up, repeat the steps in the preceding list until your debits and credits equal out.

You can always go back and correct the books and prepare another trial balance before you draft the financial statements and reports. Don't close the books for the fiscal year until you complete the financial statements and the owner accepts and approves them. We talk more about the closing process in Chapter 22.

Testing Your Balance by Using Computerized Accounting Systems

If you use a computerized accounting system, that system automatically generates your trial balance for you. Because the system allows you to enter only transactions that are in balance, the likelihood that your trial balance won't be successful is pretty slim. But that doesn't mean your accounts are guaranteed to be error-free.

Remember the saying "Garbage in, garbage out"? If you make a mistake when you enter transaction data into the system, even if the data's in balance, the information that comes out is also in error. Although you don't have to go through the correction steps covered in the section "Dealing with trial balance errors," earlier in this chapter, to reach a successful trial balance, you still may have errors lurking in your data.

In QuickBooks, the Trial Balance report is the first report on the Reports, Accountant & Taxes menu (see Figure 16-2). In addition to the trial balance, you can request a report showing the General Ledger, transaction detail by account, journal detail, voided/deleted transactions, and transactions by date.

Your business's accountant probably uses many of the report options on the Accountant & Taxes page to double-check that you entered transactions correctly and that no one is playing with the numbers. In particular, the accountant may use a report option called *Audit Trail,* which reveals what changes affected the business's books during an accounting period and who made those changes.

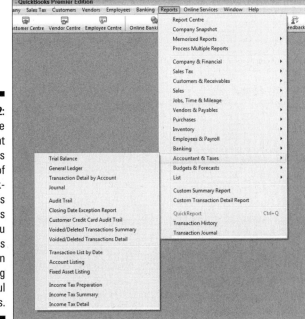

Figure 16-2:
The Accountant & Taxes section of Quick-Books's Reports menu provides the option of creating many useful reports.

Although it doesn't match the trial balance done manually in Figure 16-1, the QuickBooks trial balance shown in Figure 16-3 uses several General Ledger accounts and gives you an idea of what a computerized accounting trial balance looks like (though only the top portion is shown).

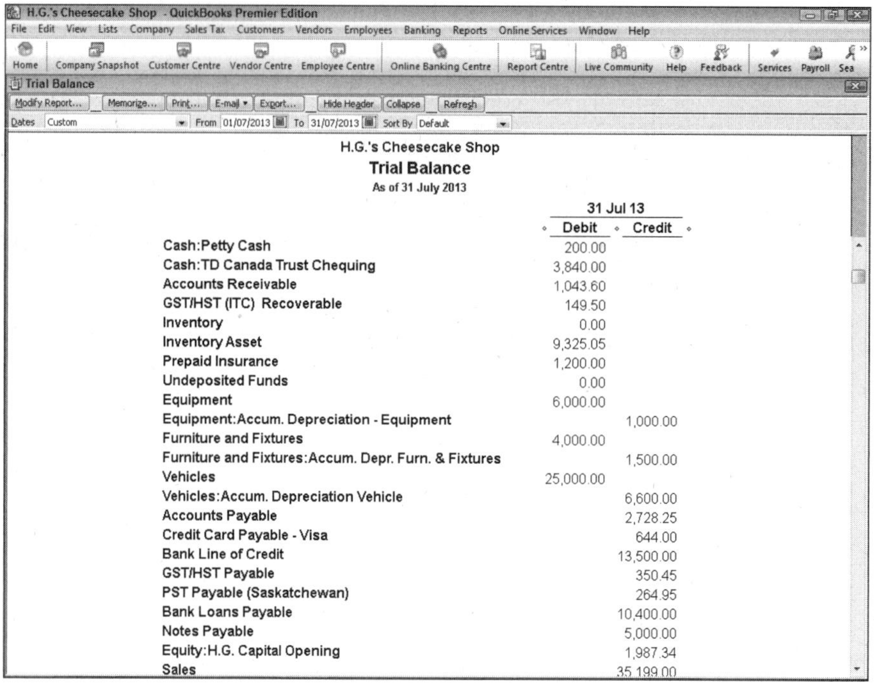

H.G.'s Cheesecake Shop

Trial Balance

As of 31 July 2013

	31 Jul 13	
	Debit	Credit
Cash:Petty Cash	200.00	
Cash:TD Canada Trust Chequing	3,840.00	
Accounts Receivable	1,043.60	
GST/HST (ITC) Recoverable	149.50	
Inventory	0.00	
Inventory Asset	9,325.05	
Prepaid Insurance	1,200.00	
Undeposited Funds	0.00	
Equipment	6,000.00	
Equipment:Accum. Depreciation - Equipment		1,000.00
Furniture and Fixtures	4,000.00	
Furniture and Fixtures:Accum. Depr. Furn. & Fixtures		1,500.00
Vehicles	25,000.00	
Vehicles:Accum. Depreciation Vehicle		6,600.00
Accounts Payable		2,728.25
Credit Card Payable - Visa		644.00
Bank Line of Credit		13,500.00
GST/HST Payable		350.45
PST Payable (Saskatchewan)		264.95
Bank Loans Payable		10,400.00
Notes Payable		5,000.00
Equity:H.G. Capital Opening		1,987.34
Sales		35,199.00

Figure 16-3: Top portion of a sample trial balance report produced by QuickBooks.

Developing a Financial Statement Worksheet

After your accounts successfully pass a trial balance test (see the section "Building your trial balance," earlier in this chapter), you can then take your first stab at creating *financial statements,* including balance sheets and income statements. The first step in producing these statements is using the information from the trial balance and its corrections to develop a worksheet that includes the initial trial balance, the accounts that normally appear on a balance sheet, and the accounts that normally appear on an income statement.

You create a worksheet that includes these seven columns:

- **Column one:** Account list, including account numbers, if available
- **Columns two and three:** Trial balance (one column for debits, one column for credits)

✔ **Columns four and five:** Income statement (one column for debits, one column for credits)

✔ **Columns six and seven:** Balance sheet (one column for debits, one column for credits)

In Figure 16-4, you can see a sample of a worksheet developed from trial balance numbers. The bookkeeper has transferred the numbers of the trial balance to the appropriate financial statement; for example, the Cash account (which is an Asset account) appears in the debit column of the balance sheet. (We talk more about developing financial statements in Chapters 18 and 19.)

H.G.'s Cheesecake Shop						
Worksheet						
Month ended June 30, 2013						
	Trial Balance		Income Statement		Balance Sheet	
Account	Debit	Credit	Debit	Credit	Debit	Credit
Cash - Petty Cash	500				500	
Cash - Bank Chequing	2,500				2,500	
Accounts Receivable	1,000				1,000	
Inventory	1,200				1,200	
Equipment	5,050				5,050	
Vehicle	30,000				30,000	
Furniture	5,600				5,600	
						5,000
Accounts Payable		2,200				2,200
Bank Line of Credit		600				600
Bank Loans Payable		20,650				20,650
H.G. Capital		15,500				15,500
H.G. Drawings	0				0	
Sales		21,600		21,600		
Sales Returns & Allowances	150		150			
Purchases	12,300		12,300			
Purchase Returns & Allowances		180		180		
Automobile Expense	370		370			
Computer & Internet Expenses	220		220			
Depreciation Expense	600		600			
Insurance Expense	400		400			
Interest Expense	70		70			
Office Supplies Expense	140		140			
Payroll Benefits Expense	270		270			
Rent Expense	1,000		1,000			
Salaries and Wages Expense	3,600		3,600			
Telephone Expense	310		310			
Utilities Expense	450		450			
Totals	65,730	65,730	19,880	21,780	45,850	43,950
Net income			1,900			1,900
Total	65,730	65,730	21,780	21,780	45,850	45,850

Figure 16-4: This sample worksheet shows the first step in developing a business's financial statements.

After you transfer all the accounts to their appropriate balance sheet or income statement columns, you total the worksheet columns. Don't panic when you see that the totals at the bottom of your columns aren't equal — you haven't calculated the net income yet. However, the difference between the debits and credits in both the balance sheet and the income statement totals needs to be the same. That amount represents the net income that appears on the income statement. (You can see what we mean about net income when we develop the income statement in Chapter 19.)

In Figure 16-4, the $1,900 difference for the balance sheet appears as a credit, representing an increase in equity. The Equity account reflects the profits that the owner has reinvested into the business's assets in order to grow the business. If your business is incorporated, the Equity account that increases with profits is called Retained Earnings. You can find out more about Equity and Retained Earnings accounts in Chapter 18.

In some incorporated businesses, owners take out some of the Retained Earnings in the form of dividends paid to shareholders. *Dividends* are a portion of the earnings divided up among shareholders as a reward for their investment. The board of directors of the corporation sets a certain amount per share that the corporation pays to shareholders.

Many other small businesses that haven't incorporated pay out earnings to their owners by using a Drawings account. Amounts recorded to the Drawings account are not expenses of the business. This account tracks any cash or other assets that the owners take out of the business. Each owner of a partnership has her own Drawings account so that a history exists of how much each owner withdraws from the business's resources. Figure 16-1 and Figure 16-4 both show the H.G. Drawings account with a nil balance for the month ended June 30, 2013 because no cash had been withdrawn by the owner H.G. You will note that the Drawing account is listed immediately after the H.G. Capital account, the same as in the Chart of Accounts. We talk about the partnership business structure in Chapter 21.

Replacing Worksheets with Computerized Reports

If you use a computerized accounting system, you don't have to create a worksheet at all. Instead, the system gives you the option of generating many different types of reports to help you develop your income statement and balance sheet.

One of the advantages of your computerized system's reports is that you can easily look at your numbers in many different ways. For example, Figure 16-5 shows the way you access the Company & Financial list of reports in the Reports drop-down menu in QuickBooks. To get the report you want, just scroll down the list and click the appropriate report title.

Figure 16-5: The Company & Financial list in the Reports menu in QuickBooks gives you access to many key financial reports.

You can generate a number of different reports within the following categories:

- ✔ **Profit & Loss (income statement):** Key reports include
    - A standard report that shows how much the business made or lost during a specific period of time
    - A detailed report that includes all the year-to-date transactions
    - A report that compares year-to-date figures with the previous year (provided you kept the accounts by using the computerized system in the previous year)
- ✔ **Income and Expenses:** Key reports include
    - Income by customer (both a summary and a detailed report)
    - Expenses by vendor (both a summary and a detailed report)

- ✔ **Balance Sheet:** Key reports include

    - A standard balance sheet that shows a summary of assets, liabilities, and equity

    - A detailed report of assets, liabilities, and equity

    - A report that compares the assets, liabilities, and equity levels with those of the previous year

- ✔ **Cash Flow:** Key reports include

    - A statement of cash flows for the year

    - A forecast of cash flows during the next few weeks or months, based on money due in accounts receivable and money to be paid out in accounts payable

Computerized accounting systems provide you with the tools to manipulate your business's numbers in whatever way you find useful for analyzing your business's results. And if a particular report isn't quite right for your needs, you can customize it. For example, if you want to see the profit and loss results for a particular week during an accounting period, you can set the dates for only that week and generate the report. You can also produce a report looking at data for just one day, one month, one quarter, or any combination of dates.

You can also take the time to custom-design reports that meet your business's unique financial information needs. Many businesses customize reports to collect information by department or division. You're limited only by your imagination!

While you, the bookkeeper, work with your computerized system, various people, including the business owner, will ask you for information that you can't easily find by using standardized reports. The first few times you pull that information together, you may need to do so manually. But when you get used to your computerized accounting system and its report functions, you can design customized reports that pull together information in just the way you need it.

You have the option to export financial reports from QuickBooks to a popular worksheet software application with a click of the mouse. By clicking the Export button at the top of your trial balance report (refer to Figure 16-3), you get the report in worksheet format on your computer screen, including formulas and formatting. This worksheet can be saved on your computer, and you can then use the capabilities of the worksheet software to prepare additional reports. The exported worksheet also contains a page of QuickBooks Export Tips. You can save a great deal of time when you prepare customized reports by using this export feature.

Chapter 17

Adjusting the Books

. . . .

In This Chapter

▶ Making adjustments for cash and non-cash transactions

▶ Taking your adjustments for a trial (balance) run

▶ Adding accounts to and deactivating accounts on the Chart of Accounts

▶ Making adjustments in QuickBooks

. . . .

During an accounting period, your bookkeeping duties focus on your business's day-to-day transactions. When it comes time to report those transactions in financial statements, you must make some adjustments to your books. Your financial reports are supposed to show your business's financial health, so your books must reflect any significant transactions that have occurred — even ones that haven't yet been recorded because the transaction doesn't involve the exchange of cash. You must also make adjustments to the book value of some of your assets that have been used up or that have lost some value.

This chapter reviews the types of adjustments that you need to make to the books before preparing the financial statements, including calculating asset depreciation, dividing up prepaid expenses, updating inventory numbers, dealing with bad debt, and recognizing salaries and wages that your business hasn't yet paid. You can also find out how to add and deactivate accounts.

Adjusting All the Right Areas

Even after testing your books by using the trial balance process that we explain in Chapter 16, you still need to make some adjustments before you can prepare accurate financial reports with the information you have. These adjustments don't involve the exchange of cash, but rather deal with recognizing the use of assets, loss of assets, increases in expenses, or future asset obligations that aren't reflected in day-to-day bookkeeping activities.

The key areas in which you likely need to adjust the books include

- **Asset depreciation:** To recognize the use of assets during the accounting period.

- **Prepaid expenses:** To match a portion of expenses that your business paid at one point during the year but from which your business used benefits throughout the year, such as the cost of an annual insurance premium. You should apportion out the benefit and record an expense each month.

- **Inventory:** To update inventory to reflect what you have on hand.

- **Bad debts:** To acknowledge that some customers will never pay and to adjust accounts receivable.

- **Unpaid salaries and wages:** To recognize salary and wage expenses that your business has incurred but not yet paid.

- **Unpaid services:** To recognize that the business has received some services that it hasn't paid for nor recorded in the books.

- **Unpaid interest:** To recognize that the business has incurred interest expense that it hasn't paid for nor recorded in the books.

- **Accrued revenues:** To recognize the service revenue that the business earned but has not yet recorded or collected.

- **Unearned revenues:** To recognize service revenue that has been earned but for which the business previously recorded unearned revenue when collecting cash from the customer.

Depreciating assets

The largest non-cash expense for most businesses is *depreciation*. Depreciation is an accounting exercise that's important for every business to undertake because it reflects the use and aging of assets. Older assets need more maintenance and repair, and also need to be replaced eventually. While the depreciation of an asset increases and the book value of the asset dwindles, the need for more maintenance or replacement becomes apparent. (For more on depreciation and why you record it, check out Chapter 12.)

The time to actually make this adjustment to the books is when you summarize the books for an accounting period. Recording depreciation expenses every month is best, so that you more accurately track the reduction of the book value of the asset. If you're going to look at your bottom-line results each month, you have to look at the complete picture, which includes all your expenses. Don't leave out the depreciation expenses and just wait until the end of the year when you prepare your annual financial statements to record them. Failing to record this expense from month to month may cause the business owner to think that she's doing much better than expected. Depreciation expenses are typically pretty large, and will result in a big reduction in profits — and a big surprise for the business owner — if left until the very end of the year. However, if you aren't going to prepare financial statements monthly, then making a monthly entry for depreciation expense isn't necessary. A year-end entry will suffice.

Depreciation doesn't involve the use of cash. By accumulating depreciation expenses on an asset, you're reducing the book value of the asset as it appears on the balance sheet (see Chapter 18 for the lowdown on balance sheets).

Readers of your financial statements can get a good idea of the health of your assets by reviewing your accumulated depreciation. If a financial report reader sees that a business's assets are close to being fully depreciated, she knows that the business probably needs to spend significant amounts of cash on replacing or repairing those assets sometime soon. While she evaluates the financial health of the business, she takes that future obligation into consideration before making a decision to loan money to or possibly invest in the business.

Often, you calculate depreciation for accounting purposes by using the *straight-line depreciation method.* This method calculates an equal depreciation amount for each year, based on the anticipated useful life of the asset. For example, suppose your business purchases a car for business purposes that costs $25,000. You anticipate the car will have a useful lifespan of five years and will be worth $5,000 after five years. By using the straight-line depreciation method, you subtract $5,000 from the total car cost of $25,000 to find the depreciable value of the car during its five-year useful lifespan ($20,000). Then, you divide $20,000 by 5 to find your depreciation expense for the car ($4,000 per year). When adjusting the assets at the end of each year in the car's five-year lifespan, your entry to the books should look like this:

Account	*Debit*	*Credit*
Depreciation Expense	$4,000	
—Accumulated Depreciation: Vehicles		$4,000

   To record depreciation for vehicles.

This entry increases the Depreciation Expense account, which appears on the income statement (see Chapter 19). The entry also increases the Accumulated Depreciation: Vehicles account (which records the use of the asset), and this account appears on the balance sheet directly under the

Vehicles asset line. The Vehicles asset line always shows the cost of the asset at the time of purchase. By subtracting the accumulated depreciation from the cost, you can show the net book value of the asset. This net figure shows the value of the asset that your business is going to depreciate in the future.

You can speed up depreciation if you believe that your business won't use the asset evenly over its lifespan — specifically, that your business will use the asset more heavily in the early years of ownership. We talk more about alternative depreciation methods in Chapter 12.

Allocating prepaid expenses

Most businesses have to pay certain expenses at the beginning of the year, even though they benefit from that expense throughout the year. Insurance is a prime example of this type of expense. Most insurance companies require you to pay the premiums in advance or make a large instalment payment at the start of the term of the policy.

For example, suppose your business's annual car insurance premium is $1,200. You pay that premium in January in order to maintain insurance coverage throughout the year. Showing the full cash expense of your insurance when you prepare your January financial reports will greatly reduce any profit that month and make your financial results look worse than they actually are. That's no good.

Instead, you record a large prepayment, such as insurance or prepaid rent, as an asset called *Prepaid Expenses,* and then you adjust the value of that asset to reflect your business's use throughout the year. Your $1,200 annual insurance premium is actually valuable to the business for 12 months, so you calculate the actual expense for insurance by dividing $1,200 by 12, giving you $100 per month. At the end of each month, you record the use of that asset by preparing an adjusting entry that looks like this:

Account	*Debit*	*Credit*
Insurance Expenses	$100	
—Prepaid Expenses		$100

To record insurance expenses for the month of March.

This entry increases the Insurance Expenses account on the income statement and decreases the Prepaid Expenses account on the balance sheet. No cash changes hands in this entry because your business laid out cash when it paid the insurance bill, and you increased the asset account Prepaid Expenses at the time your business paid the cash.

Counting inventory

You need to adjust the Inventory balance sheet asset at the end of an accounting period. During the accounting period, when using a manual accounting system, your business buys inventory and records those purchases in a Purchases account without entering any change to inventory. When the business sells the products, you record the sales in the Sales account but don't make any adjustment to the value of the inventory. Instead, you adjust the Inventory value at the end of the accounting period because adjusting it with each purchase and sale would take way too much time. This method of handling inventory is based on a periodic inventory system. You adjust the ending balance of your Inventory asset account to the actual balance on hand and make the corresponding adjustment to the Purchases account. The Inventory asset account holds purchases that are unsold. When adjusted, the Purchases account shows how much inventory was sold. This is the process you follow to arrive at the amount of the cost of goods sold expense for your income statement.

Your business may have invested in a computer system that can keep track of the ins and outs of all your inventory items. In that case, you have a perpetual inventory system. We discuss the periodic and perpetual inventory systems in Chapter 8.

To make the proper adjustments to inventory in your books, follow these steps:

1. **Determine the inventory that your business still has on hand.**

    A perpetual inventory system calculates ending inventory by using the purchases and sales numbers in the books. A periodic system is not capable of keeping track of the purchases and sales of inventory. Either way, you have to do a physical count of inventory to be sure that what's on the shelves matches what's reported as the inventory asset in your books. We show you in Chapter 8 how to generate an inventory listing in QuickBooks that can help you take a physical count of your inventory. You won't be able to generate the listing of inventory items if you use a periodic system.

2. **Set a cost for that inventory.**

    The cost of ending inventory varies, depending on the cost formula that your business uses for valuing inventory. We talk more about inventory cost formulas and how to calculate the value of ending inventory in Chapter 8.

3. **Test the value of inventory against the cost.**

   The original price your business paid for the inventory (its cost), if used as the value to report on the balance sheet, may now be too high. If you determine that your business can't get at least the amount it paid for the inventory on resale, you must reduce the book value (sometimes called the carrying value, or carrying amount) of the inventory. In accounting, this process is referred to as applying the rule of the *lower of cost and net realizable value* for inventory. We discuss this issue and the need for adjustments in Chapter 8.

4. **Adjust the number of pieces remaining in inventory in the Inventory account, and adjust the value of that account based on the information collected in Steps 1, 2, and 3.**

Allowing for bad debts

No business likes to accept the fact that it'll never see the money owed by some of its customers, but in reality, that happens to most businesses that sell items on account. When your business determines that a customer who has bought goods or services on account isn't likely to pay for them, you record the writeoff of that account. After you record the writeoff, you may have other accounts receivable you won't collect. (For an explanation of sales on account, check out Chapter 9.)

At the end of an accounting period, you list all outstanding customer accounts in an aging report, which we cover in Chapter 9. This report shows which customers owe how much and for how long. After a certain amount of time, you have to admit that some customers likely won't pay. Each business sets its own determination of how long it wants to wait before including that account, or a portion of that account, as a likely writeoff. For example, your business may decide that when a customer is six months late with a payment, you're unlikely to ever see the money. In that case, you may record 100 percent of the account as a bad debt. On the other hand, you may include only 30 percent of the amount owed for accounts that are more than three months overdue in the total estimate of bad debts.

After you determine that some old accounts are likely to go bad, you no longer have to include their book value as part of your assets in the Accounts Receivable account. Including their value doesn't paint a realistic picture of your situation for the readers of your financial reports. Because the account for which you may not be able to collect no longer counts as an asset (at least, not the full amount), you adjust the value of your Accounts Receivable to reflect the loss of some of that asset.

After you calculate the total amount of accounts receivable that are likely bad debts, you can reduce the value of the Accounts Receivable account by that amount. You report this reduced value on the balance sheet. You can leave the accounts receivable in the Accounts Receivable account, as long as you think your business may receive a future collection. You reduce the book value to the realizable value by using an account called *Allowance for Doubtful Accounts*.

You can record the bad debts and increase the Allowance for Doubtful Accounts account in a few ways:

- ✔ **By customer:** Some businesses identify the specific customers whose accounts are likely to become bad debts and calculate the bad-debt expense each accounting period based on specified customers' accounts.

- ✔ **By percentage of total accounts receivable:** Other businesses look at their bad-debts histories and develop percentages that reflect those experiences. Instead of taking the time to identify each specific account that will probably be a bad debt, these businesses record bad debt expenses as a percentage of their Accounts Receivable account.

- ✔ **By percentage of sales:** And still other businesses use a percentage of the amount of sales on account in the year to estimate that year's bad debt expense. The logic in this case is that the more you sell, the more you're likely to experience a bad debt.

However you decide to estimate bad debts, you need to prepare an adjusting entry at the end of each accounting period to record bad-debt expenses and increase your Allowance for Doubtful Accounts account. Here's an adjusting entry that records bad-debt expenses of $1,000:

Account	*Debit*	*Credit*
Bad-Debt Expense	$1,000	
—Allowance for Doubtful Accounts		$1,000

To record bad debts for March.

After you have exhausted your collection efforts and your business decides that it won't be able to collect anything for a specific account receivable, you record a writeoff of that particular account. At that point, you use the Allowance for Doubtful Accounts account to absorb this reduction in assets. (We discuss recording your losses in Chapter 9.) Here's a sample writeoff entry:

Account	*Debit*	*Credit*
Allowance for Doubtful Accounts	$200	
—Accounts Receivable		$200

To record the writeoff of the Brown account.

Keep track of any GST/HST you initially charge on a sale that you have to write off. You can now recover that GST/HST. We explain how to record that portion of the accounts receivable in Chapter 9.

You can't have bad-debt expenses if you don't sell to your customers on account. You need to worry about bad debt only if you offer your customers the convenience of buying your products on account.

Also keep in mind that although you have written off an account receivable, you can still take measures to try to collect the owed money. If the amount of the account is large enough, a collection agency may take it on. You can expect the agency to give their best efforts, but you should also be ready to share the cash they ultimately collect, 50-50. Some businesses may find this cost to be steep, but after all, you have already given up on the account receivable, so any money collected by the agency is a windfall.

Recognizing unpaid salaries and wages

Not all pay periods fall at the end of a month. If you pay your employees every two weeks, you may end up closing the books at the end of a month or year in the middle of a pay period. So, for example, you may not pay employees for the last week of March until the end of the first week of April.

When your pay period hits before the end of the month, you need to make an adjusting entry to record the payroll expense that your business has incurred but hasn't yet paid to the employees. You estimate the amount of the adjustment based on what you pay every two weeks. In the case of our example, you accrue an expense in the amount of half of your payroll. The accrual causes the payroll cost for two weeks to be split between two accounting periods. At the end of March, you increase the expense for the accrual in the appropriate amount. When the business actually pays out the cash for payroll, in April, you then take into account your accrual entry made at the end of March. The cash paid to employees is paying for one week's work done in April, charged to the Wages and Salaries Expense account, and one week's work for the wages payable accrued at the end of March. For our example, the expense to accrue is in the amount of $3,000, so you make the following adjusting entry to the books to show the accrual:

Account	Debit	Credit
Wages and Salaries Expense	$3,000	
—Accrued Wages Payable		$3,000

To accrue payroll expenses for the last week of March.

This adjusting entry increases both the Wages and Salaries Expense account, which you report on the income statement, and the Accrued Wages Payable account, which appears as a liability on the balance sheet. When you finally do pay out the salaries and wages, along with the week's pay for the first week in April, you reduce the amount in Accrued Wages Payable by using the following entry:

Account	Debit	Credit
Accrued Wages Payable	$3,000	
Wages and Salaries Expense	$3,000	
—Cash		$6,000

To record April payroll.

As we mention earlier in this section, this first payroll in April is paying employees for the last week in March and the first week in April.

These extra entries may seem like a lot of work, but if you don't match the payroll expenses for March with the revenues for March, your income statement doesn't reflect the actual state of your affairs. Your revenues at the end of March would look very good because you didn't fully reflect your salary and wage expenses in the income statement, but your April income statement would look very bad because it would include the extra expenses that your business actually incurred in March.

Accruing for unpaid services

Some services, such as utilities (hydro, water, and heat), don't bill you every month, and when they do bill you, the period of services for which they're billing likely doesn't align with the end of the month. In these cases, you need to estimate and record these expenses in the books as a period-end adjustment.

For example, say that the hydro company bills you for two months at a time (which it probably does). The end of the last billing period falls right in the middle of the month (the middle of February), and the amount of the bill is $800. Now, at the end of March, you want to record an *accrual* — an expense for which an invoice has not been received by the end of an accounting cycle. You can come up with a rough estimate of the amount to accrue. Just divide $800 (the amount owed for two months) by 2 (the number of months) to get $400 per month. Now, multiply that $400 by 1½ (representing a month and a half, from the middle of February to the end of March) to get $600. Here's the entry you'd make in this situation:

Account	Debit	Credit
Utilities Expense	$600	
—Accounts Payable		$600

To accrue hydro expense for the months of February and March.

Your accrual adjusting entry increases your Utilities Expense account on your Income statement with a debit, causing your profit to decrease. Your Accounts Payable account, a liability on the balance sheet, increases with a credit.

Accruing for unpaid interest

In Chapter 13, we discuss how to calculate interest that you earn or pay on money you have borrowed or lent out. Now imagine that your business borrows money and signs a promissory note with your bank. The note calls for the business to make an interest payment every three months. But just because the payments are delayed a few months doesn't mean that you don't have an expense right away. The interest expense is adding up every minute of every day. You don't necessarily think about it that way, but when it comes time to make any necessary adjustments to your trial balance before you prepare your financial statement, you need to account for any interest you may owe.

In this example, the amount of interest the business must pay every three months is $300. The first interest payment is due on April 30. The next payment is due on July 31. At the end of May, you need to recognize that you have an expense for one month's worth of interest in the amount of $100 ($300 divided by three months), as well as a liability to the bank in the same amount.

You record the interest accrual at the end of May as follows:

Account	Debit	Credit
Interest Expense	$100	
—Interest Payable		$100

To accrue interest on promissory note for the month of May.

With this accrual adjusting entry, your Interest Expense account on your income statement increases with a debit, and your Interest Payable account, a liability on the balance sheet, increases with a credit.

Accruing for revenue

As we point out earlier in this chapter, you record accruals so that expenses are reported in the correct accounting period, so that your income statement paints a complete picture of all the expenses that you paid or will pay. Accrual adjustments take care of the timing difference between when an expense happens and when you pay for that expense.

You also need to make accruals for revenue. You have to report revenue on your income statement when your business earns it, not just when you send a bill to a customer for work you did, or when the customer pays your bill. When you're in the business of providing services to customers and the work that you do happens over a long period of time, you'll likely need to record accruals of revenue each month.

Suppose an architect is hired to prepare a set of plans for the construction of a warehouse. He negotiates with his customer to bill the work when he completes the job, after the customer's final approval of his drawings. The job may take several weeks. Even though he has arranged to bill the customer at the end of the job, he's earning his fee as he does the work.

The total price for the work is $1,000, and the architect does some of the work in the month of May and a larger part of the work in June. At the end of May, when it's time to report his income statement, the architect would be remiss if he omitted the revenue earned on this assignment. Using his past experience, he comes up with an estimate of what proportion of the total job was completed by the end of May. He concludes that 30 percent of the job was done in May, so he records an accrual for that revenue as follows:

Account	_Debit_	_Credit_
Account Receivable	$300	
—Service Revenue		$300

To accrue for revenue earned for the month of May ($1,000 × 3 ÷ 10).

The revenue accrual adjusting entry increases the Accounts Receivable account, an asset on the balance sheet, with a debit and increases the Service Revenue account with a credit.

Adjusting for unearned revenue

So far, you have taken care of adjusting your income statement numbers for non-cash transactions. You may also need to record an adjustment for unearned revenue. In the case of unearned revenue, you receive cash up front, before any work happens. We discuss in Chapter 9 how you record the collection of cash and the increase in liability in the Unearned Revenue account on your balance sheet. What you now need to worry about is how much, if any, of the amount collected in cash can be counted as revenue by the time the end of the month comes around.

Using the architect example from the preceding section (where we explain how to accrue revenue), suppose, instead, that the architect demands a deposit on the work before starting the job. The architect asks for $500 — half of the total amount of $1,000. Because none of the work has been done at this point, he can't say that the $500 represents revenue. He must wait. The question then becomes, How long does he have to wait? Well, it depends.

Bookkeepers for businesses that often collect deposits and deliver services very quickly usually assume that by the end of the month the deposits will turn out to be revenue. For the sake of expediency, the architect decides in this case to record the collection of the cash as Service Revenue right away. He records the $500 when received, the same as he would for a cash sale, as follows:

Account	Debit	Credit
Cash	$500	
—Service Revenue		$500

To record cash collected for service revenue in April.

But the architect can't get too happy just yet. Our favourite expression is "Don't count your chickens before they hatch." He has made an assumption that the work and, consequently, the service he's giving his customer will be done and over with by the end of the month of May. When he gets to the end of May, he must check that he is correct in this assumption.

At the end of the month, he needs to come up with an adjustment to Unearned Revenue. Using his past experience, he estimates the proportion of the total job completed by the end of May is 30 percent, and so $300 ($1,000 × 3 ÷ 10) can be recorded as an increase in Service Revenue with a credit. Because he has already collected $500 cash, which is greater than the value of the work that's been done, he leaves behind $200 of revenue that hasn't yet been earned in the Unearned Revenue account. The architect records the following at the end of May:

Account	Debit	Credit
Unearned Revenue	$300	
—Service Revenue		$300

To reduce Unearned Revenue for the amount of revenue earned in May.

Keep a close eye on the Unearned Revenue account in your General Ledger. If you seldom collect deposits for doing work, you won't have a problem remembering which customers the unearned revenue belongs to.

Testing Out an Adjusted Trial Balance

In Chapter 16, we explain why and how you run a trial balance on the accounts in your General Ledger. Adjustments to your books call for another trial balance, the *adjusted trial balance,* to ensure that your adjustments are correct and ready for you to post to the General Ledger.

You track all the adjusting entries on a worksheet similar to the one discussed in Chapter 16. You need to create this worksheet only if you're doing your books manually. You don't need to worry about it if you're using a computerized accounting system, because the bookkeeping software does most of the work for you.

The key difference in the worksheet for the adjusted trial balance, as compared to the manual worksheet we discuss in Chapter 16, is that you must add four additional columns to the worksheet, for a total of 11 columns:

- **Column 1:** Account Titles. With account numbers, if available.

- **Columns 2 and 3:** Unadjusted Trial Balance. The trial balance before you make the adjustments; Column 2 for debits and Column 3 for credits.

- **Columns 4 and 5:** Adjustments. You list all adjustments to the trial balance in Column 4 for debits and Column 5 for credits.

- **Columns 6 and 7:** Adjusted Trial Balance. Calculate a new trial balance that includes all the adjustments. Be sure that the credits equal the debits when you total each new trial balance. If they don't, find any errors before you add entries to the Balance Sheet and Income Statement columns.

- **Columns 8 and 9:** Income Statement. Column 8 includes all the income statement accounts that have a debit balance, and Column 9 includes all the income statement accounts that have a credit balance.

- **Columns 10 and 11:** Balance Sheet. Column 10 includes all the balance sheet accounts that have a debit balance, and Column 11 includes all the balance sheet accounts that have a credit balance.

After you feel confident that all the accounts are in balance, post your adjustments to the General Ledger so that all the balances in the General Ledger include the adjusting entries. By including the adjustments, you make the General Ledger match the financial statements that you prepare.

Changing Your Chart of Accounts

After you finalize your General Ledger for the year, you may want to make changes to your Chart of Accounts, which lists all the accounts in your accounting system generally in the numerical order of the assigned account numbers to each General Ledger account. (For the full story on the Chart of Accounts, refer to Chapter 3.) You may need to add accounts if you think you need additional ones or deactivate accounts if you think your business no longer needs them. QuickBooks allows you to deactivate accounts but you can't delete accounts that have had any transactions. You are prevented from deleting accounts for reasons of internal control. The Canada Revenue Agency requires you to retain permanent records of all transactions for seven years. You can only deactivate an account which has not been used in the current year. Deactivation only means that the account does not appear in the Chart of Accounts. You can make the account active again at a later date, if you need to use the account again.

Deactivate accounts from your Chart of Accounts only at the end of the year. If you deactivate an account in the middle of the year, your annual financial statements won't reflect the activities in that account prior to its deactivation. So, even if you decide halfway through the year to no longer use an account, you should leave it on the books until the end of the year, and then deactivate it.

You can add accounts to your Chart of Accounts throughout the year, but if you decide to add an account in the middle of the year in order to more closely track certain assets, liabilities, revenues, or expenses, you may need to adjust some related entries.

Suppose you start the year by tracking paper expenses in the Office Supplies Expenses account, but paper usage and its expense keep increasing, so you decide to track the expense in a separate account beginning in July. First, you add the new account, Paper Expenses, to your Chart of Accounts. Then, you prepare an adjusting entry to move all the paper expenses that you recorded for the year to date in the Office Supplies Expenses account to the Paper Expenses account. In the interest of space and to avoid boring you, we give you an abbreviated adjusting entry. In your actual entry, you may want to detail the specific dates that your business bought paper as an office supplies expense, rather than just tally one summary total. Here's a simplified adjusting entry:

Account	Debit	Credit
Paper Expenses	$1,000	
—Office Supplies Expenses		$1,000

To move expenses for paper from the Office Supplies Expenses account to the Paper Expenses account.

Moving beyond the catch-all
Miscellaneous Expenses account

When bookkeepers add new accounts to the Chart of Accounts, they most commonly adjust the Miscellaneous Expenses account. In many cases, you may expect to incur an expense only one or two times during the year, so you don't need to create a new account specifically for that expense. But after a while, you may find that your so-called rare expense is adding up, so you designate an account for that expense because you now feel that keeping track of that expense in the books is necessary. Now, you need to create some adjusting entries to move expenses out of the Miscellaneous Expenses account.

For example, suppose you think your business needs to rent a car only one time before it buys a new vehicle, so you enter the rental cost in the books as a miscellaneous expense. However, after renting cars three times, you decide to start a Rental Expense account mid-year. When you add the Rental Expense account to your Chart of Accounts, you need to use an adjusting entry to transfer any car-rental expenses incurred and recorded in the Miscellaneous Expenses account prior to the creation of the new account.

Using the QuickBooks General Journal

When you record adjusting entries at the end of any reporting period, none of those entries involve cash. If you use QuickBooks, you enter these transactions in the General Journal. (You also use the General Journal to record error corrections.)

To access the General Journal in QuickBooks, select Company from the top menu bar and then click Make General Journal Entries, as shown in Figure 17-1.

Figure 17-2 provides an example of the year-end adjusting journal entry that records depreciation on a business's vehicle. In the Memo column, the Make General Journal Entries page allows you to enter a short narrative explanation of the entry.

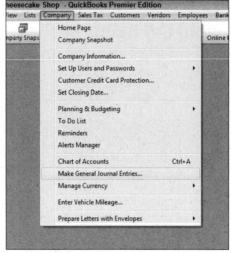

Figure 17-1:
You can access the Make Journal Entries command from the Company menu bar item.

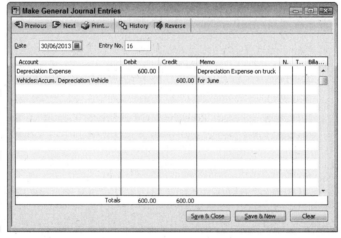

Figure 17-2:
A General Journal entry that records the depreciation expense on a vehicle.

Part V
Reporting Results and Starting Over

The 5th Wave   By Rich Tennant

"Cooked books? Let me just say you could serve this profit and loss statement with a fruity Zinfandel and not be out of place."

In this part . . .

*I*t's time to show off all the hard work that you and your employees have put into keeping your business operating and making a profit. This part explains how to use all the information that you've collected throughout the accounting period to prepare financial reports that give investors, lenders, vendors, government agencies, and your business's employees a clear picture of how well your company did during the month, the quarter, or the year.

This part also covers the year-end government reports, as well as forms that you must file with the CRA. Finally, we guide you through the process of closing out the books at year-end and getting ready for the next year.

Chapter 18

Developing a Balance Sheet

. . . .

In This Chapter

▶ Breaking down the balance sheet

▶ Pulling together your balance sheet accounts

▶ Choosing a balance sheet format

▶ Drawing conclusions from your balance sheet

▶ Polishing electronically produced balance sheets

. . . .

*P*eriodically, you want to know where your business stands. Therefore, at the end of each accounting period, you take a snapshot of your business's condition. This snapshot, which is called a *balance sheet* (or sometimes called a *statement of financial position*), gives you a picture of where your business stands — how much it has in assets, how much it owes in liabilities, and how much the owners have invested in the business at a particular point in time.

This chapter explains the key ingredients of a balance sheet and tells you how to pull them all together. You can also find out how to use some analytical tools called ratios to see how well your business is doing.

What Is a Balance Sheet?

Basically, creating a balance sheet is like taking a picture of the financial aspects of your business.

You put the business name, the title of the statement, and the ending date for the accounting period on which you're reporting at the top of the balance sheet.

Insert the proper name of the business in the titles of your financial statements. When outside readers look at your reports, they want to know who they're dealing with, and your business's name tells them a lot. For example, an incorporated business has one of the following at the end of its name: Limited (Ltd.), Corporation (Corp.), or Incorporated (Inc.).

Although a balance sheet doesn't tell the whole story about a business, it gives the outside readers some idea of the business's financial position and how it's financed at a particular point in time. For example, a bank needs to decide whether to lend your business some money. Your balance sheet reveals that you already owe a lot of money to other banks and mortgage companies, and so the bank decides that your business is too high a risk and declines your loan request. Here's another example: An outside reader may be someone interested in buying your business. In this case, the reader looks at the balance sheet to help determine the value of the business so that she can decide on a fair purchase price.

The rest of the report summarizes

- ✔ **The business's assets:** Including everything the business owns in order to stay in operation

- ✔ **The business's debts:** Including any outstanding bills and loans that the business must pay

- ✔ **The owners' equity:** Basically, how much the business owners have invested directly and indirectly in the business

Assets, liabilities, and equity probably sound familiar — they're the key elements that show whether your books are in balance. If your liabilities plus equity equal assets, your books are in balance. All your bookkeeping efforts are an attempt to keep the books in balance based on this equation, which we talk about in Chapter 2.

Gathering Balance Sheet Ingredients

You can find most of the information you need to prepare a balance sheet on your adjusted trial balance, which you can get from your worksheet or from running a trial balance with your computerized accounting system after you have calculated and recorded any necessary adjusting journal entries. (We show you how to develop a trial balance in Chapter 16 and how to adjust that trial balance in Chapter 17.)

To keep this example somewhat simple, we assume that the fictitious business H.G.'s Cheesecake Shop has no adjustments for the balance sheet as of June 30, 2013. In the real world, every business needs to adjust something (you usually need to record depreciation) every month, at a minimum.

To prepare the balance sheet illustrations in this chapter, we use the key accounts listed in Table 18-1; these accounts and dollar amounts come from a hypothetical H.G.'s Cheesecake Shop's trial balance.

Table 18-1	Balance Sheet Accounts
Account Name	*Balance in Account*
Cash	$2,500
Petty Cash	500
Accounts Receivable	1,000
Inventory	1,200
Equipment	5,050
Vehicles	30,000
Furniture	5,600
Accumulated Depreciation	(5,000)
Accounts Payable	2,200
Bank Line of Credit	2,600
Bank Loans Payable	18,650
H.G., Capital	17,400

Dividing and listing your assets

The first part of the balance sheet is the Assets section. The first step in developing this section involves dividing your assets into two categories: current assets and non-current assets.

Placing the accounts from your trial balance (refer to Chapter 16) into groups onto your balance sheet is called *classification*. After you give the proper classification to the individual accounts, you can organize your financial statements into groups of accounts, which enables you to create subtotals (such as current assets) on your balance sheet. These key subtotals allow you and your readers to make a quick comparison to other figures or subtotals within a financial statement or to another financial statement.

For example, an owner may compare the amount of profit on the income statement to the total equity appearing on his business's balance sheet to decide whether he's getting enough of a financial reward or return (profit) for his investment (equity). (We show you how to perform this calculation in Chapter 19.)

The grouping of current and non-current assets and liabilities on the balance sheet is the most valuable classification provided to outside readers. The reader can compare current assets to current liabilities to quickly and easily measure your business's liquidity. In turn, your business's liquidity is defined as your business's ability to pay the debts and liabilities that are due in the next 12 months (current liabilities) with the current assets. We show you how to calculate some key liquidity ratios later on in this chapter.

Current assets

Current assets are things your business owns that you can easily convert to cash and that you expect to use in the next 12 months to pay your bills, your employees, and any other debt that comes due. Current assets include cash, *accounts receivable* (money due from customers), short-term investments (including money market mutual funds, share, and bond investments), inventory, and prepaid expenses. (We cover cash in Chapter 14, accounts receivable in Chapter 9, inventory in Chapter 8, and prepaid expenses in Chapter 17.)

The Cash line item on a balance sheet includes what you have on hand in the cash register, as a float; what you have in the bank, including chequing accounts and savings accounts; and what's in your petty cash box. In most cases, you simply list all these accounts as one item, Cash, on the balance sheet.

H.G.'s Cheesecake Shop's current assets are

> Cash $2,500
>
> Petty Cash $500
>
> Accounts Receivable $1,000
>
> Inventory $1,200

The bookkeeper totals the Cash and Petty Cash accounts, giving her $3,000, which she lists on the balance sheet as a line item called Cash.

Non-current assets

Non-current assets are things your business owns that you expect to have for more than 12 months. Non-current assets include land, buildings, equipment, furniture, vehicles, and anything else that you expect to have for longer than a year.

H.G.'s Cheesecake Shop's non-current assets are

Equipment	$5,050
Vehicles	$30,000
Furniture	$5,600
Less: Accumulated Depreciation	($5,000)

Most businesses have more items in the Property, Plant, and Equipment category in the non-current assets section of a balance sheet than H.G.'s Cheesecake Shop. For example, a manufacturing business that has a lot of tools, dies, or moulds created specifically for its manufacturing processes would have a line item called Tools, Dies, and Moulds in this asset group on its balance sheet.

Similarly, if your business owns one or more buildings, you should have a line item labelled Land and another labelled Buildings. And if you lease equipment under certain conditions that resemble a purchase, you classify that equipment as Equipment under Capital Lease.

Some businesses lease their business space and then spend a lot of money fixing that space up. For example, a restaurant may rent a large space and then furnish it according to a desired theme. Money spent on fixing up the space becomes an asset called Leasehold Improvements that you list on the balance sheet in the Property, Plant, and Equipment category of non-current assets.

Everything we've mentioned so far in this section — land, buildings, capitalized leases, leasehold improvements, and so on — is a *tangible asset,* which is an item that you can actually touch or hold. Another type of non-current asset is the intangible asset. *Intangible assets* aren't physical objects; common examples are patents, copyrights, and trademarks (all of which are rights granted by the government). Besides these intangible assets, you may also own goodwill. All intangibles assets are useful to the business in earning revenue and have the following descriptions:

✔ **Patents:** Give businesses the right to dominate the markets for patented products. When a patent expires, competitors can enter the marketplace for the product that was patented, and the competition helps to lower the price for consumers. For example, pharmaceutical companies patent all their new drugs and therefore are protected as the sole providers of those drugs. When your doctor prescribes a brand-name drug, you're getting a patented product. Generic drugs are products whose patents have run out, meaning that any pharmaceutical business can produce and sell its own version of essentially the same product.

✔ **Copyrights:** Protect original works — including books, magazines, articles, newspapers, television shows, movies, music, poetry, and plays — from being copied by anyone other than their creators. For example, this book is copyrighted, so no one can make a copy of any of its contents without the permission of the publisher, John Wiley & Sons, Inc.

✔ **Trademarks:** Give companies ownership of distinguishing words, phrases, symbols, or designs. For example, check out this book's cover to see the registered trademark, *For Dummies,* for this brand. Trademarks can last forever, as long as a business continues to use the trademark and files the proper paperwork periodically with the governments in the countries in which it operates. Consequently, because this type of asset can have a limitless useful life, you may not record any depreciation or amortization.

✔ **Goodwill:** Exists only in relation to a business as a whole. A bookkeeper records goodwill in the books only if someone has purchased the business. Goodwill is somewhat of a specialized asset and has some unique accounting rules surrounding it. If it comes up in your Chart of Accounts, consult your business's accountant to find out what you need to know to properly deal with it.

In order to show in financial statements that the book values of non-current assets reduce over time, you either depreciate or amortize them. You depreciate tangible assets in the category of Property, Plant, and Equipment, with the exception of land; refer to Chapter 12 for details on how to depreciate. You amortize intangible assets, such as patents and copyrights (amortization is very similar to depreciation). Each patent or copyright asset has a lifespan based on the number of years the government grants the rights for it. After recording an initial cost for the intangible asset, a business then divides that cost by the number of years it has government protection and writes the resulting amount off each year as an amortization expense, which appears on the income statement. If, for some reason, the business doesn't feel like the asset will be useful during all of its legal life, then you reduce the amount of years used in the calculation to a lower, more reasonable number. You place the sum of the amortization or depreciation expenses that your business has written off to expense during the life of the asset on the balance sheet in a line item called Accumulated Depreciation or Accumulated Amortization (whichever is appropriate for the type of asset).

Acknowledging your debts

The Liabilities section of the balance sheet comes after the Assets section (see the section "Dividing and listing your assets," earlier in this chapter) and shows all the money that your business owes to others, including banks, vendors, governments, financial institutions, mortgage companies, or individuals. Like assets, you divide your liabilities into two categories on the balance sheet:

- ✔ **Current Liabilities:** All bills and debts that you plan to pay within the next 12 months. Accounts appearing in this section include any demand Bank Loan for an operating line of credit, Accounts Payable (bills due to vendors and others), Credit Cards Payable, all the Payroll Withholding Liability accounts, and the current portion of any long-term debt (for example, if you have a mortgage on your store, the amount of any principal payments due in the next 12 months appear in the Current Liabilities section).

  Whenever a business has a demand bank loan, the business has to include the unpaid principal balance of this loan with current liabilities. (With a *demand bank loan*, if at any time the bank doesn't feel comfortable with your financial position or if you overstep the limits set down in the loan agreement, the bank can demand a full principal repayment within an extremely short period of time.) Because the business has the looming possibility that it may have to repay this loan balance quickly, accounting rules require that the business groups the loan with current liabilities.

- ✔ **Non-current Liabilities:** All debts you owe to lenders that your business is required to pay with due dates beyond 12 months. Mortgages Payable (for the principal amount due beyond the next 12 months), Loans Payable, and Notes and Bonds Payable are common accounts in the non-current liabilities section of the balance sheet.

Most businesses try to minimize their current liabilities that carry interest charges because the interest rates on short-term loans, such as credit cards, are usually much higher than those on loans that have long terms. While you manage your business's liabilities, always look for ways to minimize your interest payments by seeking long-term loans that have lower interest rates than you can get on a credit card or short-term loan.

H.G.'s Cheesecake Shop's balance sheet has the following accounts in its liabilities section:

Current Liabilities:

Accounts Payable	$2,200
Bank Line of Credit	$600

Non-current Liabilities:

Bank Loans Payable	$20,650

Naming your owners' investments

Every business has investors. Even a small mom-and-pop grocery store requires money up front to get the business on its feet. You report investments that individuals or other businesses make into the business on the balance sheet as *equity*. The line items that appear in a balance sheet's Equity section vary, depending on whether the business is incorporated. (Businesses incorporate primarily to minimize the owners' personal legal liabilities; we talk more about incorporation in Chapter 21.)

If you're preparing the books for a sole-proprietorship business, the Equity section of your balance sheet should contain a single Capital account for the owner. If the business is a partnership, you need to list a Capital account for each partner, with the partner's name as part of the account title. Capital accounts record all money invested by the owners to start up the business, as well as any additional contributions they make after the start-up phase. You also have a Drawings account for each owner, which tracks all money that each owner takes out of the business during the year. You don't list the Drawing accounts on the balance sheet but you do reduce the Capital account by the amount of the Drawings account to arrive at a net investment by the owner reported on the balance sheet.

For a business that's incorporated, the Equity section of the balance sheet should contain the following accounts, at a minimum:

- ✔ **Common Shares:** Portions of ownership in the business, purchased as investments by business owners. The units of ownership are *shares*. Each share carries a voting right for the owner of the share.

- ✔ **Retained Earnings:** All profits that shareholders have reinvested in the corporation.

Sorting out share investments

You're probably most familiar with the sale of shares on the open market through the various stock market exchanges, such as the Toronto Stock Exchange (TSX). However, not all corporations sell their shares through public exchanges; in fact, most corporations aren't public companies, but rather remain private operations.

Whether public or private, you obtain ownership in a business by buying shares. If the business isn't publicly traded, you buy and sell shares privately. In most small companies, family members and close friends make these share exchanges, as well as outside investors whom the business has approached individually as a means to raise additional money.

Because H.G.'s Cheesecake Shop is a sole proprietorship, a single account appears in the Equity section of its balance sheet:

H.G., Capital $17,400

This amount represents the balance in the owner's Capital account after you close the income statement accounts and the Drawings account at the end of the year. The Capital account increases by the net profit and decreases by any drawings taken by the owner during the year. We discuss closing the income statement accounts for the profit and the closing of the Drawings account in Chapter 22.

Ta-Dah! Pulling Together the Final Balance Sheet

After you group together all your accounts (see the section "Gathering Balance Sheet Ingredients," earlier in this chapter), you're ready to produce a balance sheet. Private businesses usually choose between two common formats for their balance sheets: the Account format or the Report format. The same line items appear in both formats; the only difference is the way in which you lay out the information on the page. Publicly held corporations in Canada now use a third option (as do corporations around the globe), the Statement of Financial Position format, because of the implementation of the International Financial Reporting Standards (IFRS).

Account format

The Account format is a two-column layout that has Assets on one side, and Liabilities and Equity on the other side. Here's how the balance sheet of H.G.'s Cheesecake Shop on June 30, 2013, looks by using the Account format:

H.G.'s Cheesecake Shop
Balance Sheet
June 30, 2013

Current Assets		*Current Liabilities*	
Cash	$3,000	Accounts payable	$2,200
Accounts receivable	1,000	Bank loan payable	600
Inventory	1,200		
Total current assets	$5,200	*Total current liabilities*	*$2,800*
Non-current Assets		*Non-current Liabilities*	
Equipment	$5,050	Loans payable	$20,650
Furniture	5,600	Total liabilities	$23,450
Vehicles	30,000		
Accumulated Depreciation	(5,000)	**Equity**	
Total non-current assets	$35,650	H.G., capital	$17,400
Total assets	$40,850	Total liabilities and equity	$40,850

Report format

The Report format is a one-column layout that shows assets first, then liabilities, and then equity.

Here's the balance sheet of H.G.'s Cheesecake Shop on June 30, 2013, using the Report format:

H.G.'s Cheesecake Shop
Balance Sheet
June 30, 2013

Current Assets		
Cash	$3,000	
Accounts receivable	1,000	
Inventory	<u>1,200</u>	
—Total current assets		$5,200
Non-current Assets		
Equipment	$5,050	
Furniture	5,600	
Vehicles	30,000	
Accumulated Depreciation	<u>(5,000)</u>	
—Total non-current assets		<u>$35,650</u>
—Total assets		<u>$40,850</u>
Current Liabilities		
Accounts payable		$2,200
Bank line of credit		<u>600</u>
—Total current liabilities		$2,800
Non-current Liabilities		
Bank loans payable		<u>$20,650</u>
—Total liabilities		$23,450
Equity		
H.G., capital		<u>$17,400</u>
—Total liabilities and owner's equity		<u>$40,850</u>

Alternate format

Canadian corporations that have stock traded on any of the public exchanges, including the TSX, have the choice to use a third balance sheet format — the Statement of Financial Position format. This alternate format is consistent with the format used by many publicly traded companies in the vast majority of countries around the world that follow International Financial Reporting Standards (IFRS). The format shows the same content as the two formats we describe in the preceding sections, but the sequence of the groups of accounts is different — in each of the asset and liability sections, the order is reversed so that the non-current line items appear before the current ones. You may hear some Canadian accountants refer to this format as the *inverted format*.

Putting Your Balance Sheet to Work

With a complete balance sheet in your hands, you can analyze the numbers through a series of ratio tests to check your cash status and track your debt. Because banks and potential investors use these types of tests to determine whether to loan money to or invest in your business, run these tests yourself before you seek loans or investors. Ultimately, the ratio tests we cover in the following sections can help you determine whether your business is in a strong cash position.

Testing your liquidity

When you approach a bank or other financial institution for a loan, you can expect the lender to use two ratios to test your liquidity position: the current ratio and the acid test ratio (also known as the *quick ratio*). A business has a good liquidity position when it can show that it has the ability to pay off its bills when they're due without experiencing a serious cash crunch.

Current ratio

This ratio compares your current assets to your current liabilities. It provides a quick glimpse of your business's ability to pay its bills.

The formula for calculating the current ratio is

Current assets ÷ Current liabilities = Current ratio

The following equation calculates the current ratio for H.G.'s Cheesecake Shop:

$5,200 ÷ $2,800 = 1.86

Lenders usually look for current ratios of 1.20 to 2.00, so any bank would consider a current ratio of 1.86 a good sign. A current ratio less than 1.00 is considered a danger sign because it indicates the business doesn't have enough current assets to pay its current bills.

A current ratio greater than 2.00 may indicate that your business isn't investing its assets well and may be able to make better use of its current assets. For example, if your business holds a lot of cash, you may want to invest that money in some non-current assets, such as additional equipment, that you need to help grow the business.

Acid test (quick) ratio

The acid test ratio uses only the financial figures in your business's Cash, Short-Term Investments, and Accounts Receivable accounts. Although the acid test ratio is similar to the current ratio in that it examines current assets and liabilities, the acid test ratio is a stricter test of your business's liquidity. The assets part of this calculation doesn't include inventory because you can't always convert inventory to cash as quickly as other current assets and because, in a slow market, selling your inventory may take a while.

Many lenders prefer the acid test ratio when determining whether to give you a loan because of this ratio's strictness.

Follow these steps to calculate your business's acid test ratio:

1. **Determine your quick assets.**

   Cash + Short-term investments + Accounts receivable = Quick assets

2. **Calculate your quick ratio.**

   Quick assets ÷ Current liabilities = Quick ratio

The following calculations give you an example of an acid test ratio:

$3,000 + $1,000 = $4,000 (quick assets)

$4,000 ÷ $2,800 = 1.43 (acid test ratio)

Lenders consider a business that has an acid test ratio around 1.0 to be in good condition. An acid test ratio less than 1.0 indicates that the business may have to sell some of its short-term investments or take on additional debt until it can sell more of its inventory.

Assessing your debt

Before you even consider whether to take on additional debt, you should always check out your present debt condition. One common ratio that you can use to assess your business's debt position is the *debt to equity ratio*. This ratio compares what your business owes to what your business owns.

Follow these steps to calculate your debt to equity ratio:

1. **Calculate your total debt.**

   Current liabilities + Non-current liabilities = Total debt

2. **Calculate your debt to equity ratio.**

   Total debt ÷ Equity = Debt to equity ratio

The following calculation gives you the debt to equity ratio for H.G.'s Cheesecake Shop on June 30, 2013:

$2,200 + $600 + $20,650 = $23,450 (total debt)

$23,450 ÷ $15,500 = 1.35 (debt to equity ratio)

Lenders like to see a debt to equity ratio close to 1.0 because it indicates that the amount of debt is equal to the amount of equity. Because H.G.'s Cheesecake Shop has a debt to equity ratio of 1.35, most banks probably wouldn't loan it any money until either it lowered its debt levels or the owners put more money into the business.

Generating Balance Sheets Electronically

If you use a computerized accounting system, you can take advantage of its report function to automatically generate your balance sheets. These balance sheets give you quick snapshots of the business's financial position, but they may require adjustments before you prepare your financial statement for external use.

One key adjustment you'll likely have to make involves your Inventory account. If you're using a periodic inventory system, your computer software isn't keeping track of all the ins and outs of the purchases and sales transactions involving your inventory. You must adjust your Inventory balance sheet account to the amount left on hand after you do a physical count. We discuss how to do a physical count of inventory in Chapter 8.

Chapter 19

Producing an Income Statement

*W*ithout one very important financial report tool, you'd never know for sure whether your business made a profit. This tool is called the *income statement,* and most businesses prepare one on a monthly basis, as well as quarterly and annually, in order to get feedback on how well the business is doing financially.

Analyzing the income statement and the details behind it can reveal a lot of useful information that can help you make decisions to immediately improve your profits and your business overall. This chapter covers the parts of an income statement, how you develop one, and examples of how you can use it to make business decisions.

What Is an Income Statement?

Did your business make any money? You can find the answer in your *income statement,* the financial report that summarizes all the sales and revenue activities, costs of producing or buying the goods or services sold, and expenses incurred in order to run the business.

Income statements summarize the financial activities of a business during a particular accounting period (which can be a month, quarter, year, or some other period of time that makes sense for a business's needs).

Often, bookkeepers include three accounting periods on an income statement: the current period and two prior periods. So, a monthly statement shows the current month and the two previous months; a quarterly statement shows the current quarter and the two previous quarters; and an annual statement shows the current year and the two previous years. Providing this much information gives income statement readers a view of the business's earning trends.

Organizing the accounts from your trial balance (refer to Chapter 16) and placing them into groups in your income statement is called *classification*. Deciding which expenses belong in a particular group depends on what you want to emphasize and what the people looking at the financial statement want to see. Although you don't have to, you may choose to classify your business's expenses by either their nature or their function.

The Employee Benefit Costs item on an income statement provides an example of the classification of an expense based on its nature. On the other hand, you can group this expense with others in the more general Administrative Expenses item, classifying the employee benefits costs as an expense, in accordance with their function.

The classification and grouping of accounts allows you to create subtotals that your readers can use to make easy comparisons within a financial statement or with another financial statement. These number comparisons often result in ratios, which managers or bankers, for example, use as tools for analysis because they want a quick measure of the performance of the business. We look at some key ratios in the section "Testing Profits," later in this chapter.

The seven key lines that make up an income statement classified by function are

- **Sales or Revenue:** The total amount of money taken in from selling the business's goods or services. You calculate this amount by totalling all the sales or revenue accounts. You label the top line of the income statement as either Sales or Revenues; either is okay.

- **Cost of Goods Sold:** How much a business spent in order to buy or make the goods that it sold during the accounting period in review. We show you how to calculate cost of goods sold in the section "Finding cost of goods sold," later in this chapter.

- **Gross Profit:** How much a business made before taking into account operations expenses, calculated by subtracting the Cost of Goods Sold figure from the Sales or Revenue figure. Gross profit is a subtotal and doesn't represent an account in the General Ledger.

✔ **Operating Expenses:** How much the business spent on operations. Qualifying expenses include administrative fees, salaries, advertising, utilities, rent, and other operations expenses. You add all the Expense accounts that appear on your income statement to get this total.

✔ **Other Income:** How much a business has earned in rental revenue or interest income from some of its savings or investments.

✔ **Other Expenses:** How much the business spent on financing (in the form of interest costs).

✔ **Profit or Loss:** Whether the business made a profit or loss during the accounting period in review, calculated by subtracting total operating expenses from gross profit, adding any other income, and subtracting other expenses.

Figure 19-1 shows you the kind of detailed income statements (referred to as Profit and Loss statements by QuickBooks) that can be generated automatically in different formats by your QuickBooks software.

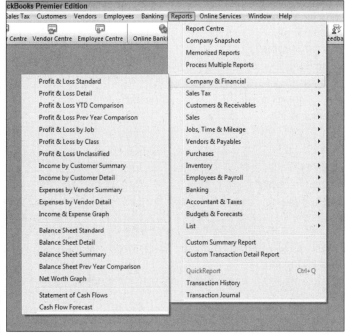

Figure 19-1:
The Company and Financial section of the QuickBooks Reports menu lets you choose from several financial statement formats.

Formatting the Income Statement

Before you actually create your business's income statement, you have to pick a format in which to organize your financial information. You have two options to choose from: the single-step format or the multi-step format. They contain the same information but present it in slightly different ways.

The *single-step format* groups all data into two categories: revenue and expenses. The *multi-step format* divides the income statement into several sections and gives the reader some key subtotals, which make analyzing the data easier.

The single-step format allows readers to calculate the same subtotals that appear in the multi-step format, but those calculations mean more work for the reader. Therefore, most businesses that sell inventory choose the multi-step format to simplify income statement analysis for their external financial-report readers.

Here's an example of a basic income statement prepared in the single-step format for H.G.'s Cheesecake Shop using imaginary amounts:

Revenues		
—Net sales	$28,500	
—Interest income	150	
Total revenues		$28,650
Expenses		
—Cost of goods sold	16,300	
—Depreciation	1,200	
—Rent	1,000	
—Salaries	3,500	
—Supplies	300	
—Interest expense	250	
Total expenses		22,550
Profit		$6,100

Using the same numbers, here's a basic income statement prepared in the multi-step format:

Revenues		
—Net sales	$28,500	
—Cost of goods sold	16,300	
Gross profit		$12,200
Operating expenses		
—Depreciation	1,200	
—Rent	1,000	
—Salaries	3,500	
—Supplies	300	
Total operating expenses		6,000
Profit from operations		6,200
Other income		
—Interest income		150
		6,350
Other expenses		
—Interest expense		250
Profit		$6,100

Preparing the Income Statement

Before you can prepare your income statement, you have to calculate net sales and cost of goods sold by using information that appears on your worksheet, or preferably on the computerized trial balance, which we explain in Chapter 16. For the illustrations that follow, we use the amounts reported on H.G.'s Cheesecake Shop worksheet that appears in Chapter 16.

Finding net sales

Net sales is a total of all your sales minus any sales discounts, returns, and allowances. In order to calculate net sales, you look at the worksheet's line items regarding sales, discounts, and any sales returns and allowances. H.G.'s Cheesecake Shop's worksheet lists Sales of $21,600 and $150 for Sales Returns and Allowances given to customers. To find your net sales, you subtract the sales discounts from your total sales amount; so, H.G.'s Cheesecake Shop has $21,450 net sales.

Finding cost of goods sold

Cost of goods sold is the total amount your business spent to buy or make the goods that you sold. To calculate this amount for a business that buys its finished products from another business in order to sell them to customers, you start with the book value of the business's *opening inventory* (the amount in the Inventory account at the beginning of the accounting period), add all purchases of new inventory (net of any purchase discounts or returns and allowances, and adding freight-in), and then subtract any *ending inventory* (inventory that's still on the store shelves or in the warehouse; it appears on the balance sheet, which we explain in Chapter 18).

The following is a basic cost-of-goods-sold calculation with imaginary amounts:

Opening inventory + Purchases = Goods available for sale

$100 + $1,000 = $1,100

Goods available for sale – Ending inventory = Cost of goods sold

$1,100 – $200 = $900

To simplify the example for calculating cost of goods sold, we assume that the book values for opening inventory (the book value of the inventory at the beginning of the accounting period) and ending inventory (the book value of the inventory at the end of the accounting period) are the same. Refer to Chapter 8 for details about calculating inventory cost formulas. So, to calculate H.G.'s Cheesecake Shop's cost of goods sold, we need only two key lines of its worksheet: the Purchases made and the Purchase Returns and Allowances received to lower the purchase cost:

Purchases – Purchases returns and allowances = Cost of goods sold

$12,300 – $180 = $12,120

Drawing remaining amounts from your worksheet

After you calculate net sales and cost of goods sold (see the preceding sections), you can use the rest of the numbers from your worksheet to prepare the income statement.

Showing three accounting periods on an income statement is standard practice (refer to the section "What Is an Income Statement?" earlier in this chapter), so Table 19-1 shows what an income statement spanning three months looks like (but shows actual numbers for only one month).

Table 19-1	Monthly Income Statement for June 2013, H.G.'s Cheesecake Shop		
Months Ended	*June*	*May*	*April*
Revenues			
—Net sales	$21,450		
—Cost of goods sold	12,120		
Gross profit	9,330		
Operating expenses			
—Automobile expense	370		
—Computer and Internet expenses	220		
—Depreciation expense	600		
—Insurance expense	400		
—Office supplies expense	140		
—Payroll benefits expense	270		
—Rent expense	1,000		
—Salaries and wages expense	3,600		
—Telephone expense	310		
—Utilities expense	450		
Total operating expenses	7,360		
Profit from operations	1,970		
Other expenses			
—Interest expense	70		
Profit	$1,900		

You and anyone else in-house are likely to want to see the type of detail shown in the example in Table 19-1, but most business owners prefer not to show all their operating details to outsiders. Remember, the more information you give to outsiders, the more they know about how your business operates and the more easily they can come up with strategies to compete with your business.

Therefore, consider summarizing the Expense section in income statements that you plan to distribute externally. For external statements, many businesses group all advertising and promotions expenses into one line item and all administrative expenses into another line item.

Gauging your cost of goods sold

Businesses that make their own products, rather than buy them for future sale, must track inventory at three different levels:

- ✔ **Raw Materials:** This line item includes purchases of all items used to make your business's products. For example, a fudge shop buys all the ingredients to make the fudge it sells, so the cost of any inventory on hand that the business hasn't yet used to make fudge should appear in the Raw Materials line item.

- ✔ **Work-in-Process Inventory:** This line item shows the book value of any products that your business is making but can't yet sell. A fudge shop probably wouldn't have anything in this line item, considering fudge doesn't take more than a few hours to make. However, many manufacturing companies take weeks or months to produce products and therefore usually have some portion of the inventory book value in this line item.

- ✔ **Finished-Goods Inventory:** This line item lists the value of inventory that a business has ready for sale. (For a business that doesn't make its own products, Finished-Goods Inventory is the same as the Inventory line item.)

If you keep the books for a business that manufactures its own products, you can use a computerized accounting system to track the various inventory accounts described in the preceding list. However, your basic accounting system software can't cut it — you need an advanced package in order to track multiple inventory types.

Deciphering Gross Profit

Business owners must carefully watch their gross profit trends on monthly income statements. Gross profit trends that appear lower from one month to the next can mean one of two things: Sales revenue is down, or cost of goods sold is up (or both).

If revenue is down month-to-month, you may need to quickly figure out why and fix the problem in order to meet your sales goals for the year. Or, by examining sales figures for the same month in previous years, you may determine that the drop is just a normal sales slowdown given the time of year, so you don't need to hit the panic button.

If a downward profit trend at a particular time of year isn't normal for your business, it may be a sign that a competitor's successfully drawing customers away from your business, or it may indicate that customers are dissatisfied with some aspect of the goods or services you supply. Whatever the reason, preparing a monthly income statement gives you the ammunition you need to quickly find and fix a problem, thereby minimizing any negative hit to your yearly profits.

In addition to sales revenue, cost of goods sold can also be a big factor in a downward profit trend. For example, if the amount you spend to purchase products that you then sell goes up, your gross profit goes down. As a business owner, you need to do one of five things if the costs of goods sold are reducing your gross profit:

- ✔ Find a new supplier who can provide the goods more cheaply.
- ✔ Increase your prices, as long as you don't lose sales because of the increase.
- ✔ Increase your volume of sales so that you can sell more products and meet your annual profit goals.
- ✔ Reduce other expenses to offset the additional product costs.
- ✔ Accept the fact that your annual profit will be lower than expected.

The sooner you find out that you have a problem with costs, the faster you can find a solution and minimize any reduction in your annual profit goals.

Monitoring Expenses

The Expenses section of your income statement gives you a good summary of all the money you spent to keep your business operating that didn't directly relate to the sale of an individual good or service. For example, businesses usually use advertising both to bring customers in and with the hopes of selling many different types of products. So, you should list advertising as an expense, rather than a cost of goods sold. After all, rarely can you link an advertisement to the sale of an individual product. You also can't directly connect the administrative expenses that go into running a business — such as rent, wages and salaries, office costs, and so on — with specific sales.

A business owner watches her expense trends closely to be sure that costs don't creep upwards and lower the business's bottom line. Any cost-cutting that you can do on the expense side can definitely increase your bottom-line profit.

Using the Income Statement to Make Business Decisions

Many business owners compare their income statement trends by using percentages, rather than the actual numbers. You can calculate these percentages easily enough — simply divide each line item by the Net Sales appearing at the top of the income statement. Table 19-2 shows a business's percentage breakdown for one month.

Table 19-2	Monthly Income Statement for June 2013 with Percentage of Net Sales — H.G.'s Cheesecake Shop	
Month Ended	*June*	
Revenues		
—Net sales	$21,450	100.0%
—Cost of goods sold	12,120	56.5%
Gross profit	9,330	43.5%
Operating expenses		
— Automobile expense	370	1.7%
— Computer and Internet expenses	220	1.0%
—Depreciation expense	600	2.8%
—Insurance expense	400	1.9%
—Office supplies expense	140	0.7%
—Payroll benefits expense	270	1.3%
—Rent expense	1,000	4.6%
—Salaries and wages expense	3,600	16.8%
—Telephone expense	310	1.4%

Month Ended	*June*	
—Utilities expense	450	2.1%
Total operating expenses	7,360	34.3%
Profit from operations	1,970	9.2%
Other expenses		
—Interest expense	70	0.3%
Profit	**$1,900**	**8.9%**

Looking at this percentage breakdown, you can see that H.G.'s Cheesecake Shop had a gross profit of 43.5 percent in June, and its cost of goods sold was 56.5 percent. If the prior month's cost of goods sold was only 52 percent, for example, the business owner would need to find out why the cost of the goods used to make his product likely went up. If the owner doesn't take action to change the trend of increasing cost of goods sold, the business will make a lot less profit.

You may want to see how your income statement results compare to industry trends for similar businesses that have similar revenues; this process is called *benchmarking.* By comparing results, you can find out whether your costs and expenses are reasonable for the type of business you operate, and you can identify areas in which you have room to improve your profitability. You also may spot some red flags related to line items for which you spend much more than the average.

You may find locating financial information truly comparable to yours that you can use for benchmarking more difficult than you may expect. The vast majority of small businesses are privately owned, so you don't find their information readily available. Some of the information that you can find concerns businesses that are much larger than yours and can consequently achieve huge economies of scale for some of their expenses. Take any information that you find with a grain of salt and use it only as a guide, rather than a rule.

To obtain industry trends for businesses similar to yours, for a fee, visit www. bizminer.com. To use the statistics tool on this website, select the industry that best matches the one your business operates in, such as Retail: Vehicle Dealers, and review the resulting average profitability and expense percentages for businesses in the same industry.

Testing Profits

With a completed income statement, you can do a number of ratio calculations of your business's profitability. You certainly want to know how well your business did in comparison to other similar businesses. You also want to be able to gauge your *return* on your business.

Three common tests are return on sales (ROS), return on assets (ROA), and return on equity (ROE). These ratios have much more meaning if you can find industry averages for your particular type of business so that you can compare your results.

When you're looking at the profit of a small, owner-managed business, ask yourself this question: Did the owner get paid for her work? Many mom-and-pop operations have few, if any, employees. The owners don't take a salary from the business. Instead, they live off the profits of the business. If that's the case for your business, you need to make some adjustments to the numbers in order to make a comparison with another business that has employees (or vice versa). You want to level out the playing field between the two businesses in your comparison. You can either add a salary to the non-salaried business or reduce the wages and salaries expenses from the business that has employees.

When looking at apparently comparable income statements, watch for another line item: Income Taxes. If one of the businesses is incorporated and therefore must pay income taxes, and the other business isn't incorporated (so it doesn't pay income taxes), you can't compare the results of the two businesses. If you want to compare your unincorporated business with an incorporated one, use that business's subtotal of profit before taxes to make your comparisons (or compare your incorporated business's subtotal with an unincorporated business's total profit).

Return on sales

The return on sales (ROS) ratio tells you how efficiently your business runs its operations. Some accountants and investors use the term *profit margin,* which is essentially the same ratio. Using the information on your income statement, you can measure how much profit your business produced per dollar of sales and how much extra cash you brought in per sale.

You calculate ROS by dividing profit (before income taxes) by net sales. H.G.'s Cheesecake Shop had profit of $1,900 and net sales of $21,600. (If your business isn't a corporation, you don't have to factor in any business income taxes because only corporations pay income taxes. We talk more about business taxes in Chapter 21.) Here's H.G.'s Cheesecake Shop's calculation of ROS:

Profit before income taxes ÷ Net sales = Return on sales

$1,900 ÷ $21,450 = 8.86%

As you can see from this calculation, H.G.'s Cheesecake Shop made around 9 cents on each dollar of sales. To determine whether the ROS that you calculate for your business calls for celebration, you need to find the ROS ratios for similar businesses.

Return on assets

The return on assets (ROA) ratio tests how well your business uses its assets to generate profits. If your business's ROA is the same as or higher than similar companies' ROA ratios, you're doing a good job managing your assets.

To calculate ROA, you divide profit by total assets. H.G.'s Cheesecake Shop has on its balance sheet (which you can find in Chapter 18) and in its worksheet (in Chapter 16) total assets of $40,850. H.G.'s Cheesecake Shop's profit was $1,900. Here's H.G.'s Cheesecake Shop's calculation of ROA:

Profit ÷ Total assets = Return on assets

$1,900 ÷ $40,850 = 4.65%

This calculation shows that H.G.'s Cheesecake Shop made around 4.6 cents or 4.65 percent on each dollar of assets it held.

ROA can vary significantly, depending on the type of industry in which you operate. For example, if your business requires you to maintain a lot of expensive equipment, such as a manufacturing firm, you have a much lower ROA than a service business that doesn't need as many assets. ROA can range from less than 5 percent for manufacturing companies that require a large investment in machinery and factories to as high as 20 percent or even higher for service companies that have few assets.

Return on equity

To measure how successfully your business earned money for its owners or investors, calculate the return on equity (ROE) ratio. This ratio almost always looks better than the return on assets (refer to the preceding section) because ROE doesn't take debt into consideration.

You calculate ROE by dividing profit by shareholders' or owners' equity. The balance of the H.G., Capital account, which represents the only owner's equity on H.G.'s Cheesecake Shop's balance sheet of June 30, 2013, can be obtained by adding the beginning balance of $15,500 and the profit for June of $1,900 to get $17,400. As was the case for the revenue and expense accounts used for preparing the income statement, these amounts appear in the worksheet given in Chapter 16. The following shows H.G.'s Cheesecake Shop's calculation of ROE:

$$\text{Profit} \div \text{Shareholders' or owners' equity} = \text{Return on Equity}$$

$$\$1,900 \div \$17,400 = 10.92\%$$

The ROE for H.G.'s Cheesecake Shop is 2.3 times larger than the ROA, demonstrating a relatively high level of liabilities compared to equity on its balance sheet.

Branching Out with Income Statement Data

The income statement you produce for external use — banks and investors — may look very different from the one that you produce for in-house use by owners or managers. Most business owners prefer to provide the minimum amount of detail necessary to satisfy external users of their financial statements. For instance, they prefer to deliver summaries of expenses, rather than line-by-line expense details; a net sales figure without reporting all the detail about discounts, returns, and allowances; and a cost of goods sold figure without reporting all the detail about how you calculated that figure.

Internally, the contents of the income statement are a very different story. With more detail, a business's managers can better make accurate business decisions. Most businesses develop detailed reports based on the data collected to develop the income statement. Bookkeepers commonly pull items such as discounts, returns, and allowances out of income statements and break them down into further detail:

✓ **Discounts:** Reductions on the retail price as part of a special sale. Discounts may also be in the form of volume discounts provided to customers who buy large amounts of the business's products. For example, a store may offer a 10 percent discount to customers who buy 20 or more of the same item at one time. In order to put their net sales numbers in perspective, business owners and managers must track how much they reduce their revenues to attract sales. We discuss how to track down the amount of volume discounts in Chapter 9.

✔ **Returns and allowances:** Transactions in which a significant reduction in price is granted to resolve a dispute or in which items are returned by your customer for any reason — not the right size, damaged, defective, and so on. If a business's number of returns increases dramatically, a larger problem may be the cause; therefore, business owners need to track these numbers carefully in order to identify and resolve any problems with the items that they sell.

Another section of the income statement that you're likely to break down into more detail for internal use is the Cost of Goods Sold line item. Basically, you present the detail collected to calculate that line item — including beginning inventory, ending inventory, purchases, freight-in costs, purchase discounts, and purchase returns and allowances — in a separate report. (We explain how to calculate the cost of goods sold in the section "Finding cost of goods sold," earlier in this chapter.) We also discuss inventory costs in Chapter 8.

You can generate an unlimited number of internal reports from the detail that goes into your income statement and other financial statements. For example, many businesses design a report that looks at month-to-month trends in revenue, cost of goods sold, and income. In fact, you can set up your computerized accounting system (if you use one) to automatically generate this report and other custom-designed reports. Using your computerized system, you can produce these reports at any time during the month if you want to see how close you are to meeting your month-end, quarter-end, or year-end goal.

Many businesses also design a report that compares actual spending to the budget. On this report, each of the income statement line items appears with its planned budget figures and the actual figures. When you review this report, you flag any line item that's considerably higher or lower than expected, and then research that item to find a reason for the difference.

Figure 19-2 shows the input screen in QuickBooks for entering budget information by month for the next fiscal year's income statement. To access this feature in QuickBooks, click the Company command on the top menu bar, click Planning and Budgeting, and then click Set Up Budgets. After you have entered your budget information, you can generate several reports, including graph depictions of financial performance versus budgets. From the Reports command on the top menu bar, click Budgets and Forecasts to choose from several formats involving the budget information you set up earlier.

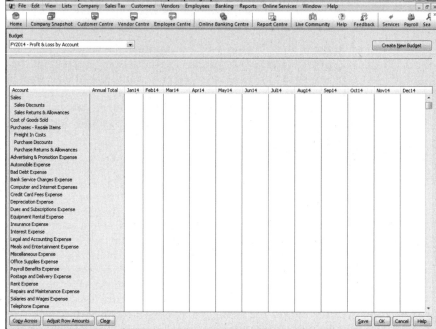

Figure 19-2:
Set up
budgets
with
QuickBooks,
including
profit and
loss by
account.

Chapter 20

Completing Year-End
Payroll and Reports

. . . .

In This Chapter

▶ Mastering employee payroll reporting

▶ Balancing and reconciling annual payroll summaries

. . . .

*E*ven though you diligently file all your monthly or quarterly remittance
vouchers with the federal government throughout the year, you still
have a lot of paperwork to complete at the end of the year. You need to file
forms for each of your employees. Yes, you guessed it — end-of-the-year
government paperwork takes a lot of time. To help make it as painless as possible, though, this chapter reviews the forms you must complete, the information you need for each form, and the process for filing your business's
payroll information return with the federal government.

Year-End Employee Reporting

You may think that you have to do a lot of government paperwork related to
your payroll throughout the year, but you haven't seen anything yet. End-of-
year payroll reporting requires a lot of forms and a lot of time.

Although the federal government doesn't require that you prepare a separate
wage and tax statement for each employee during the course of the year, you
do have to prepare this statement at the end of the year for each employee.
The rules are clear. You must issue a Statement of Remuneration Paid, commonly referred to as a T4 slip, if you had to deduct CPP/QPP contributions, EI
premiums, or income tax from an employee's gross pay, or if the employee's

gross pay for the year was more than $500. If you provide employees with taxable group term life insurance benefits, you always have to prepare T4 slips, even if the total remuneration paid in the calendar year is less than $500.

You base T4 amounts on payments in the calendar year. (Your business's fiscal year-end doesn't matter to the CRA — it bases requirements on the calendar year.) Whatever payroll your business paid to employees in the calendar year is the amount you need to report on T4s.

Preparing T4s

You should keep most of the information that you need to put together an employee's T4 as part of your payroll records so that you can easily pull it together.

For each employee, you must complete four copies of a T4: Two copies go to the employee, one copy stays in your business's permanent records, and one copy goes to the CRA, along with the T4 Summary (which we discuss in the section "Preparing the T4 Summary," later in this chapter). If you're filing the T4 electronically (see the sidebar "Filing T4s online," in this chapter, for more about this process), you don't have to worry about filing paper copies of these documents with the CRA.

Here are some tips about filling in certain individual boxes on the T4s (Figure 20-1 shows you where these boxes appear on the form):

Filing T4s online

You can fill out T4s on the CRA's website (www.cra-arc.gc.ca). The site even makes filling out T4s for multiple employees easy by automatically entering information that's consistent on the forms for all your employees (such as the year, the employer name and address, and the employer business number).

If you're using the PDF fillable form, instead of printing off versions of the form to fill by hand, make sure you print the results before you move on to enter the next employee's information.

You can't save CRA's online forms in an electronic format.

If your business needs to file more than 50 T4 slips, you must file your return electronically with the CRA by using the Internet File Transfer (XML) service (www.cra-arc.gc.ca/esrvc-srvce/rf/xml/menu-eng.html), which transmits the information in Extensible Markup Language (XML). Check the CRA website for more details about file sizes and other specifications.

Employer's name – Nom de l'employeur	Canada Revenue Agency / Agence du revenu du Canada **T4** STATEMENT OF REMUNERATION PAID ÉTAT DE LA RÉMUNÉRATION PAYÉE

Year / Année

Employment income – line 101 Revenus d'emploi – ligne 101 **14**	Income tax deducted – line 437 Impôt sur le revenu retenu – ligne 437 **22**

54 Payroll account number / Numéro de compte de retenues

Province of employment Province d'emploi **10**	Employee's CPP contributions – line 308 Cotisations de l'employé au RPC – ligne 308 **16**	EI insurable earnings Gains assurables d'AE **24**

Social insurance number Numéro d'assurance sociale **12**	Exempt – Exemption CPP/QPP EI PPIP **28** RPC/RRQ AE RPAP	Employment code Code d'emploi **29**	Employee's QPP contributions – line 308 Cotisations de l'employé au RRQ – ligne 308 **17**	CPP/QPP pensionable earnings Gains ouvrant droit à pension – RPC/RRQ **26**

Employee's EI premiums – line 312 Cotisations de l'employé à l'AE – ligne 312 **18**	Union dues – line 212 Cotisations syndicales – ligne 212 **44**

Employee's name and address – Nom et adresse de l'employé

Last name (in capital letters) – Nom de famille (en lettres moulées)   First name – Prénom   Initials – Initiales

RPP contributions – line 207 Cotisations à un RPA – ligne 207 **20**	Charitable donations – line 349 Dons de bienfaisance – ligne 349 **46**

Pension adjustment – line 206 Facteur d'équivalence – ligne 206 **52**	RPP or DPSP registration number N° d'agrément d'un RPA ou d'un RPDB **50**

Figure 20-1: The CRA form T4 — Statement of Remuneration Paid.

Employee's PPIP premiums – see over Cotisations de l'employé au RPAP – voir au verso **55**	PPIP insurable earnings Gains assurables du RPAP **56**

Other information (see over) Autres renseignements (voir au verso)	Box – Case [ ] Amount – Montant [ ]	Box – Case [ ] Amount – Montant [ ]	Box – Case [ ] Amount – Montant [ ]
	Box – Case [ ] Amount – Montant [ ]	Box – Case [ ] Amount – Montant [ ]	Box – Case [ ] Amount – Montant [ ]

T4 (11)

✔ **Box 10 – Province of employment:** Use the standard two-alpha-character abbreviations — ON for Ontario, for example.

✔ **Box 12 – Social Insurance Number:** You obtain this nine-digit number from the TD1 signed by your employee when your business hired him and enrolled him on your payroll. Refer to our discussion of the enrolment of employees in Chapter 10.

This number confirms your employee's eligibility for employment, and the government uses it to keep track of the money you handle on behalf of your employee as his agent. Consequently, you absolutely must check the accuracy of the SIN when you prepare a T4.

✔ **Box 14 – Employment income:** Report the gross earnings, which include all salary, wages, bonuses, vacation pay, tips and gratuities, honorariums, director's fees, and management fees. Include in this amount the taxable benefits. We discuss taxable benefits in Chapter 10.

✔ **Boxes 16 and 17 – Employee's CPP or QPP contributions:** Enter the amount you deducted from the employee's pay for contributions to the Canada Pension Plan (CPP) or Québec Pension Plan (QPP). Make your entry concerning CPP (Box 16) or QPP (Box 17), depending on the province or territory of employment. Don't include the employer's share of contributions to these plans. Also, the amount you enter in the appropriate box shouldn't exceed the annual maximum. If it does, don't reduce the amount that you enter on the T4 because that figure won't match what you've remitted using your PD7A remittance voucher. We discuss the regular remittance of payroll deductions and benefits using this voucher in Chapter 11. The employee receives any excess over the maximum as a reimbursement when she files her personal tax return.

- ✔ **Box 18 – Employee's EI premiums:** Enter the amount of Employment Insurance (EI) premiums that you deducted from the employee's gross pay. Don't include the employer's share of the contributions. Like with CPP (or QPP), if you over-deducted and the total exceeds the maximum for the year, don't change the amount to the maximum on the T4. The employee receives a refund of the excess contribution automatically when filing his tax return.

- ✔ **Box 20 – RPP contributions:** Enter the total amount the employee contributed to a registered pension plan (RPP). Don't include the employer's share of the contributions made to the RPP.

- ✔ **Box 22 – Income tax deducted:** Enter the total income tax that you deducted from the employee's gross pay, including the federal, provincial (except in Québec), and territorial taxes.

- ✔ **Box 24 – EI insurable earnings:** Enter the total amount you used to calculate the employee's EI premiums, up to the maximum insurable earnings for the year.

- ✔ **Box 26 – CPP/QPP pensionable earnings:** Enter the total amount you used to calculate the employee's CPP withholdings, up to the maximum pensionable earnings for the year.

- ✔ **Box 28 – Exempt (CPP/QPP, EI, and PPIP):** PPIP stands for provincial parental insurance plan (PPIP) premiums on self-employment income. In most cases, you leave this box blank.

- ✔ **Box 29 – Employment code:** In most cases, you leave this box blank.

- ✔ **Box 44 – Union dues:** Enter the amount you deducted from the employee's earnings for union dues. Use this box only if you and the union agree that the union won't issue receipts for union dues to employees.

- ✔ **Box 46 – Charitable donations:** Enter the amount you deducted from the employee's earnings for donations to registered charities in Canada. In many cases, the charity issues the receipts and mails them directly to the employee. If charities to which your employees donate use this method, leave this box blank.

- ✔ **Box 50 – RPP or DPSP registration number:** Enter the seven-digit registration number issued for a registered pension plan (RPP) or deferred profit-sharing plan (DPSP).

- ✔ **Box 52 – Pension adjustment (PA):** If your business offers employees a registered pension plan (RPP) or a deferred profit-sharing plan (DPSP), enter the amount of the employee's PA for the year (in dollars).

- ✔ **Box 54 – Payroll account number:** Enter the 15-digit business number (BN) that you use at the top of the PD7A when you send your employees' deductions to the CRA. We discuss the PD7A filing form in Chapter 11.

- ✔ **Box 55 – Employee's PPIP premiums:** Enter the PPIP premiums that you deduct for employees who work in Québec.

- ✔ **Box 55 – Employee's PPIP insurable earnings:** For employees who work in Québec, enter the total amount that you used to calculate the employee's PPIP premiums.

- ✔ **Other information:** This area at the bottom of the T4 slip provides blank boxes into which you can enter codes and amounts that relate to employment commissions, taxable allowances and benefits, deductible amounts, and other entries, if they apply. You can find an explanation of each box number on the fifth page of the PDF fillable T4 form.

When you prepare the T4 forms, if you discover that you've over-contributed as an employer to either the CPP or EI programs, complete Form PD24, *Application for a Refund of Overdeducted CPP Contributions or EI Premiums,* to apply for a refund of your CPP or EI overpayment. You can obtain a copy of the form on the CRA website (www.cra-arc.gc.ca). You can request a refund for up to four years from the end of the year in which you made the CPP overpayment and up to three years from the end of the year in which you made the EI overpayment.

Producing T4s with QuickBooks

If you're using QuickBooks, you can generate T4s automatically. Click the Employees command on the top menu bar, and then click Payroll Forms to access the Process T4s link. A pop-up window appears, asking you to select the form that you want to produce. Alternatively, you can obtain all the summary data from the QuickBooks T4 Summary Report by clicking Employees and Payroll in the Reports drop-down menu. You can transcribe the information from this summary report onto the CRA T4 Summary form, shown in Figure 20-2.

Filing T4s

As an employee, you've probably noticed that every business you ever worked for waited until the last possible day to provide you with your T4. Now that you're preparing these documents for your business's employees, you have a better understanding of your employers' delay. It takes time to put T4s together, especially when you want to make sure they're correct.

Figure 20-2:
The CRA
form T4
Summary —
Summary of
Remuner-
ation Paid.

© *Canada Revenue Agency. Reproduced with permission of the Minister of Public Works and Government Services Canada, 2012*

If you use a computerized accounting system's payroll software package to prepare your T4s, you can definitely do the task much more easily than by hand, but running the reports and reviewing them to be sure that everything's accurate before you print the final forms still takes time. Although you can send out amended T4s, if necessary, filing the additional forms takes a lot of extra work, so you want to avoid correcting a T4 whenever possible. You can best eliminate the need for corrections by very carefully checking all information on the forms before you distribute them to your employees.

The filing deadline with the CRA for the T4s and the T4 Summary is the last day of February following the calendar year to which the information return applies. If you fail to file these forms by the deadline, you have to pay a penalty for each failure of $10 to $75 per day, with a minimum penalty of $100 and a maximum penalty of $7,500, depending on the number of T4 slips that are late. So, you definitely don't want to miss the deadline, especially because you can't claim your penalty payments as business expenses.

The CRA isn't totally inflexible. If you miss a T4 filing deadline, you can find some avenues of relief. The CRA can sometimes cancel or waive all or part of any interest charges and penalties. They can consider extraordinary circumstances that may have prevented employers from fulfilling their filing obligations. For example, your business may have experienced a power failure that made obtaining the information from your accounting system or preparing the forms impossible, or your business may have lost records in a flood or fire.

Based on our experience, if something prevents you from filing on time, you should communicate your problem to the CRA immediately. After you warn them, the CRA can give you advice about how to make the best of the situation. Also, if you tell them ahead of time, the CRA may be far more understanding if you miss a deadline, particularly because they know that it happened for reasons out of your control and not because of neglect on your part.

If you fraudulently file a T4 claiming you paid wages that you didn't actually pay, you can be hit with a lawsuit for civil damages. The person whom you claimed you'd paid may sue you for any damages incurred because of this fraudulent T4.

Preparing the T4 Summary

After you complete a T4 for each employee, you must prepare a T4 Summary. This summary provides the totals of all monetary information on the individual T4s. The T4s and the T4 Summary make up your T4 information return that you need to file with the CRA. The totals you report on your T4 Summary have to agree with the totals you report on your employees' T4 slips. Errors or omissions can cause unnecessary processing delays.

Figure 20-2 shows a copy of CRA's T4 Summary.

The T4 Summary has the same box reference numbers as the individual T4s. In addition to that data, however, the Summary also includes the amounts that the employer contributed for the CPP/QPP and EI. (Refer to Chapter 10 for information on how much an employer must contribute.)

All contributions that the employer and employee made must match the total amount of the monthly (or possibly quarterly) remittances that you sent in to the CRA by using the PD7A Remittance Voucher (which we discuss in Chapter 11).

Before preparing the T4 Summary, total up the data and make sure that the sums of Boxes 16, 18, 19, 22, and 27 correspond to the year-to-date total of the remittances. You enter the remitted amount in Box 82 of the T4 Summary. If the entries in Boxes 80 (Total deductions reported) and 82 (Remittances) don't match, your business has to pay any shortfall in remittances when you file your T4 return.

If you're using software to calculate your payroll, you may want to test the accuracy of the payroll records around the middle of the calendar year. Compare your individual employee record totals against the total of the remittances that your business has sent to the CRA to date. If the figures don't match, you can track down the source of the problem to any discrepancies and make the necessary corrections before the end of the calendar year, when the error can cause you a great deal of headaches and possibly CRA penalties.

Chapter 21

Satisfying the Taxman

· ·

In This Chapter

▶ Sorting out business structures

▶ Filing sole proprietor taxes

▶ Reporting taxes on partnerships

▶ Filing taxes for corporations

▶ Reporting and paying provincial sales tax and GST/HST

▶ Finding tax information in QuickBooks

· ·

*P*aying taxes and reporting income for your business are very important jobs, and the way in which you complete these tasks depends on your business's legal structure. From sole proprietorships to corporations and everything in between, this chapter briefly reviews business types and explains how you have to handle income taxes for each type. You also get some instruction on collecting and remitting provincial sales tax and retail sales tax (PST/RST) and goods and services tax and harmonized sales tax (GST/HST) on the products that your business sells.

Finding the Right Business Type

You need to know a business's type when you do tax preparation and reporting for that business. If you work as a bookkeeper for a small business, you need to know the business's legal structure before you can proceed with reporting and paying income taxes on the business income. Not all businesses have the same structure, so they don't all pay income taxes on the profits they make in the same way.

But before you get into the subject of tax procedures, you need to understand the various business structures that you may encounter as a bookkeeper. The following sections outline each type of business.

Sole proprietorship

The simplest legal structure for a business is the *sole proprietorship,* a business that's owned by one individual. An individual can be the sole proprietor of several businesses. As far the Canada Revenue Agency (CRA) is concerned, each business is a separate entity. So, you need to separate the bookkeeping and tax reporting for each business, as well. That separation may sound simple, but sometimes transactions get tricky when separate businesses share assets.

Most new businesses start out as sole proprietorships. Some of those businesses never change their statuses, but others grow by adding partners and becoming partnerships. Some businesses add a lot of staff and want to protect themselves from lawsuits, so they become corporations. We cover these other structures in the following sections.

When you begin a business, consider obtaining a business number (BN) right away. We discuss the needs and uses of this CRA account in Chapter 1. Although a sole proprietorship doesn't have to pay income taxes directly and may not have a payroll, it most likely needs a BN for when it remits GST/HST that it charges its customers for goods and services.

Partnership

Whenever more than one person owns a business, you must consider the business a partnership for accounting and tax reporting. A partnership doesn't need a formal written agreement to exist. Also, a partnership may exist for a very short period of time, particularly if its formation is connected to a particular event or activity that doesn't repeat.

Like a person can have several sole proprietorships (discussed in the preceding section), an individual can be a partner of several businesses. The partnership is the most flexible type of business structure involving more than one owner. Each partner in the business is equally liable for the activities of the business. This structure is slightly more complicated than a sole proprietorship, and partners should work out certain key issues before the business opens its doors. These issues include

- ✔ How the partners will divide the profits and losses
- ✔ How each partner can sell his share of the business, if he so chooses
- ✔ What will happen to each partner's share if a partner becomes sick or dies
- ✔ How the partnership will be dissolved if one of the partners wants out

Limited partnership (LP)

Partners in a partnership don't always have to share equal risks. A partnership may have two different types of partners: general and limited. The *general partner* runs the day-to-day business and is held personally responsible for all activities of the business, regardless of how much she has personally invested. *Limited partners,* on the other hand, are passive owners of the business and aren't involved in its day-to-day operations; they view their ownership in the business as an investment only. If someone files a claim against the business, the limited partners can be held personally liable for only the amount of money that matches how much they each individually invested in the business.

Partners usually relate the amount of investment risk they are taking in a business to the balance of their individual Capital account. In Chapter 2, we explain that the Equity account of an owner of an unincorporated business is called the Capital account.

Limited liability partnership (LLP)

Professionals, such as accountants, lawyers, and doctors, often form a limited liability partnership (LLP). Because these professions provide services to customers who rely on the professionals' expertise, the risk exists that the negligence of some partners can hurt all the partners in the partnership. Partners in an LLP have unlimited liability for their own negligence but have limited liability for other partners' negligence. These types of businesses need to obtain professional liability insurance because they need to address claims of damage from customers.

Corporations

If your business faces a great risk of being sued, the safest business structure for you is the *corporation.* Courts have clearly determined that a corporation is a separate legal entity and that its owners' personal assets are protected from claims against the corporation. Essentially, no one can sue or demand collections from an owner or shareholder in a corporation because of actions taken by the corporation. This veil of protection is the reason many small-business owners choose to incorporate, even though it involves a lot of expense and a lot of government paperwork.

In a corporation, each share represents a portion of ownership, and the business must split profits based on share ownership. You don't have to sell shares on the public stock markets, such as the Toronto Stock Exchange

(TSX), in order to be a corporation, though. In fact, most corporations are private entities that sell their shares privately among friends, family, and investors.

If you're a small-business owner who wants to incorporate, you first must form a board of directors. Boards can include both owners of the business and non-owners. You can even have your spouse and children on the board — we bet you'd have some interesting board meetings.

Check with your accountant to determine whether incorporating your business makes sense. Incorporating has important tax implications that you must consider. Operating a corporation also increases administrative, legal, and accounting costs. Be sure that you understand the costs before you incorporate.

In Canada, you can have a federally incorporated business or use the provincial or territorial incorporation statutes. The federal statute, called the Canada Business Corporation Act (CBCA), allows the incorporation of federal corporations. Here are a couple advantages of incorporating federally:

- ✔ You can conduct business and use your corporate name across Canada, so if you decide to expand your business to other provinces or territories, you don't have to register in those provinces or territories.

- ✔ Your business has a degree of flexibility in choosing a location from which to operate. An Ontario corporation, for example, needs to file forms and pay additional fees if it wants to operate in Québec as well as Ontario.

Businesses that incorporate have start-up costs directly related to the process of setting up the corporation, which involves legal services. Although you don't have to obtain legal advice when you incorporate, we encourage you to do so, especially if you're considering setting up a business that has a complicated share structure.

Corporations can have fiscal year-ends other than calendar year-ends. Proprietorships and partnerships (which we talk about in the preceding sections) usually report their business year-ends on December 31 each year.

If you're a sole proprietor or if you are a member of a partnership in which all the partners are individuals, you can elect to have a non-calendar year fiscal period. To do this, you need to file your election by using Form T1139, Reconciliation of Business Income for Tax Purposes, which you obtain from the CRA website (www.cra-arc.gc.ca).

Corporation role call

Because a corporation is a separate legal entity that has no physical form, individuals who have an interest in the corporation and have the authority to make decisions for the corporation must carry out the corporation's activities, such as borrowing money. You can divide these individuals into three categories:

✔ **Shareholders:** The people who own the corporation. They make decisions by voting and passing resolutions, generally at a shareholders' meeting. Most important, they elect the directors of the corporation.

✔ **Directors:** Supervise the management of the corporation's business. A corporation must have at least one director. Directors appoint the corporation's officers.

✔ **Officers:** A corporation's officers hold positions such as president, chief executive officer (CEO), secretary, and chief financial officer (CFO). Although a corporation's directors appoint the officers, the corporation's by-laws (which were originally filed to incorporate the business) normally set out the officers' duties. In general, officers are responsible for managing the day-to-day activities of the business.

An individual may hold more than one of these positions in a corporation. For example, the same individual may be a shareholder, a director, and an officer — someone can even be the sole shareholder, sole director, and sole officer.

Tax Reporting for Sole Proprietors

The law doesn't consider sole proprietorships to be individual legal entities, so they're not taxed as such. Instead, sole proprietors report any business earnings to the CRA on their individual tax returns — that's the only financial reporting they must do for the income their businesses earn.

Sole proprietors or individuals who earn any type of business income report this income as part of the annual personal tax return called T1 General. You need to fill out specific schedules that outline the revenues and deductible expenses of the business. These forms also help when you calculate the business and personal portions of some assets that you may use in the business, such as a house or a car.

You report on Form T2125, Statement of Business or Professional Activities, the income for each business that you, as an individual taxpayer, own. The form requires you to provide details about the business use you may claim for home office expenses.

In the following sections, we consider some of the reporting that you need to do for Form T2125, along with information about paying income taxes.

Capital cost allowance

You calculate the capital cost allowance (CCA) claim on Form T2125. (In Chapter 12, we discuss how the government lets you claim CCA, which is the tax equivalent of depreciation on long-term assets.) When you calculate your CCA, you can deduct relatively high amounts of the costs of these long-term assets against your revenues, which lowers your taxable income. The government wants to encourage you as a business to invest in assets, thereby stimulating the economy.

Unfortunately, this help from the government doesn't go on forever. The amounts that you can claim are high when you first use the assets, and then the amounts taper off in subsequent years. The amounts that you can claim supposedly work out to the same total amounts that you record as depreciation in your books. The bias in the timing of the additional tax deduction gives you a postponement or deferral in paying income tax at the beginning of the life of the long-term assets. In later taxation years, after the asset has helped generate some extra revenue and cash for the business, the deduction of CCA becomes smaller and so the amount of tax grows to a larger amount, at a time when the business can afford it.

The depreciation method that you choose can't help you avoid paying income tax. Whichever amount of depreciation you record in your books, CRA disallows it as a tax deduction. CRA determines precisely what you can claim, which is limited to the amount in the capital cost allowance calculations.

Business expenses

As a bookkeeper for a sole proprietor, you probably need to pull together the gross business or professional income, the cost of goods sold and gross profit (if applicable), and the expenses of the business so that you can record them in the Expense categories on Form T2125.

In Chapter 10, we outline how employers need to deduct Canada Pension Plan (CPP) or Québec Pension Plan (QPP) contributions from employees' gross pays. The employer also has to pay an amount to the plan equal to what her employee does. Because a sole proprietor is in effect her own employee, she has to pay both halves of the CPP contribution when she files her personal income tax return. Also, a sole proprietor can't participate in the Employment Insurance program.

Tax instalments

Proprietors don't receive paycheques. Because no paycheques exist to deduct income taxes from, the CRA requires that proprietors make income tax instalments. The CRA issues reports every six months that outline how much money a taxpayer has to pay in instalments if he wants to avoid any penalties and interest charges. (The CRA determines the amount of the first two quarterly instalments by dividing the total amount of taxes paid in the second year by four.) CRA typically assesses T1 personal tax returns in May or June each year. The required instalment amounts change in the middle of the year for the two remaining quarterly instalments. These adjustments take into account the actual amount of tax paid as assessed for the previous taxation year.

Keep close track of the tax instalment deadlines: March, June, September, and December 15. Make sure that you have enough money in your bank account to make these payments on time.

Filing Tax Forms for Partnerships

If your business is structured as a partnership (meaning it has more than one owner), your business doesn't pay taxes. Instead, you split all the profit that the business earns among the partners, who report those earnings on their personal tax returns.

As a bookkeeper for a partnership, you may need to collect the data necessary to file an information schedule called a Partnership Information Return (PIR). However, as long as a partnership has fewer than six partners for the whole fiscal year and no partner who's in another partnership, you don't have to file a PIR for that partnership.

If the partnership doesn't have to file a PIR, you calculate the partnership's income and expenses by using the same rules you use for a proprietorship. You calculate the partnership's income and expenses like the partnership was a separate person.

A partnership can own depreciable property but it can't claim capital cost allowance (CCA). The partnership's individual partners claim their share of CCA on their personal income tax return along with their share of the partnership's income.

The PIR includes a summary (T5013 SUM, Information Slips Summary) of the individual returns or slips for each partner, called Form T5013, Statement of Partnership Income. You can use this form for all types of partnerships and for several types of income. The filing deadline for the T5013 is generally March 31 each year because partnerships usually have a December year-end. It's a daunting form, but don't worry: The accountant normally prepares more-complex calculations.

After your business files the PIR, each partner reports her income on her individual tax return, the T1 General.

Paying Corporate Taxes

All corporations must pay federal and provincial income taxes. You need to file corporate tax returns within six months of the end of the corporation's fiscal year-end. Unsurprisingly, corporate tax returns are more complex than personal income tax returns, and each province has unique tax requirements and practices. The federal corporate tax return is called a T2 Corporate Income Tax Return, and it serves as a federal, provincial, and territorial corporate income tax return unless the corporation is located in Québec or Alberta. If the corporation is located in either of these two provinces, you have to file a separate provincial corporate tax return.

We don't go into a lot of detail about the complex calculations of corporate income taxes. Businesses often form corporations as part of estate planning so that a family business can pass down from one generation to the next. A corporate tax accountant or lawyer can devise many schemes to postpone the tax that a sole proprietor's death triggers.

You can more easily continue the life of a business by transferring shares of a corporation than by selling the business outright. Some people feel that the formal structure involved in accounting for a corporation and reporting to the government can provide additional safeguards over assets and stronger internal control for the business. The more structure and discipline that enters into business transactions, the more care you apply to make sure that you're making sensible decisions that can get you a good result.

Taking Care of Sales Taxes Obligations

Keeping up to date on provincial and federal tax requirements and rates, as well as paying your business's share of those taxes to the government, is complicated. As we discuss in Chapter 5, a business is an agent of the federal and provincial governments, and it must collect sales taxes on the sale of most goods and services. In addition, businesses pay taxes on most purchases.

After you record in your books the amount of the different taxes that you charge on sales, you need to remit the taxes you've collected as an agent of the governments by the deadlines that those governments set.

The government doesn't care whether you've sold goods or services to your customers on credit and haven't yet collected the accounts receivable. The government wants its money by its deadline date, no matter what. So, you may have to use your own cash to pay the taxes if you haven't collected the cash from your customers yet. This arrangement may sound unfair, but the law is the law. For tax (and many other) reasons, you want to make prompt collection of your accounts receivable.

All businesses operating in Canada need to understand how sales taxes apply to their particular business in their particular province or territory. For the provincial sales tax remittances, each province has a helpful website that provides instructions on how to remit the applicable provincial sales tax and retail sales tax (PST/RST) by the deadline. In the case of harmonized sales tax (HST), where the GST and PST are combined, you need to file only one return.

When you become a GST/HST registrant with the CRA, the CRA gives you a reporting period (monthly or quarterly, for example) and sends you a personalized pre-printed Goods and Services Tax/Harmonized Sales Tax Return, Form GST34. This form isn't available on the web, and it will already have your name, mailing address, registrant number, and reporting period filled in. After you work through the amounts that need to appear on the form, you can sign and mail the bottom stub return portion, along with a cheque made payable to the Receiver General. Remember to write your business number on your cheque.

You can file your GST/HST return online by using NETFILE. The CRA provides a four-digit access code that gives you an easy and quick alternative to mailing in the return. Electronic filing of the GST/HST return is mandatory for businesses with large amounts of sales or revenues. You can also file returns and remittances electronically though a participating bank using electronic data exchange (EDI). You can make online payments to the CRA using CRA's My Payment option. Refer to CRA's website at www.cra.gc.ca/mypayment for more details.

Be careful about how you round your numbers. When it comes to sales taxes, all the pennies count (though you may find this particularly challenging now that the penny is being eliminated from Canada's coinage system). If you rely on a cash register to calculate taxes, make sure that it correctly rounds the amounts — otherwise, you could end up in big trouble.

Using QuickBooks

If you're using QuickBooks, you can quickly and easily obtain a lot of the numbers you need to file and pay your tax remittances. From the Reports command on the top menu bar, click Sales Tax, and then click Tax Agency Report. A new screen appears, where you can select Receiver General from the drop-down menu next to the Tax Agency box to generate the GST/HST Return Report for your GST/HST remittance (see Figure 21-1).

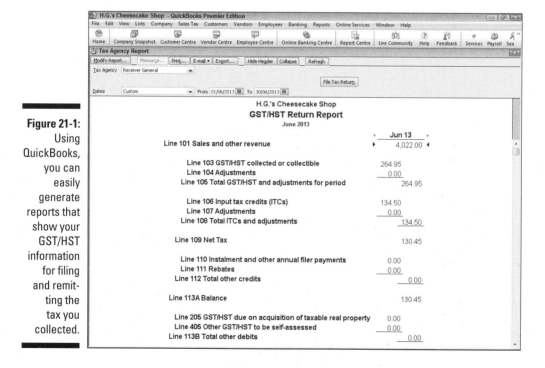

Figure 21-1: Using QuickBooks, you can easily generate reports that show your GST/HST information for filing and remitting the tax you collected.

You can also create an equivalent report for PST/RST for any province or territory. From the Reports command on the top menu bar, click Sales Tax, and then click Tax Agency Detail Report. From the next screen, select your provincial tax minister of finance from the drop-down menu next to the Tax Agency box. The report generated shows the invoice amounts and the PST/RST charged on those invoices for your reporting period. Figure 21-2 shows an example of that report.

The reports shown in Figures 21-1 and 21-2 give you the majority of the numbers that you need to fill in the PST/RST and GST/HST returns — but make sure that you fill in information in the additional boxes on the returns that relate to unusual transactions that the QuickBooks system may not have captured.

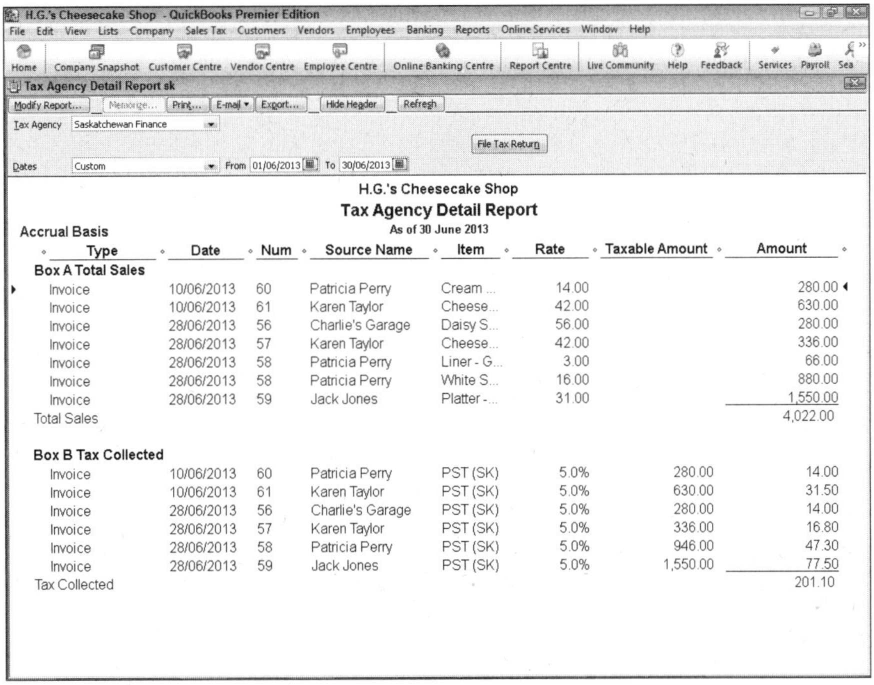

Type	Date	Num	Source Name	Item	Rate	Taxable Amount	Amount
Box A Total Sales							
Invoice	10/06/2013	60	Patricia Perry	Cream ...	14.00		280.00
Invoice	10/06/2013	61	Karen Taylor	Cheese...	42.00		630.00
Invoice	28/06/2013	56	Charlie's Garage	Daisy S...	56.00		280.00
Invoice	28/06/2013	57	Karen Taylor	Cheese...	42.00		336.00
Invoice	28/06/2013	58	Patricia Perry	Liner - G...	3.00		66.00
Invoice	28/06/2013	58	Patricia Perry	White S...	16.00		880.00
Invoice	28/06/2013	59	Jack Jones	Platter -...	31.00		1,550.00
Total Sales							4,022.00
Box B Tax Collected							
Invoice	10/06/2013	60	Patricia Perry	PST (SK)	5.0%	280.00	14.00
Invoice	10/06/2013	61	Karen Taylor	PST (SK)	5.0%	630.00	31.50
Invoice	28/06/2013	56	Charlie's Garage	PST (SK)	5.0%	280.00	14.00
Invoice	28/06/2013	57	Karen Taylor	PST (SK)	5.0%	336.00	16.80
Invoice	28/06/2013	58	Patricia Perry	PST (SK)	5.0%	946.00	47.30
Invoice	28/06/2013	59	Jack Jones	PST (SK)	5.0%	1,550.00	77.50
Tax Collected							201.10

Figure 21-2: Using QuickBooks, you can easily generate reports that show your PST information for filing and remitting the provincial sales tax you collected.

Chapter 22

Prepping the Books for a New Accounting Cycle

. . . .

In This Chapter

▶ Wrapping up General Ledger accounts

▶ Doing final bookkeeping tasks

▶ Transitioning into a new accounting cycle

. . . .

*I*n bookkeeping, an accounting period (or cycle) can span a month, a quarter, or a year (or some other division of time, if it makes business sense). At the end of every fiscal year, you need to close certain accounts and leave others open.

Like you should add accounts to your bookkeeping system at the beginning of a year (so that you don't have to move information from one account to another), you also should wait until the end of the year to deactivate any accounts that you no longer need. By using this approach, you start each year fresh with only the accounts that you need so that you can best manage your business's financial activities.

In this chapter, we explain the accounts that you must close at the end of a year so that they can start with a zero balance in the next fiscal year, such as Sales and Cost of Goods Sold. We also review the accounts that continue from one yearly cycle to the next, such as Asset and Liability accounts.

Finalizing the General Ledger

After you and the accountant complete year-end procedures and record any necessary adjusting journal entries, as we outline in Chapter 17, you need to close the books. You must zero out some accounts in the General Ledger so that they start the new fiscal year with no balances, but other accounts continue to accumulate detail and carry forward balances from one year to the next. In the General Ledger, the balance sheet accounts carry forward into the next year, and the income statement accounts and Drawings account start with a zero balance each year.

Zeroing out income statement accounts

When you and the accountant are sure that you've made all needed corrections and adjustments to your accounts, you can zero out all General Ledger accounts listed on the income statement — Sales, Cost of Goods Sold, and Expense accounts. Your accountant probably refers to these General Ledger accounts as temporary. Because the income statement reflects the activities of an accounting period, these accounts always start with a zero balance at the beginning of each year. The same rule applies to the Drawings account. If you keep your books by hand, the process requires a set of closing entries.

If you use a computerized accounting system, you may not actually have to zero out the income statement accounts and the Drawings account. For example, QuickBooks closes your Revenue and Expense accounts and puts the net result, hopefully profit, as an increase to the Equity account at the end of the year. QuickBooks maintains the data in an archive so that you can always access it to make comparisons in subsequent years' reports. You set your closing date by accessing the Company command on the top menu bar and clicking Set Closing Date and Password (see Figure 22-1). The password setup helps to ensure that someone doesn't inadvertently record a transaction in the wrong year.

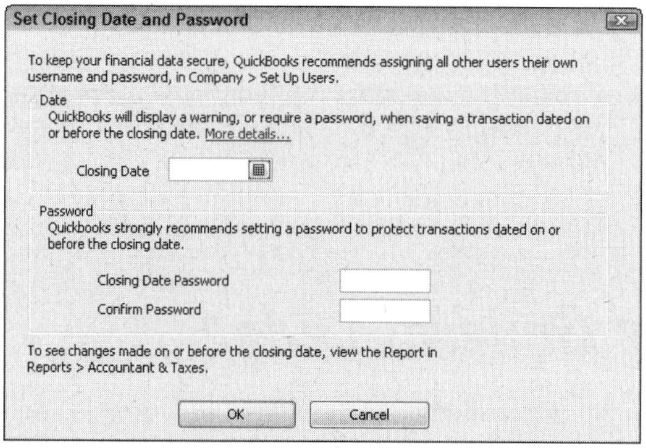

Figure 22-1:
Set the
closing
date and
password
for your
accounts in
QuickBooks.

Carrying over balance sheet accounts

Unlike income statement accounts, you never zero out the accounts listed on a balance sheet — Asset, Liability, and Equity accounts. Instead, you use your ending balances for each of these accounts to prepare a balance sheet (refer to Chapter 18), and you carry forward the data and balances in these accounts into the next fiscal year. The balance sheet just gives you a snapshot of the financial state of your business as of a particular date. From one accounting cycle to the next, your assets and (unfortunately) liabilities remain, and you also need to maintain the information about how much equity your investors have put into the business. Your accountant likely refers to these General Ledger accounts as permanent.

Conducting Year-End Bookkeeping Tasks

If you use a computerized accounting system, before you start the process of closing the books for the year, print a summary of your account information. If you make an error while closing the books, you can always use this printout to backtrack and fix any problems. Printouts also provide you with a good paper trail, in case you need to perform any account inquiry in the future.

Checking customer accounts

Before you close your books at the end of the accounting cycle, review customer accounts for possible writeoffs of accounts receivable. (We talk about writeoffs in greater detail in Chapter 9.) Now's the time to critically examine past due accounts that you truly don't expect to collect.

Assessing vendor accounts

The fiscal year-end is the perfect time to review your vendor accounts to be sure that they're current and not overdue. Also, make sure that you've entered into your vendor accounts any bills that reflect business activity in the period that you're closing; otherwise, expenses from the period may not show up in the appropriate year-end financial statements. We discuss the need to record accruals for unpaid services, such as utilities and interest, in Chapter 17.

Review any outstanding purchase orders to be sure that your vendor accounts include all orders that your business has received but for which the vendor hasn't yet billed you. For example, if you receive inventory on December 23 but the vendor doesn't send his bill for that inventory until January, you should record the bill in December (to reflect the receipt of that inventory during that year) and increase the Accounts Payable account.

Updating your inventory records

You need to keep a close watch on transactions that involve the movement of inventory in and out of your business around the year-end date or the date you take your physical inventory count. You have to make sure the book-keeping records are up to date so that the comparison between the balances for inventory reported by your books and the physical inventory amounts represents an apples-to-apples comparison.

You need to update your records for inventory received but for which vendor invoices have not yet been entered because the entry to record the invoice and the accounts payable in a computerized system also updates your inventory records.

Also scrutinize your records involving the shipment of inventory to your customers. If you have shipped out goods from your store or warehouse but haven't yet recorded the sale in your computerized accounting system, the inventory on hand and the inventory balances reported on the computer system can't possibly match up. Don't forget that when you record a sale in your computerized system, the sales entry automatically takes care of reducing the inventory on hand.

Use the reports from your computerized system to check your physical inventory count. If you find discrepancies, you must discover the source of the problem and make corrections to your bookkeeping records. We discuss the procedure for taking a physical count of your inventory in Chapter 8.

Deactivating accounts

During the closing process at the end of an accounting year, you may want to assess all your open accounts and verify that you still need them. If an account has no transactions in it, you can deactivate it at any time. However, wait until the end of the year.

If you use a computerized accounting system, deleting an account deletes all past transactions in that account, as well. Consequently, you lose all the historical information necessary to make comparisons on financial reports. The only time you should delete an account from your Chart of Accounts is when you first create your chart. When you finish creating your chart, but before you start entering transactions, you may conclude that your business will never need a particular account. In that case, go ahead and delete the account, because you don't lose any transaction information and therefore you don't affect your bookkeeping trail.

Starting the Cycle Anew

You certainly don't want to close the doors of your business while you prepare all your year-end reports, such as financial statements and governmental reports — after all, that preparation can take two or three months. So, you need to continue making entries for the new fiscal year before you close the books for the previous year.

If you use a manual bookkeeping system, you just start new journal pages and keep up with the day-to-day bookkeeping, including posting to the detailed Accounts Receivable and Accounts Payable ledgers. If you keep your books by using a computerized accounting system, your computer software will zero out the necessary accounts to start the new fiscal year, placing the data for the previous year in password-protected accounts that appear closed but remain available for the purpose of posting year-end adjustments. You can still make changes to these prior-year accounts, but only people who know the password — most likely you, your business's accountant, and your bookkeeping manager — can access those accounts.

If you keep your books by hand, part of closing out your books involves starting new files for each of your customer or vendor accounts. Most businesses keep two years of data — the current year and the previous year — in onsite office files, and they put older files into storage. When you start a new fiscal year, box up your 2-year-old files for storage and use the newly empty drawers for the next year's new files. For example, suppose you're creating files for 2014. Keep the 2013 files easily accessible in file cabinet drawers in your office, but box up the 2012 files for storage. Then, keep your 2014 files in the drawers that used to hold the 2012 files. Following this practice helps reduce the amount of work that you need to put into getting yourself organized.

You don't need to worry about a hard and fast rule for file storage. You may find that you need to access some files regularly and therefore don't want to put them in storage. No problem. Pull out any files related to ongoing activity and keep them in the office so that you don't have to run to the storage area every time you need the files. For example, if you have an ongoing legal case, keep any files related to that matter out of storage and easily accessible.

Store the backup files of the data from your accounting software, ideally off-site. The backup file gives you the accounting data that you need to retrieve in case of loss or destruction — because of a fire, for example. In order to retrieve the data, you need to have the software, which accesses the data files. Keep your software media, as well as the data files, in offsite storage.

Part VI
The Part of Tens

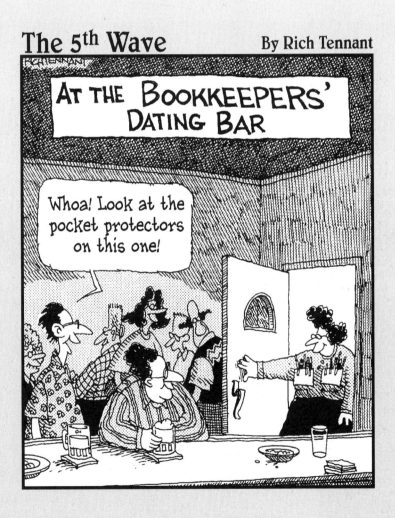

The 5th Wave   By Rich Tennant

AT THE BOOKKEEPERS' DATING BAR

Whoa! Look at the pocket protectors on this one!

In this part . . .

We join the *For Dummies* series tradition by providing you with some lists of tens. In this case, the lists contain key factors that can help you maintain your books and use the information you collect. We give you the ten best ways to use your books to manage your business's cash. We also highlight the top ten accounts that all bookkeepers must monitor in order to manage the books.

Chapter 23

Top Ten Ways to Manage Your Business Cash with Your Books

In This Chapter

▶ Keeping a handle on internal bookkeeping tools

▶ Monitoring profits and expenses

▶ Dealing smartly with vendors and customers

Many business owners think of bookkeeping as a necessary evil, but in reality, if you make effective use of the data that you collect, bookkeeping can be your best buddy when it comes to managing your cash. To really take advantage of what bookkeeping has to offer, you must understand the value of basic bookkeeping principles and use the information that you've collected. This chapter reviews the top ten ways to use your books to help you manage your business cash.

Charting the Way

You may not think that a list of accounts, called the Chart of Accounts, is worth much attention, but this chart dictates how you collect your financial data and where in the books you put your business's transactions. In order for you to be able to use the information effectively, your Chart of Accounts must define each account precisely and determine exactly what types of transactions go where. (We talk more about the Chart of Accounts and how to set one up in Chapter 3.)

Balancing and Posting Your Entries

You can figure out how your business is doing only after you balance your books. Without balanced books, you can never know whether your profit numbers are accurate. In bookkeeping, you use a process called *double-entry bookkeeping* to keep the books balanced. We talk about this basic principle and how to keep the books balanced in Chapter 2. If you want to use the information that you collect regarding your business transactions, you must accurately post those transactions to your accounts. If you forget to post a transaction to your books, your reports don't reflect that financial activity — which can cause serious problems, such as underestimating your true expenses. Or, if you post an incorrect transaction to your books, any reports that use the incorrect information are also wrong. We talk about the posting process in Chapters 4 and 5.

Reconciling Your Bank Account

In order to control your cash, you need to control access to your cash. Anyone who handles cash for your business shouldn't be allowed to record cash transactions. You must prepare your business bank account's reconciliation as a key internal control procedure. The reconciliation matches up the bank and book transactions involving cash so that you can confirm the accuracy of the cash balance in the books. If you don't have an accurate bank account balance, you risk making decisions about your business's cash that can get you into a lot of trouble. Reconciling your bank account also allows you to check that the transactions in cash come from authorized payments. We talk about bank reconciliation and its benefits in Chapter 14.

Tracking Customer Collections

If your business sells to customers on account, you certainly want to be sure that your customers pay for their purchases in the future. (You gather customer account information in the Accounts Receivable account, as well as in individual records for each customer.) Review reports based on customer payment history, called *aging reports,* on a monthly basis to be sure customers pay on time. You set the rules for credit sales, so you may want to cut off customers from future purchases if their accounts are more than 60 days past due. We talk about how to manage customer accounts in Chapter 9.

Paying Bills Accurately and on Time

If you want to continue getting supplies, inventory, and services from your vendors, you must pay them accurately and on time. Managing your payments through the Accounts Payable account ensures accuracy and timeliness, and it also saves you from mistakenly paying bills twice. To be safe, review aging reports on your payment history to make sure that you are making timely and accurate payments. We talk about managing your payments in Chapter 8.

Planning Profits

Nothing is more important to a business owner than the profits she ultimately makes. But many business owners don't take time to plan their profit expectations at the beginning of each year, so they have no way to gauge how well their business is doing throughout the year. Prevent this problem by taking time before the year starts to develop profit expectations and a budget that can help you meet those expectations. Then, develop a series of internal financial reports from the numbers in your bookkeeping system to help determine whether you're meeting your sales targets and maintaining control over your inventory costs and operating expenses. We talk about sales tracking in Chapter 9, tracking purchases in Chapter 8, and how to determine your profit in Chapter 19.

Comparing Budget to Actual Expenses

Keeping a careful watch on how well your budget planning reflects what's actually happening in your business can help you meet your profit goals. Like with profits (see the preceding section), take time to develop a budget that sets your expectations for the year, and then develop internal reports that give you the ability to track how closely your actual expenses match that budget. If you see any major problems, correct them as soon as possible so that you can meet your target profit by the end of the year. We talk about internal financial reporting in Chapter 19.

Comparing Sales Goals to Actual Sales

In addition to watching your expenses, you also need to monitor your actual sales so that they match the sales goals you set at the beginning of the year. Designing an internal report that tracks sales goals versus actual sales allows you to monitor how well your business is doing. If you find your actual sales are below expectations, correct the problem as early in the year as possible in order to improve your chances of meeting those year-end goals. To find out how to use internal financial reports to track your sales activity, check out Chapters 9 and 19.

Tracking Cost Trends

You need to be aware of the costs involved in purchasing the products you sell or the raw materials you use to manufacture your products, because these cost trends can have a major impact on whether your business earns the profit you expect. If the costs are trending upward, you may need to adjust the selling prices of the products that you sell in order to meet your profit goals. We talk about tracking purchases and cost trends in Chapters 8 and 19.

Making Pricing Decisions

Properly pricing your product can be a critical factor in whether your product sells. If you make the price too high, you may not find any customers willing to buy the product; if you make it too low, you risk losing money.

When determining what price to charge your customers, you must consider a number of different factors, including how much you pay to buy or manufacture the products you sell, market research about what customers will pay for a product, what price your competition is charging, what you pay your employees, and advertising and administrative expenses that you incur. All these items factor into what you have to spend to sell that product. We talk about tracking costs and expenses in Chapters 8 and 19.

Chapter 24

Top Ten Most Important Accounts for Any Bookkeeper

In This Chapter

▶ Thinking about key Asset accounts

▶ Understanding critical Liability accounts

▶ Taking in money

▶ Monitoring costs and expenses

▶ Tracking the owners' equity in the business

*E*ach and every account has its purpose in bookkeeping, but all accounts certainly aren't created equal. For most businesses, some accounts are more essential than others. So in case you're having trouble figuring out where to start setting up your accounts and what you need to include in your Chart of Accounts, this chapter looks at the top must-have accounts for bookkeepers.

Cash

All your business transactions pass through the Cash account, which is so important that you actually need two journals — Cash Receipts and Cash Disbursements — to track the activity. (We discuss these journals at length in Chapter 5.) As the bookkeeper, you have the responsibility to properly record all cash — whether it's coming into the business or going out — in the Cash account.

Accounts Receivable

If your business sells its goods or services to customers on account, you definitely need an Accounts Receivable account. In this account, you track all money due from your customers. As the bookkeeper, you need to keep Accounts Receivable up to date so that your business can send timely and accurate invoices and reminder statements to customers. We talk about how to handle Accounts Receivable in Chapter 9.

Inventory

Every business that has products to sell must carefully account for and track those money-making products so that it knows what it has on hand to sell. As the bookkeeper, you contribute to this process by keeping accurate inventory records in an Inventory account. You should periodically test the numbers that you have in your books by doing physical counts of the inventory on hand. We talk about how to manage inventory and Inventory accounts in Chapter 8.

Accounts Payable

No one likes to send money out of the business, but you can ease the pain and strain by tracking and paying bills in your Accounts Payable account. You certainly don't want to pay anyone twice, but you also want to pay bills on time — otherwise, your business may no longer get the supplies, inventory, or other things it needs to operate. Suppliers often penalize late-paying businesses by cutting them off or putting them on cash-only accounts. On the flipside, if you pay your bills early, you may be able to get discounts and save money with suppliers, so the early bird definitely gets the worm. For more on the Accounts Payable account, check out Chapter 8.

Payroll Taxes Payable

As the bookkeeper, you need to make sure that your business makes payments to the Canada Revenue Agency (CRA) on time. The money that you withhold from the gross pay of employees doesn't belong to the business. Your business acts as an agent of the government by following the laws that the government has established concerning payroll. These laws require that you deduct from an employee's gross pay a combined federal and provincial withholding income tax. These laws also require that both the employer and the employee make contributions to the Canada Pension Plan (CPP) and/or Québec Pension Plan (QPP), as well as the Employment Insurance (EI) program. Bookkeepers must remit the amounts due to the proper authorities by the deadline dates. We discuss these responsibilities as an employer in Chapters 10 and 11.

Loans Payable

Your business is bound to need to purchase major assets such as equipment, vehicles, and furniture at some point. Unfortunately, you may find that your business doesn't have the money to pay for such purchases. In that case, your business can take on long-term loans by signing promissory notes payable that it will repay over longer than a 12-month period. The Notes Payable account allows you to monitor the activity on these loans so that you can get and keep the best rates by making all loan payments on time and accurately. We talk about bank loans and the Notes Payable account in Chapter 13.

Sales

No business can operate without taking in cash, mostly through sales of the business's goods or services. In the Sales account, you track all incoming revenue collected from sales of inventory. You must record sales in a timely and accurate manner because, otherwise, you can't figure out how much revenue your business generates every day. To find out more about sales and the Sales account, refer to Chapter 9.

Purchases

In order to have a tangible product to sell, if your business has sales instead of service revenue, it has to either manufacture the product (in which case, you have to purchase a raw materials inventory) or purchase a finished product from a supplier. You track all your purchases of inventory in the Purchases account. The Purchases account is a key component in calculating cost of goods sold, which you subtract from sales to find your business's gross profit. We talk about the Purchases account in Chapter 8.

Wages and Salaries Expense

It's a fact of business that you must pay employees to get them to stay around. No matter how much you beg, few people want to work for nothing. To keep up with what is, for many businesses, the biggest expense, you track all money paid to employees in the Wages and Salaries Expense account. Accurate maintenance of this account ensures that your business files all governmental reports and pays all payroll withholding taxes and benefits. And if you don't take care of these responsibilities to the government, you can find yourself in some serious hot water. We talk about payroll obligations and the related accounts in Chapters 10, 11, and 20.

Equity

Accounts related to owners' *equity,* which is the amount each owner invests into the business, vary depending on the type of business for which you keep the books. When one person or a group of partners own a business, and that business isn't incorporated, no common shares exist to apportion ownership. Instead, you add money put into the business by each of the owners in Capital accounts (one for each owner), and you deduct from the Capital accounts any money taken out of the business by the owners in Drawings accounts (again, one for each owner). In order to be fair to all owners, you must carefully track all owners' Equity accounts. We talk about business structures and types of ownership in Chapter 21. We discuss owners' Equity accounts in Chapter 18.

The Retained Earnings Equity account exists only for incorporated businesses. It tracks any profits made by the business that it reinvests to grow the business (instead of paying those profits out to business owners as dividends). This account is *cumulative,* which means it shows a running total of earnings that the business has retained since it opened its doors. Although managing this account doesn't take you a lot of time, you need to keep the Retained Earnings account accurate. Investors and lenders want to track how well the business is doing and know how much money the shareholders, as investors, have put in or left in to finance the business. We talk about retained earnings in Chapter 18.

Appendix

Glossary

· ·

accounting equation: Assets = Liabilities + Equity.

accounting period: The time period over which the books track financial information. The period can be a month, a quarter, or a year.

accounts payable: Money due to vendors, suppliers, contractors, and consultants for products or services purchased by the business.

accounts receivable: Asset in which revenue is recorded on products sold or services provided to customers, and the business collects it at a later date.

accrual accounting: The accounting method that requires a bookkeeper to record transactions when they actually occur, even if cash hasn't yet changed hands. The bookkeeper records revenue when the business earns it (not when the business actually receives payment for the products or services) and counts expenses when the business receives goods or services, even if the business hasn't yet paid for the goods or services.

accrued expenses: Expenses that a business has incurred by receiving services, but for which the business hasn't yet received an invoice or paid any cash. Accrued vacation pay earned by employees but not yet paid out is included in accrued expenses and recorded to accrued liabilities.

accrued expenses payable: Liabilities for unpaid expenses that a business has incurred by receiving services or products, but for which the business hasn't received an invoice. Accrued interest payable is an example.

accrued revenues: Revenues that a business has earned by delivering goods or services, but for which the business hasn't yet sent an invoice or received any cash.

accumulated depreciation: The total amount of depreciation expense that the bookkeeper has recorded since the business purchased the fixed assets being depreciated.

adjusting entry: An entry that the bookkeeper prepares and posts at the end of an accounting cycle or reporting period to adjust the accounts in order to implement accrual accounting.

amortization: An accounting term similar to depreciation used to show the portion of an intangible asset's book value that has been expensed each year.

arm's length transaction: An exchange of assets, products, or services between two unrelated or unaffiliated parties or, if the parties are related, conducted as if the parties were unrelated to avoid the appearance of conflict of interest.

assets: All things owned and controlled by the business, such as cash, inventory, buildings, vehicles, furniture, and any other item that the business uses to earn revenue.

average costing: An accounting method used to assign cost to inventory by calculating an average cost per unit purchased.

bad-debt expense: An estimated expense for customer accounts receivable that the business likely won't be able to collect.

balance sheet: The financial statement that presents a snapshot of the business's financial position (assets, liabilities, and equity) at a particular date in time. This statement is also called the statement of financial position.

bank overdraft: A negative position of a bank account; also referred to as being *overdrawn* at the bank.

book value of assets: The amounts of assets that the bookkeeper reports in a business's balance sheet; also referred to as the carrying amount.

buildings: The account that tracks the cost of any buildings that a business owns, controls, or uses in the business.

Canada Revenue Agency (CRA): The CRA administers the tax laws for the Government of Canada and most provinces, and controls various programs delivered through the tax system.

capital: An equity account followed by (or preceded by) the name of the person to whom the capital account belongs; used in a sole proprietorship or partnership.

capital cost allowance: A depreciation technique used by the Canada Revenue Agency (CRA) for depreciable assets.

cash basis accounting: An accounting method that's based on actual cash flow. The bookkeeper records expenses only when the business actually pays out cash for the goods or services, and records revenue only when the business collects cash from the customer.

certified general accountant (CGA): A CGA belongs to the Certified General Accountants Association of Canada. CGAs work within organizations, providing their expertise in varying roles besides accounting.

certified management accountant (CMA): A CMA belongs to the Society of Management Accountants of Canada. CMAs are generally known for their management roles inside organizations.

Chart of Accounts: A listing of the General Ledger accounts, usually in numerical order, organized in the following sequence: Asset, Liability, Equity, Drawings, Revenue, and Expense accounts.

chartered accountant (CA): A CA belongs to the Canadian Institute of Chartered Accountants (CICA). People generally think of a CA as the independent auditor for organizations, although that's only one of many roles the CA plays.

classification: The process of grouping General Ledger accounts on financial statements based on those accounts' nature or function (in the case of the income statement) or by their liquidity (in the case of the balance sheet).

common shares: The ownership shares issued by a corporation for capital that owners invest in the business; also referred to as capital stock.

copyright: An intangible asset that protects original works — including books, magazines, articles, newspapers, television shows, movies, music, poetry, and plays — from being copied by anyone other than their creators.

corporation: A business organized as a separate legal entity under corporation law. The unit of ownership of a corporation is a common share.

cost of goods sold: All money spent to purchase or make products that a business plans to sell to its customers.

credits: Accounting entries that increase Liability, Revenue, or Equity accounts and decrease Asset, Expense, or Drawings accounts. Credits always appear on the right side of an accounting entry.

current assets: All items owned by the business that it expects to use or convert to cash in the next 12 months. These assets include items, such as cash, that a business can easily liquidate. Other examples of current assets include cash, accounts receivable, inventory, marketable securities, and prepaid expenses.

current liabilities: All financial obligations that the business needs to pay in less than 12 months, such as accounts payable (money due to vendors, contractors, and consultants) and credit cards payable (payments due on credit card balances).

current ratio: A test of a business's short-term liquidity (debt-paying capability). A business calculates the current ratio by dividing its total current assets by its total current liabilities.

debits: Accounting entries that increase Asset, Expense, or Drawings accounts and decrease Liability, Revenue, or Equity accounts. Debits always appear on the left side of an accounting entry.

depreciation: An accounting method used to reduce the book value of a long-term asset over a the number of years that the business uses that asset.

dividends: Amounts distributed from the Retained Earnings account to shareholders as a reward for their investment. Dividends represent a distribution of equity.

double-entry bookkeeping: A system of recording transactions that uses debits and credits to keep the accounts in balance.

drawings: An account that records the amount of money or assets that the owner takes out of or withdraws from the business for personal use. The account's name includes the name of the owner.

electronic funds transfer (EFT): An electronic transaction at a bank that doesn't require a deposit slip or cheque. Businesses often use EFTs to make preauthorized payments, such as monthly mortgage payments, and to make automatic deposits to employees' bank accounts for their net pay.

employee benefits: Payments made by the business, in addition to wages and salaries, that provide pensions, medical insurance, or other fringe benefits to the employees.

equipment: The account that tracks equipment purchased for more than one year's use, such as computers, copiers, tools, and cash registers.

equity: Account used to track the value of things owned by the business owners or shareholders after deducting for liabilities.

expenses: All costs of operating a business that aren't assets, including financing costs and income taxes.

fidelity bond: A type of insurance that covers a business against the risk of employees stealing cash or other assets.

financial statement: Generally refers to one of the three primary accounting reports of a business: the balance sheet (also called the statement of financial position), statement of cash flows, or income statement.

first in, first out (FIFO): An accounting cost formula used to assign cost to inventory. This formula assumes the first items available for sale are the first items sold.

fiscal year: An accounting period, generally 12 months long. Usually ends on December 31 for unincorporated businesses, and at any chosen date (usually a month's end) for a corporation.

fixed assets: A category of long-term assets — sometimes called property, plant, and equipment — that the business uses in its operations.

furniture and fixtures: Chairs, desks, store fixtures, and shelving needed to operate the business.

general journal entries: Any entries made to correct or adjust balances in the general ledger accounts or to record accruals at the end of an accounting period.

general ledger: A summary of all historical transactions that occurred since the business first opened its doors. This ledger is the granddaddy of a business's financial information.

generally accepted accounting principles (GAAP): The authoritative standards and approved accounting methods.

goodwill: A non-current intangible asset that the bookkeeper records when a business purchases another business. Goodwill represents aspects such as business reputation, store locations, customer base, and other items that increase the value of the business bought as a going concern.

gross margin (profit): The total of sales revenue less cost of goods sold for the period.

gross pay: The amount that an employee earns in a pay period, before the business takes off deductions (which results in net pay).

impairment loss: The amount by which an asset's book value exceeds the amount that can be recovered by using the asset in the business.

income statement: The financial statement that summarizes all revenues and expenses for a period and reports the net earnings or profit of a business.

intangible assets: Anything the business owns that has value but can't be touched, such as licenses, patents, trademarks, brand names, and goodwill.

interest: The charge that a business must pay when it borrows money (principal) from a bank or other business; this form of interest is an expense. Interest can also be revenue when the business makes loans to others as investments and therefore collects interest on those investments.

inventory: All products that the business manufactured or purchased, which it plans to sell to customers.

journals: Where bookkeepers keep records (in chronological order) of daily business transactions.

land: The account that tracks the land owned, controlled, and used by the business. Land can be inventory if a business's operations involve selling land. Land can be an investment if the business has the intent to sell the land at a gain.

leasehold improvements: Improvements, which last longer than 12 months, that the business makes to buildings or other facilities that it leases (rather than purchases).

liabilities: All debts the business owes, such as accounts payable, bank loans, unpaid bills, and mortgages payable.

limited liability partnership (LLP): A partnership structure in which partners have unlimited liability for their own negligence but have limited liability for other partners' negligence.

limited partnership (LP): A partnership that has two different types of partners: general and limited. The general partner runs the day-to-day business and is held personally responsible for all activities of the business.

liquidity: The ability of a business to pay its expected debts and liabilities in the next 12 months, as well as meet unexpected needs for cash.

lower of cost and net realizable value (LC & NRV): An accounting method used to value inventory based on whichever is lower: the actual cost of the inventory or the value expected on resale net of selling costs.

net pay: An employee's gross pay less payroll deductions.

net profit or net earnings: The bottom-line results of a business after subtracting from revenues and gains all costs and expenses, including interest, depreciation, losses, and amortization (and possibly income taxes). Net profit reflects how much money the business makes and how much equity has increased in the period.

non-current assets: All things a business owns that it expects to use or convert to cash in more than 12 months, such as buildings, factories, vehicles, and furniture (property, plant, and equipment); intangibles; and long-term investments.

on account: On credit. A bookkeeper records purchases and sales on account with the understanding and agreement that the business will make cash collections and payments at a later date.

operating cash flow: The cash generated by a business's operations to produce and sell its products or deliver its services.

operating expenses: Expenses incurred by a business in its operations, such as advertising, equipment rental, store rental, insurance, legal and accounting fees, entertainment, salaries, office expenses, repairs and maintenance, travel, utilities, possibly taxes, and just about anything else that goes into operating a business.

operating line of credit: A preauthorized approval to borrow money from a bank when needed, at a preset limit.

operating profit: A measure of a business's earning power from its ongoing operations; excludes interest expense, interest revenue, and unusual gains and losses.

partnership: An unincorporated business structure in which two or more people are owners and do business with the intention of making a profit.

patent: An intangible asset that guarantees the inventor or the owner of a product or process's patent the exclusive right to make, use, and sell that product or process over a set period of time, determined by law.

payroll: The way a business pays its employees.

periodic inventory system: Tracking inventory that a business has on hand by doing a physical count of inventory on a periodic basis, whether daily, monthly, yearly, or any other time period that meets a business's financial reporting needs.

perpetual inventory system: Tracking inventory that a business has on hand by adjusting the inventory counts after each transaction. A business needs a computerized inventory control system to manage inventory if the business uses this method.

petty cash: Small amounts of cash kept on hand at business locations for incidental expenses that don't require payments by cheque.

point of sale: The location where customers pay for products or services that they want to buy, such as a cash register or service counter.

posting: The process of entering summarized transactions to the General Ledger that first appeared in a journal in chronological order.

prepaid expenses: Expenses that a business pays up front, such as a year's worth of insurance or property taxes.

profit: The amount by which revenues exceed expenses. See also *net profit or net earnings.*

promissory note: A written promise to pay a specified amount of money at a later date. Generally, promissory notes carry interest.

property, plant, and equipment: See *fixed assets.*

proprietorship: Sometimes referred to as sole proprietorship to indicate that this type of organization structure involves a single owner.

quick (acid test) ratio: The number calculated by dividing the total of cash, accounts receivable, and short-term investments (if any) by total current liabilities.

residual value: The value that the business intends to receive when it sells a used asset to another business that plans to use that asset for essentially the same purpose.

retained earning: An Equity account used by corporations to track any net profits left in the business from accounting period to accounting period, which the business reinvests in itself for future growth. Dividends paid to shareholders reduce this account.

return on assets (ROA): A ratio that tests how well a business uses its assets. A business calculates this ratio by dividing profit by total assets.

return on equity (ROE): A ratio that measures how well a business earns money for the owners or investors. A business calculates this ratio by dividing profit by shareholders' or owners' equity.

return on sales (ROS): A ratio (also referred to as *profit margin*) that determines how efficiently a business runs its operations. A business calculates this ratio by dividing profit by net sales.

revenue: All money earned in the process of selling the business's goods and services or from interest on loans or investments and renting property to others.

salvage value: The value that the business intends to receive when it gets rid of a used asset at the end of that asset's useful life.

sole proprietorship: See *proprietorship.*

solvency: Refers to the ability of a business to pay all of its liabilities on time.

specific identification: An accounting cost formula used to keep track of the cost inventory based on the actual items sold and their individual costs.

statement of cash flows: One of the three primary financial statements of a business, which summarizes its cash inflows and outflows during a period according to a threefold classification: cash flow from operating activities, investing activities, and financing activities.

straight-line depreciation: A depreciation technique that assigns the cost of a fixed asset, less any residual value for that fixed asset, in equal amounts to each year of its useful life.

tangible assets: Any items owned by the business that a person can hold or touch, such as cash, inventory, or vehicles.

trademark: An intangible asset that gives a business ownership of distinguishing words, phrases, symbols, or designs that can be legally protected.

trial balance: A listing of the General Ledger account balance at a point in time. The total of the debits must equal the total of the credits.

unearned revenue: The receipt of cash recorded as a liability until the revenues become earned.

unincorporated: Unincorporated business entities, such as partnerships and proprietorships, aren't legal entities separate from their owners in the way that corporations are.

unusual gains and losses: Nonrecurring gains and losses that happen infrequently and that are aside from the normal, ordinary sales and expenses of a business. **useful life:** The time period a business intends to use a productive long-term asset (either tangible or intangible), regardless of the physical or legal life of the asset.

vehicles: Cars and trucks used by the business to earn revenue.

workers' compensation programs: Programs administered by the provinces to protect employees who are injured on the job or become sick or disabled because of the job.

Index

• C •

• F •